CHARLOTTE H. BRUNER was born in 1917 in Illinois, USA. Having obtained a BA in English and an MA in Comparative Literature, she began her academic career in 1954 at Iowa State University where she remained until her retirement as Professor Emeritus in 1987.

Bruner has pioneered the teaching and researching of contemporary African writing and has taught and written on French, English, African and Caribbean literatures. For fourteen years she co-ordinated an interdisciplinary course in Third World Cultures for the College of Liberal Arts and Sciences.

Her extensive travels on four continents have brought her into contact with a number of writers as yet largely unrecognised, many of them women. In collaboration with her husband, David Bruner, she produced a weekly radio series 'First Person Feminine' for over six years.

In addition to over fifty articles on Diaspora literature and women's writings, her literary achievements include *Unwinding Threads* (Heinemann, 1983), which she edited, and *The Feminist Companion to English Literature* (1990) for which she was the African consulting editor.

As a much respected leader in her fields, Bruner won the Iowa Women's Political Caucus Award in 1981 followed by the Iowa State University Human Relations Award in 1985.

THE HEINEMANN BOOK OF
AFRICAN WOMEN'S WRITING

Edited by Charlotte H. Bruner

HEINEMANN

To
Charles and Nell

Heinemann International Literature and Textbooks
a division of Heinemann Educational Books Ltd
Halley Court, Jordan Hill, Oxford OX2 8EJ

Heinemann : A Division of Reed Publishing (USA) Inc.
361 Hanover Street, Portsmouth, New Hampshire, 03801-3912, USA

Heinemann Educational Books (Nigeria) Ltd
PMB 5205, Ibadan
Heinemann Educational Boleswa
PO Box 10103, Village Post Office, Gaborone, Botswana

LONDON   EDINBURGH   PARIS   MADRID
ATHENS   BOLOGNA   MELBOURNE   SYDNEY
AUCKLAND   SINGAPORE   TOKYO

First published by Heinemann International Literature and Textbooks in 1993

Series Editor: Adewale Maja-Pearce

British Libary Cataloguing in Publication Data
A catalogue record for this book is available from the British Library.

ISBN 0435 906739

Phototypeset by Cambridge Composing (UK) Ltd, Cambridge
Printed and bound in Great Britain
by Cox & Wyman Ltd, Reading, Berkshire

93 94 95 96 10 9 8 7 6 5 4 3

308.809
HEI
993

CONTENTS

Preface   vii
Acknowledgements   ix
Map showing location of contributors   x

WESTERN AFRICA

EASTERN AFRICA

SOUTHERN AFRICA

NORTHERN AFRICA

PREFACE

'The African woman writing fiction today has to be somehow exceptional', prefaces *Unwinding Threads*, the anthology of writing by women in Africa (1983), to which the present collection is a companion piece. The assertion holds, nonetheless, but now African women writers are no longer isolated voices crying from a 'wilderness.' They are reaching an audience at home and abroad. They are aware of each other. Those who published earlier and are still writing provide role models for others, new and as yet unheard. And their wilderness is no bleak desert nor isolated jungle. It can be the bulldozed shanty town of a Capetown coloured suburb, the work-a-day world of the exploited serving girl in a middle-class Kenyan neighbourhood, the horror-strafed sidewalk of a war-torn Lebanese city, or the turmoil of frustration and inhibition in the inner world of the woman behind the veil. There is also joy: the comfort of enduring friendship, the satisfaction of academic achievement and social power, the independence of thought, the affirmation of personal identity.

Each writer selected has her own gift. Her style reflects her unique perspective on her own time and culture. Hopefully, the stories included here will not only delight the readers at home and abroad but also encourage other women as yet unrecognised to write as well.

The creation of the first anthology was a challenge and a joy. When Heinemann editors asked me to do a follow-up collection, I was delighted and at first astonished because only a few years had gone by. But by common consent we decided that new writers, or hitherto unpublished ones, were not only writing fiction but were recording the *new* Africa. They know the Africa since independence, since 'modernisation', since westernisation, since the feminist movement. It seems appropriate to seek new voices, and new perspectives from a new generation. The writers who were approached responded with enthusiastic understanding. Several wrote short stories for our consideration.

One novelist decided to try out the short-story format for the first time. In rare cases, a chapter of an autobiography served as a story unit as it stood.

Narratives complete in themselves were preferred, although some fine novelists had to be omitted. Generally, the writers already featured in *Unwinding Threads* were not included again unless they had very recent stories or were just now becoming available in English translation. Not all areas in the vast continent are mentioned, though women may well be writing there too. Any such collection as this can be at best representative, not inclusive.

Naturally I could not have succeeded without the encouragement and guidance of the Heinemann editors, John Watson and Lisa Barnett, whose idea it was and whose friendship urged me on. The writers themselves have been most responsive and enthusiastic. The many letters we have exchanged about them and their writings have strengthened my belief in their talents and their warmth. Scholars and translators have often guided me to works I could not otherwise have known. Evelyne Accad, Dorothy Blair, Mildred Mortimer have helped me to discover new North African writers. Don Burness and Gerald Moser suggested Orlanda Amarílis's Portuguese story. Peter Nazareth introduced me to Aminata Maïga Ka and to the work of Violet Dias Lannoy. My husband, David, translated 'The Stone Bench' at my request. So this anthology represents not just the editor's expertise but also that of some of the outstanding scholars in the field. I do hope all who have worked with the book will find it as gratifying to read and to ponder as I do.

Charlotte H. Bruner

ACKNOWLEDGEMENTS

The editor and publishers would like to thank the following for permission to use copyright material:

Catherine Acholonu for 'Mother was a Great Man'; Zaynab Alkali for 'Saltless Ash'; Awuor Ayoda for 'Workday'; The Centre for the Portuguese Speaking World for 'Disillusion' by Orlanda Amarílis; Editions de L'Ocean Indien Ltee. for *Lakshmi's Gift* by Ananda Devi; Sheila Fugard for 'Lace'; Heinemann for 'Cardboard Mansions' from *Coming Home and Other Stories* by Farida Karodia; John Johnson Ltd for 'Women From America' by Bessie Head; Daisy Kabagarama for 'The Rich Heritage'; Richard Lannoy for 'The Story of Jesus – According to Mokuba, the Beloved Tribesman'; Librarie Ernest Flammarion for 'Death in Slow Motion' by Andrée Chedid; Prof. Bruce Merry for 'Regina's Baby' by Jean Marquard; Ifeoma Okoye for 'The Paypacket'; Pantheon Books, a division of Random House Inc. for 'Bowl Like Hole' from *You Can't Get Lost in Capetown* by Zoë Wicomb; Présence Áfricaine for the chapter from *La Voie de Salut* by Aminata Maïga Ka; Quartet Books for 'Three Cloistered Girls' and 'My Father Writes to my Mother' by Assia Djebar, and 'God on Probation' by Gisèle Halimi; Reed International Books for 'She was the Weaker' from *She Has No Place in Paradise* by Nawal El Saadawi; Syros Alternatives for 'Le Sofa en Pièrre' (The Stone Bench) by Leïla Sebbar); The Women's Press Ltd for the extract from *Nervous Conditions* by Tsitsi Dangarembga.

The publishers have made every effort to trace copyright holders, but in some cases without success. We shall be very glad to hear from anyone who has been inadvertently overlooked or incorrectly cited, and make the necessary changes at the first opportunity.

Map of Africa showing the location of contributors

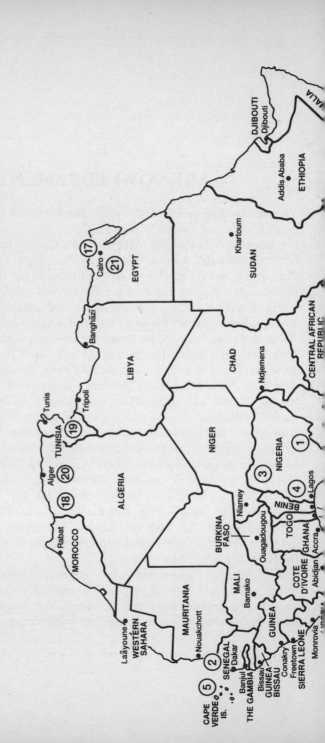

1 Ifeoma Okoye
2 Aminata Maïga Ka
3 Zaynab Alkali
4 Catherine Obianuju Acholonu
5 Orlanda Amarilis
6 Awuor Ayodo
7 Violet Dias Lannoy
8 Lina Magaia
9 Daisy Kabaragama
10 Ananda Devi
11 Bessie Head
12 Tsitsi Dangarembga
13 Jean Marquard
14 Zoë Wicomb
15 Sheila Fugard
16 Farida Karodia
17 Nawal El Saadawi
18 Assia Djebar
19 Gisèle Halimi
20 Leila Sebbar
21 Andrée Chedid

WESTERN

AFRICA

WESTERN AFRICA

The thirty or so years after West Africa's independence from colonial governance have seen a new generation grow up to face the new problems of self rule. They must cope with the continuing neo-colonial influence on language, education, family patterns, economic dominance as well as the internal problems of tribalism, separatist movements, corruption, etc.

For women authors today the scene is very different from the environment in which the 'pioneer' writers like Adelaide Casely-Hayford and Mabel Dove Danquah wrote. The establishment of elementary and secondary schools and of local universities and publishing houses makes it possible for more women to receive higher education. Now they can even read literature written by African women before them. They can publish at home for an indigenous audience instead of catering to tastes abroad.

Nevertheless, in anglophone West Africa, for example, the traditional cultural expectations for women to be primarily mothers and wives still inhibit them, and the overlay of imposed colonial values adds to their constraints. Noted Nigerian critic Molara Ogundipe-Leslie[1] says:

> The effect of the world-wide concern about the woman's position in Nigeria has been varied . . . It is . . . multi-faceted and contradictory when it is not totally false and misleading. The male-dominated society reacts in the usual fashion by denying that there is any oppression of women in Africa, glorifying an unknown pre-colonial

[1] Molara Ogundipe-Leslie is known as an outstanding literary critic and as a leader in women-and-development. She has written many books, monographs and articles, many on women's issues. Her statement here is taken from her interview with Adeola James in *In Their Own Voices: African Women Writers Talk*.

past where our African mothers were totally happy; accusing conscious women activists of being victims of western ideas and copycats of white women; claiming that 'the family' is more important than the fate of the individual woman; brushing aside women's concern with the hypocrisy that 'national development' is a greater priority now than women's liberation; asserting that women anyhow do not need to be liberated because they have never been in bondage. So you have a compounding of historical and sociological falsification, all to the end of frightening women into quietude. The most vocal and courageous who continue to talk and act socially and politically are stigmatised.

Nigeria, in particular, with its population of over 115 million and its occasional prosperity from oil, has been able to produce a more favourable climate for women writers than many other West African countries. There are several regional universities and some publishing houses. Flora Nwapa, the first black African woman novelist to publish in England, starting in the fifties, is still writing, and she has been a role model for many others. Alert to the need for local outlets for women writers, she established a publishing house for women as well as a children's literature press. Buchi Emecheta, expatriate in London, has won several prizes for her fiction and considerable international recognition. Rebeka Njau's novel and plays, Mabel Segun's satire and children's literature, Adaore Ulasi's novels, Zulu Sofola's plays, are all well regarded in their Nigerian homeland. Eno Oblong's first novel, *Garden House*, won instant recognition by receiving honourable mention for the Noma Award in 1988. There are also new writers from Nigerian areas and ethnic groups not heard from before, such as Zaynab Alkali from Hausa territory.

Because France extended its rule, culture and language over much of Western Africa, some francophone literature by women is appearing, largely since 1980 when Mariama Bä won the Noma Award. However, little of their writing is known or available abroad, and only a few works have been translated into English. *A Dakar Childhood*, Nafissatou Diallo's charming autobiography of her early years, was a landmark book when it appeared in 1975, and is translated into English. Aminata Sow Fall, also from Senegal, has an international reputation for her three ironic novels. Marie Ndiaye has written four novels, and is concerned with the pressures exerted by the entire extended family on its subservient women members.

In Cameroon, thanks to CLE magazine and publishing house and its editor's, Bernard Fonlon's, promotion of Cameroon literature, very recently some women writers have started to become known there. Like Diallo, Jedida Asheri in *The Promise* writes of her childhood, in the Banso area of the Northwest Province. Government minister Delphine Zanga Tsogo has written simulated autobiographical novels of women desiring change: *Vies des femmes* and *L'Oiseau en cage*. Lydie Dooh Bunya's *La Brise du jour* 'recounts the maturation experience of a young woman . . .' Calixthe Beyala has written two novels, *C'est le soleil qui m'a brûlée* and *Tu t'appelleras Tanga* from the point of view of a lesbian protagonist, something of a departure in African literature. Werewere Liking has experimented with various forms and genres, produces ritual drama, and has founded a cultural museum and puppet theatre in Abidjan. Her dialogue-novel, *A la rencontre de . . .* features the western world and the African continent personified as two women. They discuss their many differences and likes: language, colour, tradition, orality versus literacy, lyricism versus logical control, etc. However, it requires specialist scholars like Richard Bjornson[2] or Eloise Brière[3] to bring these Cameroonian works to public attention, or to translate them, because they are little known outside Western Africa.

It is even more difficult to find translations of African women's writings in Portuguese. Portugal had permitted its African colonies very little in formal educational institutions: a limited number of elementary schools, almost no high schools, and no universities. Lusophone literature by indigenous men and women is just now gaining recognition abroad, and little is translated into English.

Despite the many difficulties they face, women are changing the direction of West African literature. As they travel, study, and work abroad, they see new patterns emerging and they face new issues at

[2] Richard Bjornson lived and worked in Cameroon and translated works by many of the authors there. *The African Quest for Freedom and Identity*, 1991, is a definitive work, and I am indebted to him for much of the material given here on Cameroon women writers and on his critical appraisal of their works.

[3] Eloise Brière has lived in Cameroon and written much on her research on Cameroonian writers. A chapter on women writers there is included in her forthcoming study of Cameroonian literature.

home. No longer is the expected scope of their fiction domestic only. Often highly trained as sociologists, anthropologists, linguists, historians, scholars of world literature, they bring a broad perspective to their work. Their female protagonists are as often educated urban women as they are illiterate villagers. Their characters and their problems may be African, but these writers put them in global perspective.

CATHERINE OBIANUJU ACHOLONU

Mother was a Great Man

It was on a dry Harmattan evening. The leaves were already falling from the trees and the wind blew them this way and that. But for the rustling whisper of trees bending to the wind, a big hush pervaded the village square as Oyidiya and her two daughters, Mmema and Ikonne, moved past and into the family compound. None of the three women spoke. Their heads were bowed low. Their minds were occupied by the same nagging feeling of guilt. They had gone too far. They had tried to rearrange the destiny imposed on Oyidiya by her chi and now they were learning the hard way.

Mmema and Ikonne were both married to prosperous and well-to-do husbands. Their husbands were both in the beer business. They were agents of several beer and mineral drink manufacturers and this yielded much money. Oyidiya was lucky with her daughters; they were rich and easily came to her assistance whenever she needed them. Mmema had been given to her husband Kaka twenty years earlier. Kaka was about thirty when he paid her bride price. Oyidiya still remembered the day she and Mmema went to the big Orlu market to sell palm kernels. Orlu[1] people live on top of the hill about seven miles away from Mmema's people of Umuma who live in the valley. In those days if one wanted to get to the big Orlu market called Orie early enough, one set out at the first cock-crow. Then one would be sure to arrive there before the sun was overhead. Now the motor car has made every thing easy, Oyidiya thought. The Orlu people were queer people. The people of Umuma did not trust them, they regarded them as semi-strangers who could not be trusted because they had opened up to the white man without reserve. Why, they would even sell off the wares on your head while they talked and drank with you. The Orlu people on the other hand regarded the Umuma people as

[1] A small town in the Igbo heartland.

enemies of progress. Umuma people were timid and hateful; they hated to see progress and happiness in others. If an Umuma man saw that his neighbour's or brother's children were doing well in trade, he would quickly go to the witch-doctor to prepare some poisonous concoctions to kill them with. In Umuma, if you made progress, you would keep it secret; an Umuma man who owned a car would never drive it home or that would be the last day his eyes would glimpse the sun.

These notwithstanding, Oyidiya had given her first daughter, Mmema, a young girl of barely fourteen years in marriage to Kaka. Many said it was because of Kaka's wealth, others said it was witchcraft. But Kaka had been spellbound by the beauty of this little tender thing whose skin was as smooth as a water pebble and as light as ripe banana fruits, and whose eyes twinkled as they told countless exciting stories. He had quickly paid the bride price and Mmema had been escorted to his home with Ikonne to keep her company. Then they had sealed the relationship by being wedded in the church. Ikonne grew into a very attractive young girl resembling Mmema as she grew, only she was taller and stronger looking. Kaka wanted to make sure that this little girl who had been almost a daughter to him would not get into wrong hands, so he got her attached to his bosom friend Odili, from a neighbouring village, who was also in the beer business. Now, both men were rich and their wives wielded economic power in their respective homes. Oyidiya was proud of her daughters and grateful that their high financial standing made it possible for her to realise her plans; and even though she had no son of her own, people respected her because of the prosperity of her daughters which was always felt around her. She had even taken the title of Lolo which was reserved only for rich women of high social standing.[2]

As Oyidiya remembered the events of the past years, it struck her that she and her husband had almost exchanged roles. Nekwe, her husband, was a man who surpassed every woman in beauty. He was tall and skinny, with a skin as light as ripe udala fruits; and, as if to crown his beauty, Nekwe even had *mbibi* patterns on his face and arms – *mbibi* were elaborate sketches carved into the skin and darkened with

[2] In Igboland, women who wielded much influence and power in their communities were rewarded with the Lola title, especially if such women commanded respect and high regard.

some black substance to enhance beauty. These scarification marks were often associated with vanity. Now, as the thought occurred to her, Oyidiya wondered why her husband, who was now dead, did not instead, go for the *ichi* facial marks that were emblems of manhood, valour and productivity. But it would hardly have become him, she thought. Nekwe was not the manly type. Was it not she, Oyidiya, who had to stand on her feet and defend her family whenever another family challenged it? How often did she have to defend her husband against his fellow men? Yes, the gods knew what they were doing. They always joined together in marriage people of opposing qualities and thus ensured harmony.

Oyidiya did not want to admit it, but now as she went through her life in her mind, she saw clearly that she had been the man of the house while her husband, Nekwe, had been the woman. Yes. She had even indulged in excesses, for which she was now paying. She felt a strong pang of guilt and remorse. She, Oyidiya, had gone too far. She had not accepted her lot. She had forced the hand of her chi. And now this was the result.

Oyidiya walked faster. She thought her own guilt feeling surpassed those of her two daughters, who, in fact, had no hand in the decision that was now costing her her peace of mind, except perhaps in so far as they had given her the financial support with which she had realised her plans. Oyidiya walked faster still, then she stopped and turned round to face her two daughters.

'But I did the only thing any woman would have done under the circumstances. You are not blaming me, are you?' she burst out.

'Nne[3], nobody is blaming you. Humphrey will come back. We shall do all in our power to see that they release him soon.' Mmema did not even believe herself. Humphrey, she was sure, was going to face the firing squad for armed robbery.

'Kompin will die in that place, my spirit tells me he will not come out of it alive. And it is all my fault. If I had heeded to my chi.'

Humphrey was Oyidiya's last child and only son. As the old woman could not pronounce the complicated white man's name, she called him Kompin. The tears were now running down her cheeks. Oyidiya was now very old, and she had suffered a lot, chasing after a male issue which always eluded her. She had had the misfortune of bearing

---

[3] Igbo appellation for 'Mother'.

exceptionally beautiful children, for the understanding was that such children were water spirits and never lived long. Oyidiya knew this, but what she could not understand was why it was only the male issues that turned out to be water spirits while her female issues all lived and bustled with excessive vitality. No, something else was responsible for the early deaths of all her male children. She was sure her husband's second wife, Njido, was responsible. Njido was a witch and was clearly eating off all her boys hoping to lay claim to their husband's property. Even now the cold war had begun. Njido and her wretched boys were claiming everything, and they had ensured that her only son Kompin was safely behind bars. They had bewitched him, she was sure of it. Why did I not think of this before? she questioned her mind. My chi has definitely fashioned me for great things, but Njido is bent on foiling it. Yes. My chi has fashioned me for greatness . . .

Oyidiya remembered, as she took the last steps towards her family compound, that she was a woman of no ordinary birth. Her parents had been rich and very prosperous. But what made her more proud was the fact that she was of royal birth. She was from a family of chieftains, and her father, Uloka, had earnestly desired her birth. In her village, no prospective chief would even attain his royal stool unless he begot a daughter. A man's first daughter was his constant companion and bosom friend. When his wives quarrelled, his first daughter would be called in to descend sternly on them and sort out the quarrel. The first daughter of every Igbo family còmmanded a high position and pride of place, she was her father's 'two legs' while the first son was his 'right hand.' In many parts of Igboland it was the first daughter who ate the best part of the meat whenever an animal was slaughtered in her father's compound. Oyidiya remembered the story her mother had told her of how her father had had to marry her as a second wife in the bid to get a daughter to complete the requirements of his chieftaincy title.

'Your father was rich, he had a large yam barn, a hard-working wife, four able-bodied sons and, above all, the royal blood of his ancestors flowed through his veins. But the elders were adamant. They would not hear of a chieftain without a daughter. "That is the custom of Ikeduru," they insisted, "and nobody will change it." '

Ada still remembered how she shook with fear as she stood by her father while he made his pledge to the elders; how she, a mere child of six, had had to put up with the discomfort of the heavy jigida[4] strings on her hips and the ivory armlets and anklets that had darkened with age; she remembered, too, the discomfort of having to pronounce the difficult words that would give credence to her father's solemn pledge to the people of Ikeduru. 'But why a daughter?' Oyidiya had asked her mother. 'Surely a son would have been of greater importance. Our people only want sons.'

'Yes, they want sons, but they always say that to beget a daughter first is a blessing to the family. A daughter caters for the well-being of her parents in their old age, sons only care for their immediate families. They care little for their ageing parents. A son caters for continuity of the family-name and external image, but a daughter caters for love, understanding and unity within the family circle. She brings the brethren together and sorts out their differences. Our people believe that it is a curse to beget only sons and no daughter. They will not put up with a chieftain who has no daughter. They say that his homestead is standing on spikes and sooner or later will be razed to the dust.'

So, whereas other girls of her age felt inferior to the boys, Oyidiya was treated with special preference. She did not have to put up with the absurdities that forbade women to whistle, or to climb trees, and because none of these sanctions were placed on her, she grew up with the exuberance and freedom that was allowed only to boys. She did not realise the difference in the sexes until the day she bled between her legs. She had gone on a cricket-hunting session with her friends most of whom were boys. Oyidiya sighted a ube tree[5] full of ripe fruits, and made straight for it climbing with youthful abandon. Then somebody, one of the boys, shouted:

'Oyidiya is bleeding. Oyidiya is bleeding between her legs.' She could not remember how she got down from that tree. The boys jeered at her all the way home. That was how she parted ways with her male companions, especially after she discovered from her mother that that awful experience would be repeating itself every seven market weeks.

That was many many years ago. Looking back, Oyidiya thought what an irony of fate it was that she who had been a highly desired daughter, should afterwards hang in the balance because she had no male issue.

---

[4] A string of disc-like beads worn round the hips by young maidens.
[5] The native pear, the fruits of which ripen by becoming darker on the surface.

Oyidiya was left with no choice but to do what in Igboland was reserved for women of high social and financial standing to which class she rightly belonged. She must have her own son and if he would not come from her own womb then some other woman would do so in her name and on her behalf. She summoned her husband's kinsmen and told them she was going to take a wife. The men said they were surprised she had waited so long to take that inevitable step. And so after a series of visits with kegs of palm wine and presents to the Umuado village, Nekwe's kinsmen brought home to Oyidiya a young girl of sixteen, looking so ripe and full that one would have expected from her only male issues. But that was not to be, or maybe she did not stay long enough to find out. When her first two issues turned out to be girls, Oyidiya got impatient and sent her home to her parents. Then Oyidiya married again, but this time the young woman was having difficulty in conceiving. Oyidiya invited a witch-doctor to administer treatment to her, but, to her dismay and shame, the healer eloped with the young bride. Oyidiya was not to brood over a shameless woman when she could marry as many as she could. So she quickly married again, but this time, there was no Nekwe to supply the male seed. Nekwe was bitten by a snake on his way to the farm and died soon afterwards. But the new development did not dissuade Oyidiya from keeping the new wife. After all, what were a husband's male relations for, if not to see to it that their dead brother's name was not buried with him? So the new wife bore her first issue which turned out to be twin girls; and she and her new babies did not outstay the night. They were quickly bundled back to the girl's parents. It was a pity the white man had put his nose in everything, otherwise mother and daughters would have been killed and thrown into the bad bush, Oyidiya had fumed.

Oyidiya was now quite old and physically weak, but her heart was strong. She was bent on leaving behind her, after her death, a son to claim her own share of her husband's property and to retain her homestead. She, Oyidiya daughter of Uloka, would not leave this world without a son to repair and breed life into her hut. It was a pity that girls had to marry and leave their fathers' houses to breed life into other men's homes. If she did not have a son before her death, her hut would be demolished and soon the children of the other wife of her husband would begin to farm on it. That was not to be. She, Oyidiya, was going to prevent that. After all was her name not Oyidiya – the one that resembled her husband – or rather the woman that resembled a man, she quickly corrected herself.

She had long forgotten about her second wife who had escaped with the witch-doctor, and was recovering from the ill luck of the twin girls when, one day, a distant relative of her husband, who lived almost buried and forgotten in the far away town of Asaba across the great river about which she had only heard in stories of adventure, came home with the story that changed everything. Oyidiya's forgotten wife, Chitu, was living there and had long given birth to a baby boy by her witch-doctor lover. Oyidiya smiled to herself. The gods had blessed her at last, for the son was hers. In fact all Chitu's children were hers, but she was not interested in the girls; all she wanted was the boy. In spite of his questionable breeding and heritage, Oyidiya wanted to hold him in her arms, to feel his young muscles, to smell his boyhood. Gradually the feeling grew into an ache, a longing. Oyidiya summoned the kindred of her husband and told them of the new development. Some thought it was not wise to bring in a son from the lineage of wizards, it would not go well, they argued. But there were many others who thought that the gods had finally heard Oyidiya's prayers. It was therefore agreed that the boy should be brought home, if necessary, he would be abducted.

Oyidiya sent word to her daughters inviting them to give her financial support. She had to pay out a lot of money to the young men who undertook the journey. And so Humphrey was abducted and brought home to Oyidiya, who performed several sacrifices of appreciation to her chi and to Ogwugwu, the god of the village that catered for justice and fair play. Oyidiya remembered it all so vividly, now, as she pushed open the carved wooden door that led into the compound. Yes, she now had a son, but she had something else in addition, she had misery, frustration, even more – anxiety, for Kompin was an embodiment of all vices. He was a cheat, a liar, a thief, a glutton. Right from the first day he was brought into Oyidiya's home, the little boy, who was then barely four years old, had been caught eating the fish from the soup-pot and since that day he had never ceased to be in trouble. Now he was locked up in the white man's prison at Orlu. As soon as she heard the news, Oyidiya had sent for her daughters, and though they had tried to bribe him out, it was all to no avail. Oyidiya was sure this was going to be the end of the boy and of the dream that had spurred her on and filled her with hope even at the most trying periods. He was going to be shot by the soldiers who now ruled the country. She too was tired, she had lost interest in living, but she would not give up the fight. She was going to retaliate from the grave against her husband's second wife who had taken the ground from under her feet. Oyidiya pushed at the carved wooden gate of the dwarf mud-wall which creaked open to allow them in. As she took the last few steps and disappeared into the cold dark interior of her thatched, mud-walled hut, she was oblivious to everything around her – she did not see her dog, Logbo, whimpering its welcome, she did not hear her two daughters calling her from behind, she was only conscious of a dry ache somewhere inside her head. Then she swooned and was about to fall, when Ikonne caught her and, tenderly, the two women laid their aged mother on to her bamboo bed. Oyidiya the fighter, the husband of three wives, the manly woman, was no more. But before she breathed her last, Oyidiya gave her last instructions to her daughters.

'I have fought a good fight. You two should not give up now. Before they shoot him, be sure to keep a wife here in his name. Then my life shall not have been in vain. The gods and my chi have fashioned me for great things.' The two women exchanged glances.

'Mother was a great man,' they both agreed. 'We must prepare for her a befitting burial.'

IFEOMA OKOYE

The Pay-packet

Iba's heart fell. She had just learnt on arrival at the City Primary School where she was teaching, that the June salary which was a week overdue was to be paid that day. Surprisingly, she had come to dread pay-days and was a little glad when the payment of June salary was delayed.

Only six months before, she had got married to a perfect gentleman, debonair and handsome, and had moved from the village primary school where she was teaching to the City Primary School, one of the exclusive schools in Enugu, the town where her husband worked. Before her marriage, she had always looked forward to receiving her salary, and weeks before it was due she would begin to make plans on how to spend the money, would draw up lists of what to buy, deleting from and adding to them, and would visit shops and markets looking for the items on her lists and comparing prices to make sure of good bargains.

But these days pay-days had become a great terror to her, something that she longed for and dreaded at the same time. The blissful pay-days were gone – gone for ever, she thought, unless she summoned up courage to do something about the cause of her problem.

It was now the last lesson of the day and Iba sat on her chair in the fairly large classroom, her elbows on the table and her narrow chin resting on her slightly cupped hands. With her mind preoccupied with the problems that for months now had accompanied her pay-packet, she was unconscious of the din made by her eight-year-old pupils who were supposed to be reading their books silently under her supervision. As a single person, she was used to dealing with problems and had more often than not succeeded in solving them, but the problems she was now having with her pay-packet had defied any peaceful solution, at any rate one that was acceptable to her.

A piercing scream brought Iba back to reality. Ebele, one of her pupils and a spoilt child, was screaming and stamping her feet in frustration. Four girls were surrounding her and trying to calm her down in vain. Iba rushed to the scene, almost tripping over a red satchel carelessly dumped on the floor near her table.

Ebele was too distraught to say why she was screaming but her protectors came to her rescue. They spoke in quick succession.

'The five kobo belongs to Ebele,' one of the girls said.

'Boys always fight for things that are not theirs.'

'Yes, they are all greedy things.'

'And I dislike them all – they're all horrible!'

After some investigation, Iba discovered the cause of the little war. A boy had wrenched Ebele's five kobo from her and had beat her up in the process. Once again Iba played the judge, declared the boy guilty, rescued Ebele's five kobo for her, and banished the offending boy to a corner of the classroom as his punishment.

As Iba walked back to her table, she thought how true the statement of one of Ebele's defenders was: 'Boys always fight for things that are not theirs.' From her own experience, the word *boys* could be substituted by *men*. Yes, men, or at least some of them, always fight for things that are not theirs, she thought, and wished she could solve her own problems as easily as she had solved Ebele's.

At half past one, the school closed for the day. Iba dismissed her pupils after a short prayer, tidied up her table and left for the headmistress's office to collect her pay-packet. In those days teachers' salaries were paid to them in cash after they had signed a voucher. Half way to the headmistress's office, she met her friend and colleague, Ezuma.

'Are you going straight to the H. M.'s office?' Ezuma asked.

'Yes,' replied Iba, 'and what about you?'

'I'll be coming later. No need for all of us to go and squeeze ourselves into that small room at the same time. We'll roast like ground-nuts before we sign the voucher.'

'Of course you don't need the money, Ezuma,' Iba teased her friend.

To Iba, Ezuma's husband was a model life-partner. Although he wasn't rich, he never asked Ezuma to hand over her salary to him. He didn't even know exactly how much she was paid and gave Ezuma enough housekeeping money, or 'food money' as he called it, from his own salary and occasionally he bought clothes and jewellery for her. So far as she knew, they'd never quarrelled over money and Ezuma once said to her friend, 'Of course I don't spend my pay entirely on myself. I often buy presents for members of the family and contribute to the food, but that is of my own volition.'

Iba had come to know all this when she had casually asked Ezuma what she did with her salary. Ever since, she had often found herself comparing her husband with Ezuma's.

As Iba walked alone to the H. M.'s office which was situated near the school gate, she began to think of her marriage and her problems.

It was at the village school where she was teaching after her teachers' certificate course that she had met Bertrand, her husband, for the first time. In fact, it was her girlfriend's brother who, playing at match-making, brought Bertrand to her one-room apartment at the teachers' quarters behind the village school. She had earlier rejected many suitors for one flimsy reason or another, but had found herself attracted to Bertrand and accepted his proposal of marriage without thinking twice.

At that time Bertrand had just resigned his job in Lagos and had taken up a new one as a deputy chief lands officer in the Ministry of Works, Lands and Survey at Enugu. He had a large flat in an area of the town inhabited by middle-class families. A graduate in Estate Management, he had good prospects and was quite popular among his friends and colleagues who had nicknamed him 'Gentleman B'. To Iba, he was 'Darling'.

Their wedding was a society one, attended by many socialites of the town. There was more than enough to eat and drink, and the expensive Police Band was in attendance from the bachelor eve till the end of the wedding reception the following day. Iba spent all her savings on her wedding gown and all the paraphernalia that went with it. As a single woman, she was earning what she thought was enough for her. In those days she spent her money as she wished, occasionally sending some to her parents. She was the last child of the family and had no younger siblings to cater for.

Her problems actually began about a month after the wedding, although she did not quite realise it at the time. When she received her first salary as a married woman, her husband had demanded all of it. Basking in the euphoria of the newly married, she had failed to notice the implications and consequences of such a demand and had gladly complied with it. From her salary, Bertrand had given her some housekeeping money and a small amount as pocket-money.

By the end of the second month after her marriage she had begun to question the wisdom and propriety of handing over her entire salary to her husband to manage. For one thing, it bordered on slavery and for another, the pocket money she received from him was barely enough for her, what with the rising cost of make-up, clothes and jewellery as well as the little things she liked to spend her money on. Besides, she had thought her husband earned a good salary and therefore would have no need of her modest pay-packet.

When her husband demanded the third month's salary she had quietly refused to surrender it. She was then six weeks pregnant and had decided to begin buying the layette bit by bit.

'I must have the money,' her husband had repeated, his lower lip sticking out as it always did whenever he was frustrated or angry.

'I don't think it's proper for me to hand over my entire salary to you every month,' Iba had said in a conversational tone. 'I have every right to spend my salary the way I want to.'

Bertrand had become angrier. 'I see you're now getting ideas into your head. Some women in that bloody school of yours are teaching you how to grow wings, but I'll clip your wings before ever they start growing.'

'I've not discussed the matter with anyone,' Iba had said. 'Not even with my mother.'

'I want the money this minute before I lose my temper, Iba.'

When she would not comply, he had begun to beat her. She had tried to fight back, but he was much too strong for her. He was nearly six feet tall and weighed 80 kilograms, while she was only five feet four inches and 55 kilograms. Unable to take any more beating, she surrendered the money to him.

•

When she arrived at the H. M.'s office, Iba was thinking about the subsequent beatings she had received from Bertrand at the end of each month as she tried to assert her individuality. The headmistress was not in the office; the small room could only accommodate half of the forty teachers in the school while the other half loitered in the long corridor that spanned the whole top floor. They were chatting in groups, their faces radiant with the expectation of receiving some well-earned money.

As Iba watched her colleagues – they were all females – she wondered how many of them handed over their salaries to their husbands to spend as they liked. She had done a little investigation into what working married women did with their pay-packets, and what she had learnt from the few who were ready to discuss the matter freely was shocking.

First, she had asked Phoebe, a classmate at the teachers' training college. Standing there in the corridor, she could hear Phoebe's lamentation:

'My husband insists that I use my salary to feed the family. That leaves me with nothing for myself. My husband argues that he is responsible for the rent, for maintaining the family car and for paying the children's school fees. But all these put together are still less than what I spend feeding the family. And my husband is always asking for expensive meals. Men are terrible. Either way, they cheat you. My husband gets tax rebates for having me and the kids. He gets rent subsidy, but I don't. Is all this fair?'

Uzo, another of Iba's friends, had a different story to tell. Her parents had decreed that her salary for three years from the day of her wedding must be sent to them whole as part of her bride price. Her husband, who was forced to accept this arrangement in spite of the high price he had already paid, took it out on her.

'My father wouldn't dream of doing such a thing to me,' Iba had said to Uzo after listening to her story.

Uzo had continued her story after Iba's interruption. 'Because of his greed, my father has made me a slave to my husband. I beg for every kobo I spend on myself even though I earn a good salary. And it's not that my father is so poor that he can't survive without my salary.'

'I can't understand how he could do such a thing,' Iba said.

'I do. Having spent a lot of his money on my education, he doesn't want my husband to reap where he did not sow.'

'I'd react badly if Father did that to me,' was Iba's conclusion.

Ukachi, of all Iba's friends, had the saddest story to tell. She taught in the same school as her husband who was the headmaster. Ukachi had bemoaned her fate to Iba.

'The worst thing about my case is that I don't even touch my salary. My husband makes me sign the voucher while he spends the money as he likes. I am sure he keeps mistresses and perhaps spends some of my money on them. Twice I refused to sign the voucher if I wasn't going to collect the money, but on each occasion he made life so miserable for me that I've decided to forget that I earn a salary. I have to accept I'm like his housemaid who receives an allowance at the end of every month. That's the only way there'll be peace between us.'

After a long wait, Iba signed the voucher and received her salary. Leaving the school compound, she took a taxi to the main market. There she spent one third of her salary on foodstuffs, the second third on herself, and some of the rest on baby things. She bought herself two maternity dresses, some underwear, a pair of shoes and a handbag to match, and a long-sleeved shirt for her husband. The assertion of her individuality by going on a spending spree made her feel on top of the world, but underneath the elation was the fear of the consequences when she got home. She felt like one condemned to death but allowed to satisfy some of her desires before meeting her fate.

●

Iba arrived home late. With the help of her twelve-year-old niece, Ginika, who lived with her, she unpacked the food and put it into the store next to the kitchen. Theirs was a comfortable three-bedroom flat on the top floor of a two-storey block.

Walking into the sitting-room, Iba looked at the clock on the wall opposite the dining table, a wedding present from her husband's town union in Enugu.

'Three-thirty already,' she said and sank into one of the deep brown armchairs. She was hungry, tired and apprehensive.

'Have you had lunch, Ginika?' she asked her niece.

'No, Auntie,' answered the girl. 'I was worried because you were a long time coming home.'

'I'm back now, so no need to worry any more. Make us some *garri* as quickly as possible, and remember to warm the soup. My stomach has been rumbling for the past hour.'

'Auntie, I forgot to tell you that Master telephoned.'

'When?' enquired Iba, a little startled.

'A few minutes before you came back.'

'What did he say?'

'He wondered why you were late coming home and said I should tell you he'll be home around six.'

Iba heaved a sigh of relief. That would give her time enough to eat and rest and get ready for the bombshell. Before her husband left for work that morning, he had wondered aloud why her salary was overdue and she had informed him that the headmistress was ill and had been away from school for a few days but she might be in school that day to pay the salaries.

'Hurry up with the lunch, Ginika,' Iba said to her niece. 'I'm tired and I need some rest before Master gets back.'

Left alone in the sitting-room, Iba began to think over her planned course of action. First, she saw her spending spree as reckless and began to blame herself for not really considering the consequences of such an action before embarking on it. In the same breath she praised herself for her new-found courage in asserting her freedom.

Her husband's action over her salary had never ceased to baffle her. After all, he could do without her entire pay packet as he earned a good salary himself and didn't seem to have overburdening extended-family responsibilities. Outsiders who knew him would never believe that he was capable of lifting a finger against his wife; in fact, in his office he was seen as a perfect gentleman – civilised, suave, courteous and kind. On the few occasions she had gone to his office to see him, some of his colleagues, male and female alike, had told her how lucky she was to have such a perfect gentleman for a husband.

She had taken all these compliments with pretended glee, for how could she tell them what lay behind Bertrand's gentle façade? Once she had toyed with the idea of spilling the beans, of telling some of his friends what a brute Bertrand was, for to her any man who beat his wife was no better than a brute. However, something she could not explain held her back.

Bertrand arrived home after six. Over his meal, he asked Iba why she was late coming home.

'I stopped at the market,' she explained.

'For what?'

'We needed some food.'

'I'll be going to the village tomorrow,' Bertrand said.

'Why?'

'Your father will be wondering what is holding me up. Besides, there is an important meeting of my kindred tomorrow.'

'Is Father ill?' Iba asked. Her father was a retired railway worker. He had a good pension. Her mother had a stall in the village market where she sold provisions.

'No, not to my knowledge,' replied Bertrand, 'but since I'll be going to the village, I don't see why I can't call on him.'

'But you've just said he'll be wondering why you've not come to see him. I don't understand.'

'Nothing to understand,' Bertrand said and continued with his meal.

Iba waited for her husband to ask her if she had eventually received her salary that day. The period of waiting for the storm to erupt was torture to her and she wished the ordeal would happen as quickly as possible. What made the situation worse for her was her inability to predict what her husband's reaction would be.

After his meal, Bertrand went to the bedroom to pack a small suitcase for the following day's trip to the village. Iba watched him expectantly for a moment and then went back to the sitting-room.

Presently Bertrand called to her from the bedroom. She shuddered. She could guess what her husband wanted her for. She walked into the bedroom and said faintly:

'Yes, B?'

'Where's the money?' asked Bertrand.

Iba feigned ignorance. 'What money?'

'Your salary, of course. What other money?'

She wanted to tell a lie; to tell him that she had not received it; that the H. M. was still ill and could not come to school. But that would be postponing the confrontation. The sooner the punishment was meted out on her the better, she thought. Now that she had done what she wanted to do with her salary, she was ready for any lashing. No price was too high to pay for freedom, she told herself.

'I said, where's the money?' Bertrand repeated when Iba remained silent. His lower lip jutted out a little.

Iba said slowly, 'I've spent it.'

'Eh! What did you say?'

'I said I've spent it.'

'You've done what?'

'Spent it.' She was gathering more courage.

'You're crazy. I want the money this moment.'

'I can't give what I've spent. When you spend money, it doesn't come back to you, does it?'

'Look here, woman, I've not got time for jokes. Let me have the money at once. And don't provoke me.'

Iba said, 'Honestly, B, I've spent the money buying some food, a few baby things, and one or two items for myself. I even bought a shirt for you.'

Bertrand walked over to her and slapped her three times on the right cheek. Sparks of fire flashed from her eyes and her cheeks burned with intense heat. Something inside her told her to hit back. But what was the use: it had not helped matters before as he was much stronger than she was. 'I must not hit back, I must not hit back,' she kept saying under her breath to steel herself.

Then she heard herself saying calmly to Bertrand: 'You're a gentleman, B. A perfect gentleman.'

Bertrand appeared to be jolted by the words but soon recovered. 'I said, where's the money?' he repeated, and he hit Iba on the mouth.

She tasted blood, rubbed her lower lip with the back of her hand and looked at it. Her hand was smeared with blood. She wanted to go to the bathroom to spit it out, but Bertrand stopped her.

'You're not leaving this room until you've given me the money,' he said and began to beat her indiscriminately.

Iba refused to hit back. She merely protected her face with her arms like a poor boxer and kept on muttering, 'You're a fine gentleman. Your friends will be very proud of you when they hear this.'

Bertrand abruptly stopped beating her. Just then the doorbell rang.

'I'll answer it,' Iba said. 'Ginika has gone to fetch water.'

'No, I'll go,' Bertrand declared and stalked out of the room.

Iba called after him: 'You don't want anyone to know that you beat your wife. I won't hide the fact any longer.'

The doorbell rang again. A little while later, Iba heard Bertrand turn the latch. The front door squeaked. Shortly after, Iba heard Maka's voice.

'Hello, Gentleman B. Long time no see.' Maka was Bertrand's best friend and best man at their wedding.

She stood near the bedroom door and eavesdropped.

'My car's been letting me down,' Bertrand said in excuse.

'How's Iba?' Maka enquired.

'Fine. I think she's sleeping. Please sit down. A beer?'

Iba walked silently into the sitting-room. She was pressing a folded white handkerchief against her lower lip. When Bertrand saw her, he froze.

Maka stood up. 'Have I woken you up, Iba?' he asked gently.

Bertrand looked at her with a plea in his eyes. She wanted to tell

Maka everything – that Bertrand was not the fine gentleman everybody thought him to be. But again, much to her surprise something within her held her back. Instead, she said:

'No, you didn't wake me. I was already up before you rang the bell.' Her speech was slightly distorted because of her swollen lower lip. She walked up to Maka and stretched out her hand to him.

Maka took her hand and then looked at her. 'Good gracious, what's wrong with your lip, Iba?' he asked. Then he added good-naturedly, 'If I didn't know B as a fine gentleman I'd have thought he'd just given you a good beating.'

Again Iba thought of speaking the truth. She looked at Bertrand and noticed how uncomfortable he was in his chair. Their eyes met – again there was an urgent plea in his eyes.

Iba said, 'You know B can't hurt a fly. How could such a ridiculous idea get into your head, Maka? I bumped into the bathroom door.' She noticed Bertrand looking at her. There was gratitude in his eyes, gratitude tinged with nervousness.

'Have you treated your lip?' Maka asked in sympathy.

'Not yet,' replied Iba. 'Just applied a cold compress to reduce the swelling. But I'll apply G. V. later.'

'Better do so now to ward off infection,' Maka advised.

'I'll take her to the chemist later,' Bertrand said at last.

Maka rose from his chair. 'I think I'll take my leave now to allow you to go to the chemist right away.'

'You're not leaving, Maka, until you've had a beer,' Bertrand told his friend.

Maka was insistent. 'Oh, no, Gentleman B. Not today. Take Iba to the chemist straight away.'

Iba added to her husband's plea, 'My treatment can wait while you have your beer, Maka.'

'No, Iba,' Maka insisted, 'that'll not be fair to you. I'll call again tomorrow, perhaps.'

Bertrand saw Maka to his car parked in front of the block of flats. When he came back to the flat, Iba was still in the sitting-room, pressing the wet handkerchief on her lip. Bertrand went and sat on the arm of her chair.

After a moment, he said, 'I'm very grateful to you, Iba, for saving my reputation. I don't deserve that after what I've done to you.'

Iba remained silent. She was still wondering why she had behaved the way she did. Bertrand did not deserve the popularity he enjoyed among his friends who should have been made to know the man behind the mask he presented to them. She bit her lip for letting such an opportunity slip through her fingers. Her lip hurt, reminding her of her wound.

'I am very sorry, Iba,' Bertrand said. As she remained silent, he went on: 'I vowed not to tell you what I do with your salary because I wanted to save you some embarrassment. But I can't keep the secret from you any longer. I know it will hurt you to know the truth, but at least it will make you understand me better.'

Iba turned slowly and looked at him with some curiosity but said nothing.

Bertrand continued: 'Your father secretly made me promise to give him your salary every month for three years in spite of the huge sum he took from me as your bride price.'

'My father!' cried Iba, 'no, not him. He would not do such a cruel thing. Not my father!'

'You can find out from him if I'm telling a lie against him,' Bertrand persisted. 'I've been sending your salary to him every month since we married. The allowance I give you and the housekeeping money come from my own salary. I'm still paying back what I borrowed for our wedding, so I can't afford to send your father the equivalent of your salary from my own. I'm sorry I've been taking all this out on you, Iba.'

'I'll go to the village with you tomorrow,' Iba said with determination. 'If you're right, it will explain, but not excuse your brutality to me for which you may have to pay another bride price – this time, to me – to restore the *status quo ante bellum*.'

He gave her a peck on the cheek as if a tacit agreement had been reached between them.

ZAYNAB ALKALI

Saltless Ash

Betadam, a small quiet village in a far northern part of Nigeria, was neatly tucked away among hilly mountains and isolated from the rest of the world. The village of Betadam was once ruled by a powerful and conservative alien clan called the Turabe. Due to their strict adherence to Islamic religious doctrines, the Betadam inhabitants referred to them as a people who 'make mosques of their graves'. The Turabe however did not remain powerful. By the beginning of the twentieth century, petty rivalries and disloyalties among brothers undermined the power of the clan. They fought among themselves until the clan disintegrated, leaving only a handful of people.

The remnants of the Turabe clan, although relatively insignificant by the middle of the twentieth century, remained an arrogant race. They resorted to marrying among themselves to regenerate the power of the clan.

Young Amsa, a descendant of the Turabe clan, was well informed about her heritage. Elders took pains to educate the young people about the once-powerful clan, while in the privacy of their homes, those who were not clan members whispered to their children the reasons for the collapse of the once arrogant dynasty.

Amsa knew that one day the head of the Turabe clan would marry her to a young Turabe man, possibly her own cousin. She was well prepared, as any free-born Betadam woman should be, to shoulder her responsibilities. After all, a woman was born to please a man. She was however ill prepared for the fate that awaited her. At thirteen her father gave his promise to the head of the Turabe clan – Hassan. Amsa was young and had dreams of spending her life with someone young and single, not Hassan. The man was almost as old as her own father.

Amsa sought refuge in her mother, but was told firmly that her father alone knew what was best for her. Wasn't Amsa's own mother married to an older man whose wife had died leaving him with eleven children? Didn't her mother accept her fate without question? Amsa had to accept her fate. Men always knew what was right and 'a child that disobeys her father is cursed'.

At fourteen she became second wife to the head of the Turabe clan, an enviable position to many Turabe women. At thirty, she had borne him eight children, and as our people would say 'had her foot squarely placed on the man's neck'. She was small and slim, with a dark complexion and a crown of luxuriant hair, like tall grass by the bank of a stream. Amsa was softly spoken and not given to expressing her opinions freely, but her ways were quick and calculating, alert and cunning. Often she got her own way through matrimonial diplomacy and could wriggle out of tight situations leaving Yabutu, the senior wife, in deep water. While Amsa, being in complete seclusion, was given to manipulative strategies like an old politician, Yabutu, twenty years her senior was given to hard work. She had kicked aside all conventions in order to acquire economic independence. In different ways, the two women devised methods with which to fight for their rights as people, and none of the methods went down well with the old man.

One day Hassan decided that he needed a change in his matrimonial home. Yabutu was almost fifty and had long ceased to be attractive, with her coarse farmer's hands and feet. It was hard to believe that over 30 years ago she was the village beauty, 'Magira', and had held the position for over five years. Now the tall, good-looking, graceful gazelle of a woman was hunched up and gaunt. She had become morbidly strange and quiet like flowing water under a rocky surface.

As for young Amsa, she was either pregnant or nursing a baby. She had what our people would call 'the stomach of the pumpkin'. Soon Hassan was constructing extra rooms, longer and wider verandahs, giving the entire compound a new look. The women watched anxiously, unable to ask questions, but knowing Hassan had either stumbled on to some fortune or was contemplating marriage. In the past when he had wanted a wife, the two had united against him and had thwarted his plans. This time he confided in no one, until the issue of constructing a new kitchen cropped up. How was he to construct a new kitchen without betraying his intentions? An idea occurred to him. He would inform them about the need to build a new kitchen, as the old one was dilapidated. Unfortunately the excuse did not impress the women, so they set out to investigate Hassan's activities.

Amsa, alert as usual, got wind of their husband's plans. Quick as a flash she sought out her co-wife.

'Ya,' she called as she stepped into the older woman's room, 'the old man is at it again. The village is ablaze with news of his marriage.'

'Marriage? The village certainly thrives on gossip. Hassan cannot marry.'

'Ya, it's true, my brother told me so.'

'Amsa, put your mind at rest. How can he marry at a time like this, when money is scarce and the children are always hungry? He can't do this to us.'

'He has certainly done it to us this time. I heard the marriage is only two markets away.'

'Then the man has truly lost his head. His brain has turned to ashes. Look, pretend you haven't heard anything. Leave everything to me. A man who at seventy thinks he is but twenty needs to be hospitalised.'

Amsa crept into her own room, certain that Yabutu would literally fight out the issue. That was her way, too blunt to discuss things. That night she dutifully dished out the evening meal. She filled her husband's bowl as usual, shaped and reshaped the mound until it looked attractive. When she was satisfied the mound was shapely, she turned her attention to the soup bowl. More than half of the chunks of meat went into the master's bowl. It was her night to care for their husband. She made sure she kept him happy.

The following night, a day after the secret consultation, Yabutu's turn came. For weeks, Hassan had hardly paid attention to his wives as he was besotted with the thought of the new one. Something in Amsa's behaviour the previous night, however, kept him on the alert. He knew his wives like the back of his hand. When Amsa became flirtatious, she had something serious up her sleeve and was only biding time. As for Yabutu, she was ungraciousness personified. She had once been blessed with a beautiful physique, but had always been devoid of reason. Hassan always knew exactly where he stood with her.

He approached Yabutu's bedroom with cautious suspicion. Amsa waited in her room expectantly. If she knew her co-wife well, the proverbial day-of-reckoning had come. As thoughts passed through her mind, sleep threatened to overcome her. Just as she was giving in to a sound slumber, a bang followed by a shrill cry jerked her up. Amsa sneaked out quietly onto her verandah as the cry turned into screams. Usually nobody interferes in a midnight squabble, but she knew the cause and feared possible injury. At one point, she ran towards her co-wife's room, but remained rooted by the door, unable to knock as the terrible commotion went on. She sat and waited patiently, hoping sanity would prevail.

Then suddenly the screams died down. Almost immediately heavy footsteps, as if someone was staggering under some awful weight, followed. A muffled urgent protest, then a heavy thud-thud, preceded by a deep-throated groan and a barrage of curses – then – silence. Amsa crept quietly behind Yabutu's bedroom. The moon was treacherously bright. Under the window was an ungracious heap, unable to move a limb. She took one quick look and disappeared into her bedroom.

The next day was exceptionally quiet. An uneasy calm settled over the household. Hassan had not left his bedroom since morning. Towards evening he sent for his younger wife. It was still Yabutu's night, but she had to obey the master of the house. By the entrance to the inner gate, Yabutu watched her co-wife as she entered their husband's room. She roared with laughter. Hassan sat like a chief on a reclining chair, his feet resting on a footstool. He did not move even when the opening and closing of the door announced his wife's presence. His mouth was tightly drawn, his brows knitted. He was sulking. The master of the house and head of the Turabe clan sat like a small boy and sulked. He wanted to be taken care of by his younger wife. She protested. It wasn't yet her turn to cook; how could she infringe on Yabutu's right of ownership for the day?

'Can't a man tell his wife what to do without argument?' he thundered. 'Tell me, who is the master in this house?'

He stared at her with bloodshot eyes that could hardly open for the swelling. Amsa's insides rippled with laughter which she dared not express. The head of the Turabe clan asked who the master of his house was! 'Let him ask himself that question, foolish old man,' she said to herself.

A few minutes later, she emerged holding an expensive bottle of perfume. She smiled mischievously all the way to her room, making no attempt to conceal the precious gift. It might just wipe out that stupid laughter from Yabutu's lips.

A week later, when the women thought they had succeeded in stopping the silly marriage preparations, a neighbour turned up at Amsa's door. It was late in the evening.

'Mama Huseina, what good fortune brings you out at a time like this?'

'Lower your voice, my friend. The good fortune is yours. Don't prevent me from telling you the good news,' she cautioned.

'I am eager to hear what you have to say. For months you have not honoured me with a visit,' Amsa continued obviously nervous, as Mama Huseina was notorious for her gossiping.

Mama Huseina laughed, clapping her thighs to stress the importance of her mission. She sat on a stool close to her friend and looked her in the eyes intently. Amsa's expectations heightened. Her heart missed a beat.

'Listen my friend,' the woman began in earnest, 'nothing could have brought me out this late but for this very saucy story. How many ears have you, Amsa?'

'I am all ears,' her appetite for a little gossip had been whetted.

'Then lend them to me.'

'You have them all! Just get on with your saucy story. I can't wait to hear it.'

Mama Huseina smiled smugly and moved her stool even closer to Amsa. 'It is about your co-wife,' she said and Amsa tensed.

'What about her?'

The woman lowered her voice to a secretive whisper. 'She is in terrible trouble with her husband.'

She waited for an appreciative response, but got none.

'I am not aware of any trouble in this household,' Amsa replied icily.

'How foolish could you be? Your husband quarrels with your co-wife under your nose and you, without batting an eyelid, say you are unaware of it. You can't even use it to your advantage.'

'How?'

'Well, we shall not go into that. After all we are not young girls unschooled in the ways of the world, so I shall get on to the story itself. You see, yesterday Yabutu's father received a messenger from your husband.'

'Is that so?'

'Yes, it is so. I am surprised that your husband doesn't confide in you, being the favourite.'

'What was the message?'

'This is the message:

My in-law, I salute you. You should send men from your household to come and collect the camel of a wife with an elephant trunk.

The woman story-teller burst out in a fit of laughter, holding her sides and peering quickly through the partially closed door to see if anybody was within earshot. But Amsa's face showed controlled anger at the boldness of the woman.

'And what was our father's reply?'

'You mean . . .?' the woman faltered, blinking tears of laughter from her eyes.

'Yes, Yabutu's father, our father.' The reply had a heavy tinge of hostility.

The woman felt deflated at her friend's manner, but continued as the juicy story was not yet over.

'"Well," he said, "go and tell that diminutive imbecile Hassan that when he was marrying the camel, did he not notice the elephant trunk?"'

Again the woman collapsed with laughter and Amsa sprung to her feet.

'My friend, I heard your story. You have brought insults right to our doorstep, but our customs prevent me from repaying you here. Now get up and go! But as you go, don't think you have heard the last of this affair, for I'll not forget this. I'll find an occasion to repay you generously.'

'I am sorry, sister, I brought the corpse to the wrong house. Forgive my foolishness.' She then got up and fled, her tail between her legs, like a chicken that has fallen into a pool of diarrhoea.

Immediately she left, Amsa collapsed on her bed, clutching her sides with hilarious laughter. 'Men are foolish, empty idiots. A camel of a wife with an elephant trunk! Well Hassan, what happened to your village beauty of yesterday?' It was said years ago that he married Yabutu, the village beauty, to compliment his diminutive stature. And what trouble the woman gave him!

'Yabutu's father has the right answer,' she laughed with tears in her eyes. As for her, she would listen to anything. Whatever direction the wind blew, she would not lose. After all wasn't she the mistress of the house, a mother of eight?

Her laughter, however, was short lived. That same night Hassan visited her. It was her turn to cook, but it seemed he had come with a different mission. He cleared his throat several times as a way of introducing an important issue.

'Amsa,' he called authoritatively.

'Yes, my master, royal son of the Turabe,' she lowered her voice flirtatiously. He did not respond to her coquettishness as he usually did.

'Yabutu is going back to her people,' he announced bluntly. She showed no surprise. With her head bowed as if in submission, she asked why her co-wife had to leave.

'Nothing – she needs to rest.'

'To rest?' her voice was surprisingly bold. 'From what?'

'I do not expect questions from a daughter of the Turabe,' he retorted. There followed an uneasy silence, then he announced the much expected news.

'I am bringing into the house the daughter of the Imam.' He pushed his cap forward to rest on his forehead like a young man in the prime of youth. There followed another uneasy silence. He shuffled his feet restlessly. Amsa's reaction was not what he had expected.

'Daughter of the Turabe, the girl will be a great help to you,' he continued cautiously this time.

'You say, she is the daughter of the Imam?' she raised her eyes slowly to meet his.

'Yes, what is wrong with the daughter of the Imam?' He was defensive, his eyes were turning red, angling for a quarrel.

'Nothing.' Amsa was quick to sense her husband's mood. 'Nothing, my husband, except that Ya' is leaving for a mere child, age-mate of your grandchild, but then you are the man, master of the house and head of the Turabe clan.' She took a deep breath. 'A man must always be right, so do exactly as you wish, royal son of the Turabe, but accept a simple word of advice from me. While you are at it, marry the daughter of the Ladan as well.'

'Marry the daughter of the Ladan?' Hassan asked, frowning. 'Why?'

'Why? Simple: if Yabutu left, so would I,' she answered, looking boldly into her husband's eyes.

He sprung to his feet as if he had been stung by a queen bee. 'Who do you think you are, eh?' he trembled with anger. His fingers itched to land on her face.

'All right, you go!' he ordered with some show of dignity which wasn't much as his entire little frame shook. 'By noon tomorrow, all of you should vacate this house,' he flung his arms up in agitation. 'Carry everything that you own, including your children. Don't leave a single broom behind. Then I will think seriously about your suggestion.'

He turned abruptly and stomped out of the room, more like a spoilt child than an enraged adult. Once more that day, Amsa had a good laugh.

The ultimatum of course fell flat. The proposed marriage never got through. The people of Betadam accused the two women of dominating the old man by practising witchcraft. What did the two women think?

Yabutu was heard to have said at the market place that she feared no third wife. She was simply fighting for justice. How fair was it for their thoughtless old husband to take up a new wife at a time when there was hardly enough food in the house to go round? The only rivals she feared were poor health and poverty and those she swore to fight with all she had got.

And Amsa's reaction? Foolish, saltless ash[1]. Let him, if he was a man, bring in that bride-child and call her a wife. His own children would drive her into an asylum.

[1] The residue left after a distilling process in which all by-products are used and only the saltless ash remains.

ORLANDA AMARILIS

Disillusion

She pulls the door shut and goes down the stairs cheerfully. Her neighbours already know her by her quick, nervous step. One floor, a landing, she turns right and right again, now she's flying on in a hurry.

'Good morning. How are you?'

The breadman moves out of the way to let her pass. How good fresh bread smells! The aroma rises through the cloth. Only the wickers of the basket can be seen. Another landing, she turns right and right again and the steps fly under her low-heeled shoes.

She reaches the street in four steps and breathes in the foggy morning's cold air.

With a smile she crosses and walks a short way up the sidewalk on the other side of the street.

'Good morning. How are you?'

The lady in the light-coloured coat is at the trolley shop. The lady in the light-coloured coat frowns and she colours her hair.

The tired, faded-yellow street-car approaches noisily and lazily. 'Clang, clang,' laughs the modestly dressed street-car.

'Excuse me.'

The line is endless and the street-car rumbles off with a bellyful of passengers.

The hairdresser's apprentice raises her eyes from the book she's always reading. The little woman with the straw handbag pushes. She's in a hurry.

'Good morning. How are you?'

A smile blossoms on the clerk-typist's pale cheeks. She smiles and wrinkles the corners of her eyes. The clerk-typist dresses well. An imitation of dressing well. Everything is impeccable, without a spot or wrinkle. The clerk-typist does not use a girdle. Hidden by her coat – not a winter nor a summer coat – the well-rounded shapes of a tired woman in her thirties remain unknown.

Always the same faces every morning. Always the same ones. But they have nothing in common with anything she left behind her, with anything in the rootless life she has been leading ever since she abandoned her studies. Ever since that sunny but greatly uncertain and painful day when she wondered how she could continue to see the world with others' eyes . . . She had thought about going back. Her godmother had strongly advised her to do so. No. She could not. To have to adapt herself again, to start all over from the beginning . . . As if such a thing were possible. Go back for what? To vegetate behind the blinds of a city going nowhere and peer out at the women bringing water from Madeiral in cans on their heads or the men dragging carts loaded with sacks to the Morais warehouse?

No, no, forever, no.

With delight she had begun a new life in a foreign business establishment. No sewing, no written summons, no reluctantly prepared lessons. All she had to do was look neat and speak a little French and English.

Everything went well for a while. But she eventually quit. She stupidly quit for no apparent reason. The workmates with whom she would have coffee after lunch seemed like real comrades. Some times they would eat together at a little place near the Rua da Conceição. With them she had even learned a new vocabulary because of permanent contact with the public, a vocabulary which was new and exciting because of its newness and the flavour they could feel in it.

It is true. She, the young woman who knew where she was going, eventually got tired. She got tired of them all: of the boss, of her workmates, of the customers themselves, even though different ones were always coming in. She had turned her back on her job just when she was getting used to the life of taking orders. Getting used to things is one way of putting it. She preferred not having to do anything more than talk to this person or that, to laugh with some good friends. She never learned to look the sly customers in the eye, and they would undress her with their looks of desire. When that happened, she would blush and tremble. She did not know where to turn.

Why would she tremble? And shivers would run through her. No doubt deep inside herself she felt flattered. And if she were to show herself as she really was? Nothing bad could come of it. One time, a nice enough young man tried to make a date with her. He was saying such nice things. And why shouldn't she have gone to the movies with the fellow from work she was having a beer with at the sidewalk café? He was a fresh one. The encounter had gone nowhere. A person cannot be blamed for the way she is. What was too bad was that people do not understand the open way she and other women from her country deal with people. The result is a series of unfortunate misunderstandings which wind up putting them in a bad light. At least that is the way it has been with her. She would go from one bad time to another.

For these and other reasons and in spite of the front she tries to keep up, she is well aware of this. Her life from that point on has been a constant slide. It is as if there were a banana peel stuck to the soles of her shoes. She can guess the ending. She will wind up falling down with no one to help her to her feet.

A string of menial jobs has been her lot for all these years. So many she has lost count.

She gets off the street-car in a hurry. She crosses the square not without turning her head to protect herself against the wind. A strong north-east wind with frequent heavy gusts.

So many people behind me!

She runs and pants a little. The train is coming into the station. She cannot afford to miss it. She cannot. Who could put up with her boss? Put up with the same talk every day?

She is soaked with perspiration. She musters up one last burst of speed.

Finally. She barely made it.

'Good morning. How are you?'

Tired. Out of breath, she leans on the door, which opens only when the train pulls into a station.

But this is an express. It rolls on and whistles through the stations where it does not stop today or any other day.

She looks for a place to sit down. The other passengers look at her indifferently. The thin gentleman up front is buried in his morning newspaper.

The thin man turns the page and she behind him. Standing, she manages to read the main headlines.

'The Alvalade match was a real stunner.' Photographs. Blow-ups of last night's heroes.

Maybe she too was a heroine, an everyday heroine in this round of time-measured stages she could not escape.

She glances at the smuggled watch hidden under her sweater cuff. Everything is going well, as it does every day.

The door opens. Cais do Sodré station. Pushed along by the other passengers, she crosses the station. A sure-footed automaton. She reaches the glass exit door and goes down the steps.

'Good morning. How are you?'

She has not lived long on the route and she already knows so many people.

She quickly crosses the street and continues on nonchalantly. She bunches the scarf up closer to her nose and tosses the end over her shoulder.

By the mooring lines at dockside, the river breaks up in the green book of the cables which secure the bridge to the bank where the waters smell like mud.

The little boat of the thousand and one nights spits out a clump of people and swallows up another to take to the other side.

'Good morning. How are you?'

The lady in the fur coat makes herself comfortable on the wooden bench.

Oh, the fog! Oh, the fog!

She has to pay her godmother a visit. She has not been there for a long time. And she would have to tell everything down to the smallest detail. To rummage around in that pile of happenings. To tell so that nothing could now be changed.

The teacher wearing blue gloves is still standing and peering into the dense fog.

The same one on all those morning runs, she wraps her checkered coat more tightly around herself.

She fixes her eyes on the caulking between the boards.

The boat groans at its sides and moves forward deliberately into the fog.

In a little while, with one more stretch, it will be another stage, another run to the overbearing office on the large square filthy with papers and dry leaves.

'Good morning. How are you?'

The driver will lift his hand to the peak of his cap and he will sit down ready to start off.

She smooths out the coarse, loose, black strands of her handkerchief.

Where could he be? Her mind insistently probes forgotten memories.

It had been the girl at the tobacco shop who had warned her. She had already guessed and had dismissed the notion with distaste. The good-for-nothing. The girl at the tobacco shop had called him Bufo. Bufo was married. That was it. She had hooked up with a married man and even worse, with Bufo. It is enough to make a person laugh. If she could only wipe from her face the feel of his caresses. He would run his hand along her cheek and look deeply into her eyes waiting for something or other. The bastard. She still wondered what it was he wanted.

She calmly rolls the ticket between her fingers. The boat groans and rocks a bit. The teacher in the blue coat and the blue gloves presses her forehead against the window. She is afraid! She is afraid of the fog! And the boat of the thousand and one nights slips slowly through the dense fog bank.

She turns her head away from the man with the black hat. He looks at her insistently. It is not the first time. A widower? A married man? A wrinkle forms between her pencilled eyebrows.

No matter how bad things are, there is no way she can think about starting over again. There is no way.

And secretly her eyes seek out the eyes of the man with the black hat. Now with interest he inspects the legs of the skinny little bimbo sitting in the rear, toward the right side.

A smile spreads on everyone's face. The long-faced man stands up and holds onto his briefcase. The travelling salesman with the Jewish nose takes two steps toward the stairs. Finally. We have arrived. They have arrived.

They have arrived at their port in the storm. The fishmongers below are insistent chatterboxes.

She slips through the people in the crowd, a strange solitary figure in her checkered coat.

The man with the black hat is next to her. She can tell by the scent she recognises in those encounters. A whisper puts her on guard.

'You all right, man?'

'You sly devil, you are going after a mulatto.'

They laugh softly, and that laughter is an affront. 'Good morning. How are you?'

She goes down the stairs trembling, paying attention to each step on the way. She always avoids being seen with her dark-skinned countrymen so people will not think she is one of them and after all it turns out to be a white man who reminds her she is dark skinned.

Oh, Lord! She is a wandering Gypsy, with no friends, no affection, lost among so many familiar faces.

Translated by Gregory McNab

AMINATA MAÏGA KA

New Life at Tandia

Rokhaya was settled in her new comfortable life. Everything was a source of astonishment for her. Getting up early in the morning, the drudgery of coming and going for water, were things of the past. Now all she had to do was to make a gesture to have water flow at her command. All you had to do was light a wick underneath that white appliance to make it purr, and it gave out cool water, and kept the food from spoiling.

Illumination by means of a wood fire was pushed far back in her maze of memories. Several kerosene lamps lit up the house at night. A cook-boy did all the kitchen work and housework, while a neighbour came in twice a week to wash and iron the laundry. Rokhaya had nothing to do but to take it easy, braid her hair, tint her hands and feet with henna, and sleep.

'You are lucky to have such a husband and all this comfort. You are the only girl from our village to have married so well. Double your efforts to make your husband happy by attending to the very least of his needs.'

This was Aunt Aïsse's final recommendation before leaving her niece, after a month's stay. Rokhaya, like a good pupil, followed the advice of her relatives. She scarcely caught sight of her husband returning from work than she hurried to take his instrument bag from him. Then she took off his shoes, brought him his sandals and cool water. She served him his meal, cutting up the meat or the fish for him herself, and putting the vegetables within his reach. She sponged off the slightest drop of perspiration from his forehead, and fanned him.

She was completely happy and fulfilled.

At the end of each month Baba Kounta never failed to buy his wife a dress or some shoes. Except for the medical rounds which he made now and then, he always came directly home. Stretched out on a *chaise longue*, he would chat with his wife about everything – or nothing.

Rokhaya couldn't dream of having a stabler or pleasanter home. She was never uneasy, and she never asked her husband any questions. No worry crossed her mind. Her life consisted of submission and the gift of herself exclusively for the happiness of her husband.

The life of the young couple went along smoothly, anchored in this routine.

One day after lunch, Baba Kounta had some news for his wife: his elder brother, Omar Kounta, was coming almost immediately from far off Sudan to pay them a visit.

Rokhaya could not have felt more pleased. Finally she would get to know a relative of her husband, welcome him into her home and show by every little act towards him the love she felt for her husband. That was every good wife's dream: she hadn't just married her man but also his whole family. Her role was to take everything from her in-laws, without faltering.

A married woman is the scapegoat for all family trouble. A sad face while serving a meal, a word more shrill than usual, can earn her rejection or make the whole family gang up against her. Rokhaya undertook the cleaning of the guest room. To drive out the mosquitos and the musty smell, she had incense burned there all day long for several days.

Omar Kounta arrived unexpectedly one evening, guided by a small boy who directed him to the house. The couple had already finished eating. Introductions made and lengthy greetings exchanged, Rokhaya brought a bowl of cool water to her brother-in-law, not forgetting the customary bending of the knee. Then she went into the kitchen to prepare a meal for her guest.

Rising early the next day, she heated some water in a pail which she put in the bathroom for her brother-in-law's use.

About eleven o'clock, Amadou, the cook-boy, came into the court-yard holding a fine ram by the collar. Rokhaya had sent him to buy it in honour of her brother-in-law. All economy measures were set aside because hospitality is sacred, especially when it concerns the in-laws.

More carefully than ever, she supervised the cooking, and after getting washed, dressed, and perfumed she insisted on serving the meal herself.

Her brother-in-law should want for nothing, even the kola nuts which she got him three times a day. Omar Kounta gained weight. He spent nothing. His clothes were always well washed and ironed. He drank cool water, slept on a soft bed; when he was hungry he ate succulent dishes he had never tasted before.

When he came he had planned to stay only a few days. But the good life which he led at his brother's home made him inclined to prolong his stay. When one member of a family is successful, his success is everyone's, and all can benefit from it. Hard field work under a burning sun, a body dripping with sweat, muscles sore from wielding an axe on dead wood – all these were but far-off memories.

Here he took it easy from morning till night, ate and drank his fill, was always cleanly dressed and was spared all exertion. He dug himself more and more into the family, and had his own say on the couple's way of life. Wasn't it his right? He was Baba's older brother and knew how to push his prerogatives to the limit. So it was that he came to think that Baba spoiled his wife too much. Her trunk overflowed with dresses and jewellery: a real waste! And furthermore, he gave her too much money for the market! Doubtless the savings she kept from her housekeeping allowance had been sent away to her own family. What an idea Baba had had – to marry a stranger, who would do nothing but exploit him to enrich her own family! If *he* had known about it, such a marriage – such a misalliance – would never have taken place. He began to show a steadfast and obvious hatred towards Rokhaya. All the efforts she made to please her brother-in-law were in vain. Meals seemed late to him, too cold or too hot. He found much to say about the ironing which, according to him, was botched, and the bedroom, poorly swept. When Rokhaya greeted him in the morning, he was content just to mutter a response.

She was languished visibly. She couldn't sleep. It often happened that she stayed awake all night, wondering what she could have done to her brother-in-law, weeping, softly for fear of waking up her husband. She couldn't talk to him about it – she would then be charged with wanting to divide and rule. She suffered in silence. The more she tried to please Omar, the more rudely he treated her. She resolved to consult a marabout who would give her something to turn her brother-in-law's hatred away and make him better disposed towards her.

For a whole week she furtively poured the potion into her brother-in-law's food. But she could see no change. On the contrary, he seemed to ignore her even more and to get closer to his brother. He advised Baba Kounta on everything; he decided to rule over his younger brother's household as its master. One day, Omar came out of his bedroom like a fury, his tongue hanging out, his eyes full of tears. He had burned himself swallowing a hot mouthful too fast. Harassed by her brother-in-law's nagging about the lateness of the meal, Rokhaya hadn't had time to leave the dish out to cool.

It often happened that Omar Kounta took his meal alone, when his brother was kept late in the afternoon by his patients.

'Mean, nasty woman! You want to make me get out by serving red hot food. You must be made to understand that it's my brother's money! Everything here belongs to *him*, and I have the right to benefit from it. Anyway, it doesn't surprise me that you are so spiteful. Since your marriage two years ago, you have been unable to give him a child. You'll never know maternal love, barren woman that you are.'

Rokhaya was overcome with grief. She collapsed on the floor and wept for a long time. Her little sister helped her up, powerless when confronted with Rokhaya's despair. Realising that her husband would soon come back from work, Rokhaya ran to sponge her eyes. She did manage to show him a serene, pretty face. Baba Kounta was far from suspecting the drama which had taken place in his absence.

The Kountas' neighbour, old Mother Diouldé, had noticed that Rokhaya had lost weight. She had not missed Rokhaya's tired eyes with their dark circles, her fleeting smile. A widow without children, the old woman had found in Rokhaya the daughter she had never had. Rokhaya gave her things to eat, and had her laundry done and pressed by her own laundress.

She felt doubly indebted to Rokhaya for her kindness, and the countless little services she did for her. Mother Diouldé urged Rokhaya to confide in her, swearing she would keep everything absolutely secret. Rokhaya did find relief in telling of her bitterness, of the incomprehensible hatred her brother-in-law had turned upon her, and above all her uneasiness at not having conceived a child after two years of marriage.

What a crime it is not to bear a child! The fault is automatically imputed to the woman! Sterility is unacceptable and shameful. True death consists of leaving no image of oneself in this life. The punishment which follows for the woman is, in many cases, rejection or the likelihood of seeing a rival wife added to the household. Then if that wife conceives she will be overwhelmed with attention, coddled, praised to the skies by her husband and his family. But the 'barren' woman will find herself relegated to second place, abandoned by all, submitted to the vindictiveness and the name-calling of her rival, of her in-laws, of her husband. Is not the greatest calamity for an African woman that of bearing no children? And so all the ills of the world could be read in Rokhaya's eyes.

Mother Diouldé, nonetheless, had acquired a solid reputation in the art of dealing with sterility. Rokhaya could see young women lining up all day long at the old woman's home. Rokhaya had suspected her of withholding some knowledge, without supposing for a moment that it was precisely what she needed to know most. Didn't they say that Mother Diouldé's own barrenness was due to a pact she had made with the *djinns*? In exchange for the knowledge which they had given her, she could never give birth to a child.

The old woman reassured Rokhaya, and told her of hundreds of cases that she had treated successfully. Taking advantage of the absence of Baba Kounta and his brother, Mother Diouldé examined Rokhaya. With her knobbly fingers she touched the lower belly of the young woman, pressing upon the ovaries. Three times she threw the cowrie shells in a basket. She diagnosed the trouble from their position.

'Your husband's *djinn* is very jealous. He is the one who is preventing you from conceiving. In order to become pregnant, you must kill a red cock. You will prepare the meat from it on a Monday and give it in charity to some children. Next you will make a donation of two red kola nuts to a pregnant woman. I will give you a powder. You will soak it to a pulp which you will take on three successive days. Then we shall see the results,' added Mother Diouldé, laughing.

For his part, Baba Kounta made his wife undergo an appropriate gynaecological treatment. Which of the two methods worked? Who knows? Nevertheless, the fact remains that Rokhaya did not have her period the following month.

Translated by Charlotte H. Bruner

EASTERN

AFRICA

EASTERN AFRICA

Women writing in English in Eastern Africa came to European and American attention later than those of West Africa, although their works were published locally as early as the sixties. Less concerned with themes of polygamy and the colonial overlay of beliefs and values, Kenyan writers, for example, had stressed the anguish of being dispossessed of their ancestral land, and the mysterious, magical powers of evil, inflicted not just from the outsider but also from hidden enemies within.

Charity Waciuma, in *A Daughter of Mumbi* (1969), expresses the need to stay close to the traditional abode of her ancestors, even while accepting Christian ways and modern medicine. The titles of Grace Ogot's early works, *Land Without Thunder* (1968) and *The Promised Land* (1966), show preoccupation with the land, the earth, the legacy of a way of life and the traditional values tied to grazing and agricultural production. The latter novel also treats the subject of malevolent witchcraft: the curse of a Tanzanian terroriser neighbour ultimately drives farmers, settlers from Kenya, to return to their homeland. Grace Ogot's tales of the macabre, Bessie Head's fictional accounts of witchcraft's power to cause disorientation and mental breakdown, Ananda Devi's haunting spirits of the dead – all depict the force of the supernatural in common belief.

Leaving the land, migration, alienation, also provide an important focus for some Eastern African literature. With the independence of the new nations and the ensuing problems of corrupt home rule, the conflicting leaderships of tribal groups, many peasants have moved off the land, voluntarily, or have been forcibly driven away. Many have crossed national boundaries. Idi Amin's reign of terror in Uganda and the subsequent devastation and unrest still causes large migrations of Ugandans into Kenya. South African refugees sought refuge from the suppressions of apartheid, and often used border countries as bases for guerrilla forces who could cross the border south to attack. Drought has starved out many Sudanese, who have moved, often vainly, to distant refugee camps in search of food to survive. Outsider-backed civil wars between tribal factions have caused devastation of the land and massacres of the innocent, as Lina Magaia discovered in Mozambique.

So the movements of peoples has become a common thread in the writings of many East African women. Violet Dias Lannoy moved from Kenya to Goa to India to Paris, only to return to Kenya for the setting of many of her school stories. Hazel Mugot moved from Kenya back to her home in the Seychelles. Ananda Devi moved from Mauritius to Paris, writing in French of her East Indian origins. Kenyan scholar Micere Githae Mugo has lectured abroad and now lives in Zimbabwe. Daisy Kabagarama of Uganda and Evelyn Awuor Ayoda of Kenya are presently located in the American Midwest.

Some writers are returning, not to their land, but to their own local languages for fictional expression. Grace Ogot's latest works include a book of short stories and two novels in Luo. She urges others to write in their local languages. Martha Mvungi of Tanzania wrote a novel in Swahili. Tanzanian Penina Muhando has written nine Swahili plays. Caroline Ntseliseng Khaketla has written plays in Sesotho and some poetry in English. Some dramatists use local languages to bring local problems directly to the attention of the people. Mugo has produced plays performed by travelling troupes who use either Swahili or Kikuyu. These plays often emphasise the contribution women make to political and social change.

It is not only African women who have crossed national boundaries. Others from abroad have come to settle in Africa and to *become* Africans. Majorie Oludhe Macgoye[1] now identifies herself as a Kenyan poet and novelist. A Briton, she did not come to Kenya until after receiving her MA at the University of London. Working in Kenya as a missionary bookseller, she met and married Oludhe Macgoye and became a Kenyan citizen in 1964. Her prize-winning novel, *Coming to Birth* (1986), portrays a Luo woman's life as she lives through the growth of the new Kenyan nation from 1956 to 1978. 'I am so much enmeshed in my Luo family and community that I am not ashamed of writing from within it,' she says. Bessie Head left South Africa and

[1] Marjorie Macgoye's comment comes from a letter to C.H.B.

marvelled at the strange 'Woman from America' (see page 110) whom she met in her Botswanan village of Serowe.

So, distant as Eastern Africa may be from the Americas, its people and ideas filter through across the ocean and across the vast African continent itself. Despite geographical, cultural and language barriers, little by little we are establishing contact with some of the women there who give us a fictional portrayal of their lives and their backgrounds.

AWUOR AYODA

Workday

In the darkness of a cold five o'clock morning, Mary stirred in her bed and threw off the blanket with which she covered herself. She folded it up carefully and placed it on the chair by her side. She rolled up the mattress she had been sleeping on with the bottom sheet still inside. This she placed against the wall. She went into the bathroom and filled the tub a third full. She washed quickly, methodically, staring at the wall in front of her. When she had finished, she put on her dress – one of the two she owned. The other was for special occasions. She made her way up the narrow staircase to the children's room.

In the two metal-framed bunk beds, the children slept soundly. She shook them awake gently in order not to disturb their mother who slept in the bedroom across the narrow corridor that ran along the top of the house. They blinked vaguely at her and Otieno immediately rolled over and went back to sleep. She took Awino's hand and carried Akong'o back into the bathroom where she began getting them ready for school.

'Otieno, what are you still doing in bed? Okwach, get up! Where is that girl Mary? Mary!'

'Yes!' Mary called from the bathroom.

'Don't shout at me! When I call you, you come to where I am. Get these children into the bath! When do you think I will get them to school? Can't you, for one day, do things properly? Move!' Elizabeth shouted, giving Mary a push in the back.

Mary went back downstairs with the other two children and when the four were washed she led them back upstairs, thinking that she must not forget to mop up the bathroom later. She helped them dress: oiling them all over, fetching their clothes, putting on their shoes, brushing their hair. Then she made her way into the kitchen where she put on the eggs to cook, placed slices of bread under the grill, set the water boiling for tea. She laid the table – six places.

'Where are the children?' asked Elizabeth, coming down the stairs. 'Mary, fetch the children. Or are you waiting for me to do it? What are you doing standing there? Can't you hear me?'

'Leave her alone,' said Peter as he came into the room. 'You start shouting at her first thing in the morning, waking everyone up, and you continue until you leave. If you didn't go to work, she *would* be deaf.'

'Peter, the only thing you have to say to me is to tell me what you were doing until two o'clock this morning. You don't really live in this house. You are not a husband to me and even less a father to these children! You don't know where the money for food comes from, so don't interfere! Mary, get out of here! I'm not talking to you. Peter, if you could find the time to show some interest in your own . . .'

'Shut up!' snapped Peter. 'Don't question me as if you were the man in this house.'

'You see what I mean,' Elizabeth answered evenly. 'We can't talk to each other even when you start the argument. You know very well that I know about that woman – the reason why you never get home before midnight these days. Why do you come home at all? Why don't you just go and screw her until you get it out of your system? Why don't you . . .' A resounding slap on the side of her face silenced her.

'I said shut up and don't speak like a whore in my house. Akong'o, what are you doing standing there? Sit down and eat your breakfast. Elizabeth get the breakfast.'

Elizabeth looked at him hard for a moment, thought better of continuing, and walked into the kitchen where the smell of burning toast greeted her.

'Mary! For God's sake, can't you ever do anything right? Where are you?'

As Mary appeared Elizabeth threw at her the dish-towel she was using to remove the grill of burnt toast. 'You stupid village girl! You burn everything! Throw this mess away.'

Mary did so, while Elizabeth put the rest of the breakfast on the table.

'I just can't teach her how to do things right! And I hate bread in the morning.' No one answered as she sat down. Mary put on a fresh kettle of water to boil for tea.

'You'll have to take all the children in today,' Peter said as they finished. 'I have an early appointment and I'll be late if I take Otieno and Awino.'

'I can't,' Elizabeth shot back, 'I have already been late every day this week because you have this or you have that. When I lose my job, will you find the money for this household? This morning if you don't take them then they miss school.'

'Right. Then they have to miss school,' answered Peter as he made for the door. 'I'll see you tonight.'

'See you tonight indeed! See me tomorrow morning more like it.' The door had already slammed behind him.

'OK. Everybody hurry up. We're late! Mary! What are your bed things still doing in the sitting-room? Take them away! Quickly! What if someone were to walk in and see *that*? Have you no shame? Stand still while I'm talking to you. Cook the chicken and sukuma wiki for lunch. Make sure it's ready when we get back this time. Burn all the rubbish in the back this morning. Here's the money for milk. And when you go out, lock all the doors. And buy some bread as well. Will you children get outside? Mary! I said take your bed things out of here!' With that she was gone.

When they had driven off, Mary sat down in a chair and sighed. Her face relaxed as she settled down to enjoy the quiet. She was young, maybe about 15, but she wasn't sure. Her parents had never known the date of her birth. They didn't attach much importance to such things. Mary often missed them and looked forward to the two-week holiday which Elizabeth would let her have when she could do without her. Elizabeth! To Mary she seemed quite mad. She had worked here five months now and Elizabeth no longer made her cry. As long as she sent 300 shillings a month home to Mary's parents, this was where Mary would stay. Mary knew how badly her parents needed that money. She had eight brothers and sisters, all younger than her, at home and they had to be fed. Mary knew that her mother worked harder than she did. This helped her get through the day.

She roused herself, put away her bedclothes, she washed the bath and bathroom floor and she washed the breakfast dishes. She cleaned the bedrooms – making the beds and sweeping the floor. She made herself a cup of tea, cut a slice of bread and went out into the back yard to sit in the sun with her breakfast.

'Oh my, oh my! What a sweet thing do I see in that garden! A lovely, fresh, sweet thing that makes my blood boil! Oh, sweetie, give me just a little look.' It was Mwangi who worked next door. Mary never knew whether he was serious or just trying to make her laugh. But she was certain that he did not make *her* blood boil.

'Go your way Mwangi. I have too much work to do to talk to you.'

'Too much work . . .? But then what are you doing sitting in the sun? You only have four children to look after. I have seven. How can you have too much work?'

'There are two of you that work there and one of me here.'

'Then let me come over there and help you, so we can make time for some enjoyment. You have so much to learn about Nairobi. You just don't know it. If I teach you some things, no one will call you a country fool again.'

'Just go away! I know all the things I need to know. Elizabeth teaches me.'

'Then we are not talking of the same things,' he sighed, and went away laughing.

She went back inside the house and collected the children's school clothes from the previous day. These she washed in the bath. When she had put them all out on the clothes-line, she locked all the doors, making double sure, and headed for the kiosk at the end of the road. Although she gave the third house down from them a wide berth when passing, the dog still chased her on the way there and back. As she turned into the gate she heard Mwangi say:

'You see. I could teach you how to kick that dog in the mouth.'

She ignored him and went into the house to prepare lunch. When she heard Elizabeth's car draw up in the drive, she looked up quickly at the big kitchen clock and cursed because she had only just begun to cook the ugali. She had never got used to the idea of watching the clock while she worked. The time always caught her unawares.

'But how do you make food cook quicker than it does?' she thought to herself. At home they always ate when the food was ready.

'Will you children stop fighting!' she heard Elizabeth shout from the car. She had the two youngest with her who only attended a half day of pre-school. 'Why do you behave like animals? Be quiet!' The children continued to fight. She hit Akong'o across the back. 'Listen to me when I talk! Stop that noise and get out of here!'

'Nooo!' he screamed at her and jumping out of the car ran yelling around the house.

'Why don't you ever just do as you are told?' she shouted following him, and then stopped. 'Mary! Mary? I told you to burn this rubbish. What is it still doing here?'

'I haven't had time, Mama.'

'Haven't had time? Do you realise that the children can get cholera from this mess? Will you take them to hospital if that happens? Will you? I don't just talk for the good of hearing myself speak, Mary. I talk when I have a reason. If this rubbish is *still* here when I get back this evening there will be real trouble.'

'Yes, Mama,' she replied looking contrite.

'And what is that smell? What is burning?' She pushed past Mary, in through the kitchen door. 'Oh, no! Oh, Mary! How can you burn ugali? That is the most basic thing to cook! Why do these things happen to me? Don't just stand there! Take it off the cooker.'

She walked into the dining-room, stood there for a moment before coming back slowly into the kitchen. She looked at Mary for a long time before she said softly:

'Mary, do you know that I work? I work very hard. And I don't like it. When I was young, I thought that when I got married I would stay at home, clean my house, look after my children, and make my husband happy. But, I can't do that. Because the cost of everything is so high now that I have grown up. My husband drinks all his money. So I know that I have to go on working for the rest of my life. I don't even like my boss. He shouts at me. He insults me. But what can I do? I can't leave, because jobs are hard to find. Where would I get another job? Do you understand what I am saying, Mary?'

'Yes, Mama, I do,' Mary answered, guardedly, from where she stood washing out the pan.

'So you do just what I wanted to do. You can stay at home just to look after children, cook and do the housework.' Elizabeth's voice rose. 'So why is the table not laid? Why do I have to come home from all that and set my own stupid table, when I am paying you good money to do just that? Why don't you do your work?'

'I will finish this and . . .'

'And by then, I will have done it so that you can get away with as little work as possible. All right, Madam. Let me do this for you. You just do the cooking as though that is all you were employed to do, and let me get on with this work here.' She yanked the cupboard door open and began to drop plates on to a tray. One went crashing down to the ground.

'Now look what you've made me do!' She picked up a large piece, looked at it in agony, and flung it down again. 'Do you know how much plates cost? If you had set the table, this would never have happened! Why do you make me do these things?'

'I'm sorry,' Mary said. 'Let me set the table.'

'And by the time you have finished, I will be late for work again! Clean up this mess.' She went out of the kitchen and Mary heard her go upstairs. When Mary called ten minutes later to say lunch was ready, Elizabeth called down to just feed the children. She left again for work without having eaten. Mary felt tired when she looked at the mess the children had made.

'OK. Let me take you to bed now,' she said taking Okwach's hand.

'No, I don't want to sleep,' he grumbled.

'You have to sleep. Your mother says you must sleep in the afternoon, so you have to sleep,' she insisted tugging at his hand.

'Then I'll sleep here.'

'No, you won't. You'll sleep upstairs in bed!' His hand slipped free and he picked up a cup and threw it at her, hitting her in the stomach. He ran outside laughing. She caught up with him just outside the kitchen door.

'You will do as I say!' she said, slapping him. She stopped, looked at him in surprise as he started crying and then she sat on the kitchen step.

'What am I doing?' she asked herself softly. She picked him up, although he tried to hit her, and said, 'You can sleep in the sitting-room. You can sleep anywhere you like.'

'No, I want to sleep in the bedroom.' She took both children wearily up to bed and waited until they were asleep. She made her way back into the back yard and burnt the rubbish, washed the lunch dishes, dried them and put them away. She finished cleaning the dining-room and the sitting-room before the children woke up. She washed their faces, dressed them up again, locked the house and took them out for a walk to the city park a kilometre away. She enjoyed the park because the other ayahs were always ready for a chat while they watched the children play.

'Here's a tired one,' Priscilla said as she came up. 'But you do get tired. Children are very active.'

'Their parents can be quite tiring, too. You can never do anything right,' Mary said as she sat down.

'Humph, the parents! The women are the worst. The one I work for even gives me her underwear to wash. And I see her bringing those men home when it's time for the children's walk. So shameless!'

'The men are no better,' Mary answered.

'But they are men, and we can't compete with them. Women have a special place in the family. If they don't look after it, there can be no home. You are just young. In a few years' time you will know that all men are the same. Even the one you marry. But you will know how to look after a home.'

'That is true,' Mary said, thinking that she didn't want to get married, or to have to look after a home.

They were back home just before five. Mary let the children watch television, set the table and began to prepare tea. When Elizabeth arrived with the other two children, Mary was putting the tea and milk on the table.

'Switch the television off and come for your tea,' Elizabeth said to the younger children. 'Mary, why do you let them watch TV at this time? I always tell you they can watch it between six and seven. At no other time unless I say so.'

'Yes, Mama.'

'Now, make sure they all have a bath. I have to go out. If anyone rings, make sure you take a message. Just heat up the rest of lunch for dinner, add some sausages and make chapatis.'

'Oh, good!' Otieno shouted. 'Chapatis! Chapatis!' The other children took up the refrain. Elizabeth walked out with a look of relief on her face.

Between the nervy, tired children and the cooking, the first two chapatis were burnt. Mary decided to cook rice instead. She started bathing the children and putting on their pyjamas. It was not until Elizabeth walked in that she remembered first the unset table and then the rice. Her mind reeled and she lent against the wall.

'Oh, no!' she heard. 'Oh, no, no! This is impossible. Where is that girl? Where are you?'

She walked slowly down the stairs.

'So what do you want me to do? You want me to cook supper by myself? I talk to you! I talk and talk and talk and you don't hear me! And what is this? Rice? Rice? I say chapati, you cook rice? Do you think this is your own house just because you sit in here all day doing nothing?' She flung the contents of the pan on the floor. 'Do you know how much that costs? You can't even buy a packet of rice from your salary, but you think you can burn a whole pan of mine. Get out!' she shouted grabbing hold of Mary and grappling with her out of the door. 'Get out! Get out!' She slammed the door behind Mary.

Mary sat on the kitchen step, tears ran down her face and her skin burned from Elizabeth's hands, and from anger. Inside the house, Elizabeth stood there. Tears ran down her face too. She felt ashamed and she wondered what they would eat for dinner. As she filled a pan with water for ugali, she decided Mary could spend the night outside for humiliating her like this.

'They are all like that,' Mwangi's voice came softly over the hedge. 'It's no reason to cry. She just lost her temper.' The sobs continued.

'Look, you can come over and sleep in my room if she doesn't let you in later.'

'You think of only one thing,' Mary snapped. 'I don't want you! Just leave me alone.'

'No,' he replied.'I just want to help. It gets cold at night, and you are too young for this.' Her sobs increased. 'You can come now if you like.'

'No, I have to stay.' She rose and walked to the front of the house to get away from him. His kindness was stifling her.

When Peter came home at three o'clock in the morning, he found her sitting on the front step, shivering.

'What are you doing here?' he asked. 'Oh, don't tell me! That woman is mad. Come on. Come inside.' Because she didn't move, he put his arms around her and helped her up.

'You are cold,' he said gently rubbing her shoulders. 'Come on. Come inside and get to bed.' She leant against him and it felt good. Once inside the house, he said, 'You go to sleep now.' And went upstairs.

She looked after him for a long time, loving him. 'He is a good man,' she thought. 'If it wasn't for her, he would be happy.'

She went to the cupboard and pulled out her mattress and blanket.

VIOLET DIAS LANNOY

The Story of Jesus – according to Mokuba, the beloved tribesman

Of course Mr Simpson was deceiving them; this was not the usual essay lesson. They all knew the Big Christian was coming from Nairobi to visit the school, and, as the junior prefect told them in the dorm, 'The good students who don't talk after lights out will be chosen for baptism; and you all know what it means to become a Christian.' Yes, they all knew, and there wasn't a single student in Standard VIII who didn't aspire to become a Christian. It was more important than passing examinations at the end of the school year. If you failed one year you could always repeat – that is, if you were a Christian. The senior boys said that the missionaries didn't even tell your father if you failed examinations, for fear he might take you away from school and bring you up in the reserve as a pagan. The head missionary caned you himself for failing, and he was so strong, the senior students said, that after one of those canings you couldn't sit down for two whole weeks; some students even started bleeding down their legs like shameless girls. But John Mokuba wasn't afraid of the head mission-ary's caning; he could endure that, so long as he knew he would be able to go on to secondary school.

The class started opening desks and taking out notebooks. Some students brought out the Bible.

'No, no, put away those Bibles,' Mr Simpson waved angrily at the lucky boys. 'This is an essay lesson, not copywriting. You're to write what's in your head, and there should be plenty in it by now, after all the Bible lessons you've had. That is, if you are indeed the chosen ones.'

John smiled conspiratorially at no one in particular. So it was true they were to be chosen for the Big Christian. Some students said he was a bishop, but the head prefect said he was the Chief Missionary in Nairobi, and the head ought to know. What did it matter? So long as he was the Christian Elder and would choose students for free schooling in the secondary. The head prefect told them once that some baptised ones were even chosen to go to University in Kampala, and even to England sometimes. They would come back big men, just like the musungus.

'This is *your* story of Jesus, not the Bible version,' Mr Simpson explained.

'Question, Sir!' It was Moses Nyairo holding his hand up. He always asked questions, even when there was nothing more to explain. 'You mean, Sir, just as there is the story of Jesus according to St Mark and Luke and John, so now we must write our story also, Sir?'

The class laughed, but Mr Simpson looked angry at the interruption. 'You'd better get on with your work. You're expected to write an essay, not another lengthy Gospel.'

Some Form III students said the Big Christian is an Abaluhyia from Kakamega, and when he became a big man he was sent to Nairobi; now he was coming to the school to choose only students from Kakamega, so his people would become powerful. But that couldn't be true; how could an African become the Big Christian? They only become S1 teachers in the missionary schools, and even then they have to take their orders from those musungu missionaries who are only P1. That's because they never completed their Form VI and so could not go to University in Kampala. Even Mr Otsyula who also comes from Kakamega and has been to Makerere for two years is only a junior teacher and is never given the upper forms.

John looked pensively at the essay title on the BB: *The Story of Jesus, as I know it* – according to John Mokuba, he added to himself. That was a clever idea, to have chosen John for his school name. The head missionary had seemed very pleased with his explanation – 'because that's the name of the beloved tribesman of Jesus' – patting him on the shoulder and saying, 'that's the idea, love is the most important Christian concept of all; you've chosen well, in taking the name John.'

Jesus was a great elder. He was loved by all his tribesmen because he knew all the rules of his tribe and he followed them all. When he was six years old he refused to stay with the women and went with the men in his father's cottage. There were no boys of his age group in his father's compound, so he had to sit in a corner where the elders gathered. They noticed him there and asked him questions and he answered all their questions correctly and made his father proud of him. And all the elders said he was a true son of his father. When his mother came to take him away from the elders he said to her: 'Woman, don't you know I am a man? I must learn my father's business. Why do you come after me as if I am still a child?' And his own mother remained quiet and had great respect for him, because he passed the test she gave him: out of his own will he chose to go with the men, even though they were elders, instead of playing with the children and the women. After that, he always went out with his father, to work in the shop sawing wood and to look after his father's sheep and lambs. And like a strong man, he waited until he was thirty years old to have his initiation.

John bit his lower lip hard, his face flushed with the memory of his own initiation. His father had been very angry with him because he wouldn't wait until his time. This is what happens when we send our sons to those musungu schools; they forget the ways of their own people, he'd said. Of course he knew the ways of his own people, but how could he make his father understand the ways of the students of other tribes? His father had never been to school and had never lived with foreign tribesmen. He was already in Standard VII and even some boys from the lower standards used to call him morane, and when they were having their shower the other students would call out to him, 'John, you should face the wall, then we will forget that you're not a child.' All the others used to laugh, 'We don't need to see his thing, we can see from his ways that he's a morane, no amount of studies can make him a grown-up like us!' He could have beaten up all those students single-handed, but even then they'd never respect him. How could he face life in secondary school without being circumcised? 'Those missionaries make you afraid to face the circumciser's knife at the right age; have they told you to go to the hospital for the operation?' – his father had taunted him. He'd tried to explain to his father that a student would never tell the missionaries that he'd gone to be circumcised; the missionaries would call him primitive and pagan and would stop paying his school fees; that's why they had to get it done during the holidays. Times have changed, and once in school you're already grown up, there's no point in waiting for the traditional age. Some had even gone to the circumciser when they were ten; and they thought he was afraid and so avoided going to the circumciser by pretending that he was traditional minded and was waiting to be older. As a student in Standard VII of Primary School of course he had the right to decide for himself when he would be initiated; he didn't need his father's permission, but all the same his father's words stung him whenever he remembered his own ceremony. Though he hadn't even blinked when the knife cut him for manhood and the tree bark didn't stir on his head, even then his father wouldn't give him credit. 'At your age what can you feel?' And they hadn't yet performed his coming-out ceremony; they said they hadn't the money for buying the millet for brewing the beer.

But of course Jesus had never been to school. Because there were no schools in his time, so there were no holidays also, and so the missionaries would not punish him for reporting to school late. So he could afford to wait for the right season to go into the forest. He could also arrange to live for forty days in the forest on the mountain, according to his tradition, just like going to Mt Elgon.

'Question, Sir!'

Everyone in the class looked up and waited for Anthony Matinde to speak up. He was already a Christian; his father had had the sense to send him to the missionaries for baptism when he was only twelve years old in Standard VI, so he didn't have to worry about the essay.

'Can we write *anything* we know about Jesus? I mean, even if it's not in the Bible, like there are some things we understand but the Apostles never put it that way.'

'Look at the title on the BB. It says *The Story of Jesus as I know it.* What really matters is what *you* understand about Jesus' life. If all I'd wanted was the version of the Apostles, I'd have looked it up in the Bible myself.' Mr Simpson was in a bad mood, he didn't like taking orders from the Big Christian; as a musungu teacher he felt he should give all the orders himself.

So all his father's friends and relatives and elders gathered in his father's compound and the women brewed the beer. When the beer in the cottage where the elders of his father's age group were gathered was running low, Jesus' mother came with other women bearing six jars of hot water and poured it into the large beer pot which was standing in the centre, so the elders who were sitting round it and singing praise songs went on sipping the beer through the reeds during the whole night, and everyone was happy, singing songs praising Jesus' ancestors and the elders of his tribe, and they also laughed and made jokes about the women and told Jesus he must not behave like a girl because now he was going to become a man.

Before the sun had time to rise the next morning, the revered elder St John the Baptist, who belonged to Jesus' father's age group, held Jesus by the hand and led him to the river, and all the other tribesmen who were called Christians ran together with them, but Jesus' father remained in the cottage, as is the custom with the tribe. The Christians held their hands together as they ran, and they all began to sing the 'Song of the River' When they got to the river, St John took Jesus to the holy spot which the elders had chosen the previous evening, and began to splash the cold water all over his body, and then threw the wet mud at him, while he told Jesus how to behave when the cutting would be done, and all this time the tribesmen Christians went on singing the 'Song of the River.'

John Mokuba couldn't bear it any more. His hands started trembling, and his whole body took up the trembling. The '*Song of the River*' kept on coming over him, the words all round him, he couldn't think of anything else to write, they went on singing it to him. Even now, a whole year later, he couldn't bear to think of the '*Song of the River.*' His grandmother had told him that Peter Massienyia from the neighbouring location used to get fits whenever he heard it at a ceremony, though he was already a married man with more than three children; that's why he never joined the morning procession to the river. John used to laugh at the story, how could a man be afraid of a song? But that's just how he felt about it now. He could only think of the all-night dancing and singing and clapping the bells all the time until his hands and feet became like machines, going round and round in circles with the singing group. And running to the river early at dawn, held tight by the two men on either side. The washing in the cold water of the river, with the mud all over him like a new garment, and running back to the compound so fast that by the time he got to the stool for the cutting he could feel nothing; he was so tired and dazed that he couldn't even make out what was happening. But the Song remained imprinted in his mind. No, he couldn't go over it, not even for the Story of Jesus. Even Jesus never wrote it in his Gospels; his hand must have trembled too.

After his initiation ceremony was over, and the coming out and all that, Jesus moved around only with his age mates, according to custom. Each one of them

came to join Jesus after his own ceremony was over, which was at a ripe age;
some were twenty-four years old, and some even older than thirty. They all
observed their traditional custom and they were given the age-set name of
Apostle.

Maybe his father was right. These Christian missionaries knew all
about their initiation custom from the story of Jesus, but they wanted
the African students to have their ceremony earlier so that they would
not become powerful like Jesus and the other Apostles. Then they
would have to make an African their bishop, like the Big Christian
who was coming to the school and could even order the musungu
teachers what essays they should give to the class, and the way they
chose the school prefects from amongst the circumcised ones only. It
must have been the missionaries who set the boys to tease him in the
shower rooms when he was still in Standard VII and only fourteen
years old; just as his father said, they make you weak like a woman.

The thirteen Apostles moved around together all the time, just like brothers.
Though they played sex with women, they didn't get married even though Mary
Magdalen tried to seduce Jesus to marry her, just like these girls always try to
catch a man and oblige him to marry them, but Jesus and the Apostles knew
their custom and so they knew they had to fight for their people first, just like
warriors who must prove themselves in battle before they can come back to their
location and get their first wife. But at that time the country of Jesus was ruled
by the Romans who were just like the British so the Apostles were not permitted
to become warriors to prove their manhood, so they had to prove themselves by
serving the people.

It was his grandfather who'd explained to him how a man must prove
himself according to the chances which are given to him. As a child he
used to love to listen to his grandfather's stories about the warriors of
their clan who went out and fought the enemy tribes and brought back
their cattle and women, and only when they proved themselves in
battle were they allowed to come back to settle in the reserve and get
married and raise children, so that when the enemy came and even the
white soldiers with their guns, their people fought them off because
they'd kept up with their traditional customs and so remained strong
and knew how to fight even the most powerful army in the world. He
had announced to his grandfather that he too would become a great

warrior, but his grandfather had shaken his head sadly and told him that he couldn't become a warrior any more, because the musungus wouldn't let him fight and become strong but would catch him and put him in jail and there he would rot like an old woman. His grandfather saw the tears flow down his cheeks, and put an arm round his shoulders and explained to him calmly that there were other ways of becoming a warrior without holding a spear in his hand for all to see. A man had to learn the ways of his enemies and fight them in a way that he would win and not be caught and become a slave. It was his grandfather who first gave him the idea of joining school, even though he'd never mentioned the word school. Learn their ways, learn their language, learn to speak and write and live like them; they will never guess that you are all the time learning to become powerful like them in order to fight them and take their place one day. Our best warriors were those who walked and talked with the enemy from the other side of the border. So when he'd announced to his family that he wanted to go to school, his grandfather was the only person who did not attack him. The others accused of him of wanting to leave his own location and their traditional ways, of wanting to become like the musungu missionaries. His grandfather had looked at him for a long time and then he'd said calmly, I thought you wanted to become a warrior. And he'd replied proudly, yes, grandfather, I *am* becoming a warrior, but you taught me that it is not necessary for a warrior to hold a spear in his hand for all to see; when the time comes I'll bring out the gun and fight the enemy and chase him away and then with my school certificate I'll get a good job and bring wealth to all our people. The others had to let him go to join school, even his own father, for he'd obtained his grandfather's blessing.

Jesus dressed just like the Romans in long gowns which they called togas, and learnt to speak the musungu language, so they all thought he was one of them and permitted him to walk freely with his Apostles wherever he wanted to go. He wasn't shut in his own reserve, like the other people of his tribe who had to show a pass whenever they wanted to go out of their reserve. But Jesus was always careful, he never let the enemy see his ways. When he spoke in public to the people who gathered round him, he spoke in parables and riddles, so that the outsiders thought he was telling funny stories to the children. He never betrayed the secrets of his tribe which were hidden in those parables.

This too he'd learnt from his grandfather who used to amuse him as a child with riddles and sayings of the ancestors. It was only at the time of his initiation that his grandfather revealed to him the meaning of those sayings, but with the warning that he should never reveal them to a stranger, or he would be dead to the tribe. So when he heard the parables from the Bible, John had understood that these were the secrets of Jesus' tribe and he never asked the teacher for explanations. The other boys also had learnt all the parables and sayings by heart, because they all were trying to become Christians, but they didn't try to discover the secret hidden in them, for they knew that such things can never be revealed. And when the teacher would ask, Do you understand? they all nodded. The teachers also knew that they should never try to discover the inside meaning which must remain secret from strangers.

But even though he dressed and talked just like a Roman musungu, Jesus kept to the ways of his tribe. When his friends and relatives gathered round him he always gave them something to eat and drink.

John remembered with bitterness the time he'd gone to visit his cousin Peter Sielley in Kericho. Peter was dressed up as a musungu, with jacket and tie and polished shoes although he was only the cook's boy at the Tea Hotel. He'd even addressed John in Swahili, as if he were a stranger. When evening came, Peter kept on looking at his wristwatch, saying all the time, it's getting late, you'll miss your bus, we'd better hurry, I don't want you to miss your bus back to school. I must hurry back to the kitchen, Peter kept on saying, I have no time, when I'm free I'll send you word. As if he were a stranger and could come only on invitation. He himself hadn't learnt yet that when the men go to town they forget that they are all brothers and they must share everything alike; they remember only to look at their watches, like slaves looking up at their masters.

Even when they had very little to eat the Apostles shared it with their friends and relatives who came to visit them. One day they had only five fried fish and five loaves of bread, and some friends had come to visit them from the reserve. When lunchtime came Jesus took the basket with the fried fish and bread and said to his friends, that's all we have for lunch but let's all eat it together. He passed the basket round and each one took a bite and felt satisfied because he was sharing the food of his own friends. Jesus never looked at his watch to send his friends away. He was not a slave of time.

But Jesus was cunning with his enemies, even when they came from his own location. One day a man asked him: 'Master, shall we pay taxes to the Roman Government?' This man wanted to trap Jesus, because he knew Jesus would tell him not to give money to the musungus but to keep it for their own people, and then this man would report Jesus to the Government. But Jesus was not a fool, he knew the man's tricks. He answered calmly: 'Give to your king what belongs to your king, and to your God what belongs to your God.' He was careful never to use the word tribesman, or ancestor. He spoke like a musungu himself.

He'd learnt all about this story only recently from Alfred Onyonka, the senior prefect. Alfred told them how when he was in Form III they'd all fooled Mr Clarke, the senior English teacher. Mr Clarke was young and very friendly with all the students, and behaved just like one of them; he would never call them 'boys' like the other teachers sometimes did, as if they were just like 'houseboys'. He always addressed them as 'students' even if they were in Primary School. He used to speak in class about the coming of Uhuru, and of their own rights in their own country, and of how the English were exploiting them. Though he was a musungu himself, he said he'd come as a true Christian missionary and that it was his duty to work for their own good; Jesus himself preached that, but the missionaries forgot the teachings of Jesus and began treating them as natives, not as friends. But the students in Form IV were not so excited about Mr Clarke as the Form III students were: be careful, they warned, they're all the same; when the time comes he'll side with his own people. Not long after Mr Clarke said to them in class: let's discuss the role of Jomo Kenyatta, he's a great leader, he has fought to free you from colonialism, but he has gone about it by reviving backward customs like blood-drinking and witchcraft. What do you think of it all? No one answered; they remained silent as if they didn't know what he was talking about. But Mr Clarke had persisted. So Alfred stood up – he was always good at school debate – and said, Sir, we read of these things in the newspapers; they say such things happen in Kikuyuland, but how can we know about them? We're locked up here in the Friendship School with our books and our examinations. He never told a lie, but he also didn't speak the truth, just like Jesus with the taxman. But Mr Clarke had gone on and on: surely you admire the great Kenyatta, he's the greatest leader you've got and soon, when you get Uhuru, he'll become Kenya's first president. No one answered. After the discussion, when the time came to give the essay title for Prep, Mr Clarke wrote down on the B.B.: *The Leader I admire most.* They discussed the assignment with Form IV students; they all agreed they should choose an African to show this Mr Clarke that they were proud of their own people as leaders. So they all wrote about the Rev. Peter Habwe who used to come to the Friendship all the way from Kaimosi to preach at Sunday sermon at the school chapel once a month, and then all the English teachers would go to Kericho for Sunday service so they didn't have to receive communion from a black man and they didn't have to sit there quietly and listen to a black man tell them what to do to save their own white souls. But it was the headmaster himself who had asked the Rev. Peter Habwe to come and preach Sunday sermon because when he knew that Jomo Kenyatta was released from jail he got frightened and thought that if they had an African preacher, then an African president would let them keep their jobs and their big houses and cars; and that headmaster was right, because even though Jomo Kenyatta has become president of all Kenya, they have all kept their jobs and their houses. In the end it was the Form IV prefects who wrote the essay for the Form III students and they all copied it. And when Mr Clarke saw that they all wrote about the African preacher, whom he had never heard preaching because he also went to Kericho for Sunday service with the others, he couldn't say anything to them because he knew he was defeated in his plot, and that the Form III had behaved just like Jesus when he was asked questions by his enemies who called themselves his friends.

One day Mr Clarke came to the senior dorm after Prep, as he sometimes used to do to show that he was their 'friend'. He noticed the newspaper photograph on the wall over Alfred Onyonka's bed. Ah, Jomo Kenyatta himself, so you *do* admire him after all, Mr Clarke said, and so he betrayed that he still remembered the story of the essay. All the students gathered round Alfred's bed, silent, not knowing what to do. But Alfred was ready with his answer. 'He looks exactly like my father. We Africans cannot afford to take photographs of ourselves, so I stuck this one up to remind me of my father.' Everyone knew Alfred's father, even Mr Clarke; he was a native missionary who went around the reserves preaching the Gospel of Jesus. But this was the first time they all saw how much he looked like Mzoe Jomo Kenyatta himself. So they all knew that Alfred was not telling a lie, but they also knew that he wasn't telling the truth, even though he remained honest. That way they got rid of their great friend Mr Clarke, who never came again to the dorm. He also stopped speaking to the students outside class. In the evenings he would take his racket and play tennis with the wife of the maths teacher, who was a very smart musungu woman, though she never spoke to the students.

John Mokuba sat up with a start! it was the bell, and he wasn't even halfway through.

'Sir, we haven't finished, Sir! it's so long, this story of Jesus.'

'Go on, go on writing, you have another period. I forgot to tell you this would be a double period, as it is a rather special essay.'

Again that conspiratorial silence. Some students in the front rows looked round and smiled. There was no doubt about it now, their fate depended on this essay, that's why he was giving them a double; they usually completed the essays at Prep, but the missionaries wanted to make sure there'd be no help from the prefects this time; they wanted to test the students separately.

He must hurry, or he'd never get to the end which was the most important part of all, where he'd show he was a true Christian at heart. He kept his eyes fixed to the page of his notebook, his pen moving along furiously.

When it was time, all the Apostles went marching to their city. All the people came out to receive them, and they cried out, 'Welcome to our President, now we'll be free and we'll rule ourselves, this is the Christian Uhuru.' When the Romans heard this they got frightened, they said to themselves, so now the Christians have a President and they'll throw us out, and where shall we go? Here we have our plantations and our cattle and big houses with gardens and houseboys, we don't want to lose all this. So they decided to get hold of the ringleaders, that's how the musungus always behave; they forget that there's no ringleader, we all work with our age-mates by consensus, we're all responsible for the strike. But they didn't know our tradition, so they thought there must be a ringleader, and so they started working in their deceiving ways and got hold of one Apostle called Judas, promised him a lot of money and a good job in the office and told him to bring Jesus to the police station. Now Judas was a poor man, what could he do? He was supporting his family and paid all the school fees for his younger brothers, he could not say he didn't want the job. He was also working for the good of his tribe by sending all his younger brothers to school so that one day they would also get good jobs in the office and support their own families, instead of staying in the shambas like uneducated people. So Judas said, all right, I'll show you who Jesus is, I'll greet him just like my own brother, and you all will know then who he is; but you must not do him any harm. Judas was an ignorant man; he'd never been to school so he didn't know the ways of the musungu – they can say yes to you today and tomorrow they forget everything.

So Judas went back to his group and all the Apostles gathered together at night in secret for the oathing ceremony. First they killed a goat and roasted it and ate it together like brothers of the same family. Judas also ate the roast meat with bread. Then they drank blood. Then Jesus said, now we've drunk blood together we've become tied to our great fight to free our country from the Romans. Everyone who has drunk this blood must keep the oath to remain together and fight like brothers and if he fails he'll die, because this is a sacred oath and we cannot break it.

Maybe that Mr Clarke was right; Jesus knew the ways of their people and he even took the blood oath like the Mau Mau fighters. Mr Clarke himself said that the missionaries forgot the story of Jesus and stopped behaving like friends of the Africans. But it would be different with the Big Christian; he was himself an African and he knew the story of Jesus, so I mustn't be afraid; I must show that I know the story of Jesus also. Those senior prefects were deceiving us, they are jealous, they don't want us to become Christians and go to Secondary and become important students like them. That's why they keep on telling us to be careful, that we must not speak out what we feel; we must remain silent when they ask us questions. But I won't be fooled by those senior students, I'll speak out and then I'll be chosen to be a prefect also and I'll defeat them in their plot.

Jesus also said to the Apostles, now that you've taken the sacred oath you must go among the people and administer it to them, that they may also share our strength and our power and thus we will gain Uhuru for our country. That's just what Jomo Kenyatta did, he learnt the story of Jesus in England and took the blood oath there and when he came back he administered it to his tribesmen, and even others who are not Kikuyu took it, so now we're strong and now we've got Uhuru, just as Jesus said. But some missionaries forgot that they are Christians and they behaved just like the Romans, and when they heard that some Kikuyus were taking the blood oath they got frightened, they thought, now the Kikuyus have power and will take everything from us, our houses and plantations and big cars, and where can we go and live? So they started shooting the Kikuyus and killed their women and children and burnt their reserves, and so there was the Emergency. They forgot that all are Christians like Jesus.

When Judas drank the blood and heard the oath of loyalty by Jesus, he got confused. Was he betraying his own age-mate? But the Roman musungu promised thay would not harm Jesus. How could anyone accuse him for greeting his own brother? He was a poor man, they'd taken away his shamba during the Emergency and now he had to support his family by going fishing in the lake, just like the Luos who go to Lake Victoria. So if the musungu will give him a job in the office of course he'll take it. He can't let his family die of hunger. But he was still confused, because of the oath, so he started behaving like a mad man. When the Apostles saw this strange behaviour they said among themselves, now the oath is attacking our brother Judas, why is that? Has he been derailed, and now he will bring harm to us? Jesus remained calm and went on looking at Judas with piercing eyes; his face was like a burning spear, his long hair and beard were like on fire. With such power in his eyes he was looking straight into the heart of Judas, and he saw the confusion that was going on there. Poor Judas became so disturbed that he shook all over and left the cottage. Then Jesus said to the Apostles, one of us has been derailed by the enemy, now we must take care for they'll come and do harm to all of us. They held a consensus and decided to disperse; each one would remain in a separate place, so that when the musungu came for them, they would find only one and the others would escape and so would continue fighting for Uhuru. What was the use of everyone getting killed? There must be some elders left to rule the country.

His friends in the reserve didn't understand such things. Each time he went back during the holidays they kept on saying, so now you've joined the musungu, you don't care for your people and our freedom. They don't understand that some must fight and others must remain in school to take the jobs when the musungu have been thrown out of the country. You're learning their ways and their language and when they'll give you a job in the office you'll take it just like a houseboy. They've never been to school and they learn their Bible from native missionaries, so they think Judas is a traitor; they don't understand he had to support his family and send all his younger brothers to school; what could the poor man do?

Jesus took Peter, James, and the beloved tribesman John with him and went to the forest where the olive trees grow, because he wanted to discuss with them their secret plans, so that each one would know what to do and so they would all be responsible together. So that if one Apostle could not come out and speak to the people in one place, then another would come out in another place, and the musungu would become so confused they wouldn't know which one to catch as the ringleader and send him to prison. Just like when we have a school strike, we go and gather in the bush at the back of the school and there hold a consensus and each one of us knows exactly what to do.

But Judas knew the place where they used to meet to hold their consensus. He came to the olive forest whistling as if he was coming all alone and when he saw Jesus, he started greeting him. Now Jesus had seen the derailment in Judas' heart when they'd taken the secret oath, but he thought maybe now he's come back to his age-mates because of the piercing look Jesus had given him, so he greeted Judas the way he would greet his own brother who's come back home after a long absence in the city. Then the soldiers came out from the bush with their guns and started to get hold of him. But one of them said, this man can't be Jesus, he is the man who made all the sick people get cured and brought the dead back to life. He's got secret powers and we cannot arrest him. They were afraid that Jesus would strike them with his power and they would be like dead men. So they stood there with their guns like paralysed men, until their captain turned to Peter and asked him, Do you know this man? Is he Jesus the Christian? Peter remained calm and spoke very quietly, no, I don't know this man, I've never seen him before. The captain asked Peter the same question three times and each time Peter gave the same answer, for he didn't fall into the Romans' trap; they had their plan and the Romans couldn't defeat them. Jesus looked at the Apostle Peter with great pride and respect, for he had kept his oath. He said to Peter in the vernacular, 'When they take me you must build a church and you must become its head.' Then Peter knew he had done the right thing, even though he felt very sad that now he wouldn't be able to see his age-mate again. But he decided there and then that when he would build his church he would arrange to free Jesus from jail, just like our African ministers who were working with the musungu in Nairobi instead of fighting with the Kikuyus, but they succeeded in getting so many leaders out of jail and everyone decided that they also are our great leaders. Then the Roman captain turned to the soldiers and said, what? are you afraid of this man? With your guns his witchcraft can do nothing against you. He was right, when the musungu start firing their guns and burning the cottages in the reserves even the cleverest witch-doctor cannot do anything to stop them. So the soldiers advanced on Jesus and took him away.

The Apostles Peter, James, and John went quietly away into the bush where the musungu couldn't find them for they don't know the ways of the bush. But Judas remained there, his mind quite deranged now, for he saw that the Roman musungu did not keep their word. Like a madman he started to cry out, I've betrayed my brother, they're going to kill him now, I don't want their money, let them keep their job, my family cannot see me now because I brought the blood of a brother on their life. So he took a rope and hung himself from the olive tree. This way he showed that he was an honest man, because he was prepared to pay the fine for the crime he brought on his clan; he didn't waste more time, he released his clan from the dreadful punishment by the ancestors and did a great deed for his whole clan and tribe, and when they came to know of it they began to sing his praise and they called him Saint Judas; and even in our Friendship chapel we sing his praise songs because he set out tribe free from the punishment of a murderer.

Jesus was taken to prison and was given the usual caning, because he was a native. The Roman prisoners like Barabbas weren't caned because they were white and when Barrabbas was taken to court the judge said to the people in court, this man has not committed many crimes because he is a white man, so I must set him free, and all the people in court agreed because they were all musungus. So Barabbas was set free and was sent back to England. Then the judge started asking Jesus many questions, like, where did you administer the oath? Give me the names of all those Christians who took the oath; why are you fighting against our Government? Don't you like the way we are ruling you, and what do you mean by Uhuru? What type of language is that? and so on and so on. Now Jesus had studied the ways of the Roman musungu so he knew how to answer their type of questions just like our Jomo Kenyatta who made all the judges behave like foolish men.

So when the judge heard Jesus answer those questions just like a musungu, he got very frightened and he said to himself, this native man has learnt our ways therefore he has become powerful with his people and soon they will fight against us and throw us out of this country, and where will we·go then? England has lost her power after the war with the Germans and so there are no jobs in our country, so we must *stay here. So the judge told the people in court, this man has drunk blood in secret oath, now I must wash my hands because I don't want that blood to touch me, and I will listen to you to pass sentence on this man. For even the musungus have their consensus just as we Africans have, but they call it democracy. The people in court then all stood up and cried out: kill him, kill this native called Jesus. For they also were afraid to go back to England where the Germans had destroyed all their jobs.*

'Fifteen minutes to go!' Mr Simpson announced. A murmur of protest from the class, but they carried on writing frantically. 'Surely you should be nearing the end by now. Don't hand me a bulky volume like the Bible itself. I shan't have time to go through it all.'

Now the Romans had a very strange way of killing those natives who were criminals, they didn't shoot them with a real gun, they made a man carry a dead tree which they called a cross, all the way to the top of a mountain, there they stuck the man to the tree like he was a snake and thrust a spear into his side to let the blood run out. This was the punishment for taking the secret blood oath. So Jesus carried the cross, and there were other Uhuru fighters also carrying their crosses, and all the Christians came out to see them. The women went up to Jesus and some washed his face because it was so hot and he was perspiring, and others gave him food to eat and beer to drink. The men stood on the road quietly and saw all this, but they knew the Romans were watching them and were ready to trap them and take them also to jail, so who would be left to fight the Romans and rule the country if they also would go to jail? No one should say that this man is brave because he went away to fight and that man is not brave because he stayed back to go to the missionary school.

So when Jesus and the other Uhuru fighters were stuck to the cross on the hill, there were only women weeping round them, all the men were hiding, and his mother was there too, and also that woman Mary Magdalen. Then Jesus said to them, women, why do you weep? I know I'm going to die but

*other of our men have run away and they will go and build many churches
and they will rule all the countries of the Christians and then they will
remember me as their great ancestor who fought for them. I gave the other
Apostles a chance to escape and start their training to become great men and
this way I will be remembered everywhere as the Christian elder who has
now joined our ancestors to keep guard on all our people. So the women
stopped weeping and when Jesus died they took him down from the cross
tree and dressed him with the help of some elders, and they rubbed ghee on
his body so he looked clean and shining. And they said, we must be happy
now because our Jesus has joined the ancestors and he will help us to become
powerful.*

*Then the Apostles came out from their hiding places and went back to their
own locations and started building churches and schools and hospitals in the
name of Jesus and everyone in those locations became very proud of their
elder Jesus. When the other tribes saw this they thought among themselves,
see how the Apostles have worked for the good of the people in their
location, we also must do the same for our locations. So they got together all
the elders and the men and even the women and children in a big barazza
and everyone gave his donation of one shilling minimum and so they built
their own harambee schools and churches and local dispensaries and they all
sang songs of praise to their elders, and therefore each location called out a
different name when they sang the praises of Jesus, that's why there are
songs which the Christians call hymns which sing the praises of Christ,
and Jehovah, and Our Lord, and the Saviour and all other names. For
Jesus taught all his tribesmen and even people from other tribes to call out
the names of their own elders and to praise them and to build schools and
hospitals and churches in our harambee spirit.*

'Time's up!' Mr Simpson called out. 'Start giving up your books, and
better be quick about it or we'll all be late for lunch.'

*So when I think of this story of Jesus I also feel very proud because I also
have got a great ancestor who is my grandfather and now I know that I
must build a church and a school and afterwards a hospital for all the
Christians to come to these places and sing the praise of my grandfather.
Other men also respect their grandfathers but they never speak about their
greatness; these men are selfish and primitive, because they've never been to
a missionary school. But I have learnt the ways of the Christians and I*

know that I must become like the beloved tribesman, that's why I've chosen for my school name John, so it is my duty to go to secondary school and then to University and maybe also to England, and when I come back I will help the people in my location. Then they will sing songs in my praise and they'll say see, what a great man John Mokuba is, because he learnt how to become a Christian and in this way to help his people.

Banging of desks, rustling of notebooks, shuffling feet hurrying past. Subdued whispers echoing through the doorway. But John kept on writing.

That's why I go to chapel service every morning in school and when they all start calling out the name of Jesus, I call out the name of my grandfather, for this is the true story of Jesus; he wanted everyone to remember his own ancestor, but all these students in our school go on repeating the name of Jesus like parrots, because they think that Jesus has only got one name, and they've forgotten the names of their own ancestors.

'Come on, come on.' John felt the notebook being snatched from under his pen as Mr Simpson's voice boomed over him.

'Sir, I haven't finished!'

'Not finished! What are you up to? Reaching for the kingdom of heaven itself? Remember the baptismal font is only the first step; leave some energy for the rest.'

John followed Mr Simpson's voice as it trailed behind him through the classroom door. The kingdom of heaven itself! So even that would come to him, now that he'd been chosen by the Big Christian.

The Rich Heritage

Kemigisa's grandfather, Muntu, was a man who commanded a lot of respect. Many people believed that Muntu's family communicated face-to-face with God. They were respected by the local priests and church elders. Makune also admired her future family for their skill in business and their love of education. Keeping in mind that Muntu's father, Byensi had been born in the late 1880s, it was quite an achievement for him to attain standard three in his education. He could read and write a few words, but most of all he could write a simple letter to his relatives or friends. He even wrote and read letters that his friends and relatives brought to him. One day, an old man brought a letter from his son who was working in the copper mines, about 200 miles away. Byensi cleared his throat and started, 'To my dear father'. The old man screamed: 'I am not your father; stop playing games and read my son's letter.'

Muntu's mother, Karungi was very highly regarded by both her relatives and village-mates. In her young days, many parents discouraged their daughters from going to formal schools for fear of being spoilt. Her parents always warned her sternly in the following manner:

'Remember, our pretty girl, that you are the eyes of the village and indeed of the whole clan. Make sure to keep the wisdom of your grandparents alive. Avoid these new so-called schools and keep your dignity as a woman. God gave you everything when you came out of your mother's womb as a girl. Your future husband will take care of you. This is how the custom has been and will continue to be.'

Karungi took the message with a grain of salt. She knew deep inside that if her brothers could go to school and remain unspoilt, so could she. Although she did not have any formal schooling except for the catechism classes, she acted as someone who was well educated. She often pretended in front of her parents to be a great reader. She performed imaginary plays, created stories and told them, sang, and even imitated foreign languages. Although her actions were very amusing, her parents often worried that their pretty girl was very strange. As a matter of fact, some of the very old relatives wondered if she was in a healthy state of mind. Others thought that her behaviour could be attributed to spiritual powers from the ancestors, since her family's spiritual ancestor, known as 'omuchweezi', was a good and kind one.

Karungi grew up during the days of colonial expansion. Although the English ruled her country, many other Europeans, who were called 'Bajungu', often visited the country. This particular area was attractive to Europeans because of the copper mines, tea estates, wonderful spring-like weather and game parks. They even loved the local people very much. The women, tall and slender, reminded them of their own women back home. Although tradition discouraged the local girls from marrying foreigners, a few brave ones did venture to marry them and produced mixed-race children, commonly referred to as 'Bachotara'.

Karungi had been warned to avoid keeping company with girls who were attracted to foreigners. However, she liked the ones that ran the local parish. She very much enjoyed her catechism classes, locally known as 'Omugigi', and upon graduation, she requested permission to stay on and help out with the in-coming students. The parish priest granted her request and, through practice, Karungi became a very good teacher.

This type of work, coupled with old traditional wisdom that was passed on from one generation to the next, made Karungi a very well respected woman. Whenever the local women and sometimes even men wanted a certain issue resolved, Karungi was called on for leadership. Issues varied in scope, ranging from family disputes to concerns of the whole village. One day, Karungi was called upon to deal with a domestic situation where a man called Kyomya was threatening to marry a second wife if his present one did not bear him any sons. The woman had given birth to six daughters but her husband's clan showed her very little appreciation. They gave these girls names that indicated how they were not wanted very much. Boys were regarded as better cattle- and goat-herders. They would carry on the clan name, keep family wealth growing and, through marriage, the clan would acquire new relatives. Girls were regarded as a loss to the family because of their domestic role that did not bring an income to the family. The only income would come from bride wealth if the girl was lucky enough to marry into a rich family. This type of arrangement often made her family worried all the time for fear that they would be required to return the dowry if their daughter was found to be a bad wife or if she deserted her husband.

When Karungi arrived at the homestead, most people wondered if she was going to make any difference. 'Why bring in Karungi?' murmured an old woman. 'Does she have medicine to make Kinobi produce boys?' Kinobi was a nickname that was given to this woman, indicating her unpopularity. Her real name was Kakwanzi referring to her beady brown eyes. Because Karungi commanded a lot of respect, she was given the opportunity to solve the case.

Upon entering the house, Karungi demanded that all six girls be called to listen to what was going on. They were summoned at once. Some of the invited guests sat on wooden benches while others sat on the grass-covered floor. This particular type of grass is called 'Obugara' and the local people value it as people of other cultures value their carpets. In addition to being covered with grass, a mat made of cow hide was placed on Karungi's spot. After clearing her voice and drinking a glass of banana juice that was served to her, Karungi spoke, long and clear.

'Kyomya, I am surprised that you want to disrupt your household. This poor woman here has worked long hours to keep this family on its feet. She has produced all these wonderful children and no one appreciates it. Listen to the names that you have given them: Babaki, Bonabaana, and all the others. Imagine Banaki which means "What kind of children are these?" Would you be happy if you carried such a name around with you for the rest of your life?'

Karungi kept warning of the problems that this family would face if Kyomya introduced another wife into the already complex situation. Knocking her wooden club hard on the floor, she threatened to end her long-standing relationship with the family and to report the case to the parish priest. Although Kyomya was also a Catholic, he was so lukewarm in his faith that he was referred to as 'The one who fell asleep during his catechism classes'. But even though he was not very devout, he feared the idea of going to hell and on many nights, he would dream of it and wake up screaming. He took the idea so seriously that he often lit a fire, brought his fingers close to it and screamed, 'God, if hell's fire is like this one, please don't send me there'.

His wife often laughed long and hard, with tears streaming down her cheeks. She told her friends, on the way to collecting firewood or water, that she knew the medicine to keep her husband under control. Whenever Kyomya misbehaved, she lit a fire with big logs of wood and told him that she had just dreamt of her husband ending up in such a fire. At least she kept him well behaved for several days and sometimes weeks, until he eventually overcame his fear. Kakwanzi tried her hell trick with the children, but without much success. Kyomya was convinced that it was his wife's bad luck that had brought the girls and therefore he was clean before God. After all, he had the support of the whole clan.

Karungi did not need to use the hell trick. She told Kyomya forcefully that *he* was responsible for the birth of girls. Although she did not go into the details of the process, she was so clear that everyone understood what she meant. She had learned of this from the biology class at the local parish hospital where she worked as a nurse's aide. She said, very sternly;

'Shame on you, Kyomya. How dare you create a situation, then turn around and blame it on someone else? Can't you be responsible?'

Everyone was surprised at the news. She turned around and addressed all those present:

'I know several of you have been hurting your wives in a similar fashion. Go and ask Sister Maragalita at the hospital. I know you are too scared and ashamed to go there. From now on, I don't want to hear of such stories around here.'

Everyone present wondered at the power and poise with which Karungi spoke. Many of the women were happy but could not show it openly for fear that their husbands would take revenge when they returned home. The majority of the men admired her but some felt sorry for her husband. When Karungi was not looking, one man whispered: 'I am sure the next step for her will be to beat her husband and then grow a beard.' Those who heard the comment laughed, but Karungi simply ignored them. Kyomya thanked her and requested that a special meal be served because his family, that was falling apart, had been restored. This episode ended with a big feast in which millet and roasted beef were served.

LINA MAGAIA

Madalena Returned from Captivity

Madalena has returned, a child of fourteen suffering from rickets because of malnutrition. Fourteen years ago her father had been arrested far away in Cabo Delgado,[1] on the plateau, by puppets of the Portuguese political police, PIDE,[2] and sent to Machava. From the tough Kadjamangwana prison[3] in Machava he was sent as an unpaid labourer to Maragra, the sugar factory, where he courted a woman. From this love affair came Madalena.

Madalena was kidnapped by armed bandits near Maluna, where she was visiting relatives. For weeks and months, Madalena lived in a bandit base. The child was made forcibly into a woman for the bandits.

Madalena trembles. Talking to her is the commander of the force that found her in the bush when they were searching for bandits.

Madalena has lice all over her head, her body and her clothing. The commander orders them to cut her hair and find her a place to bathe. Madalena trembles.

The commander takes her, with her head shorn and her face washed, to the brigade commander. Others present include the local militia chief, who has known Madalena for more than a decade.

Madalena trembles and holds her legs tightly together. She remains standing. She stares with eyes moist with tears that refuse to flow at the group of people watching her. She continues to tremble.

The brigade commander askes, 'How do you feel, child?'

She looks at the ground without replying. She tries to open her mouth. Then the tears are released and they run down her lean cheeks.

---

[1] A province in northern Mozambique.

[1] The acronym for the much-hated Portuguese secret police. It stands for *Policia International e de Defesa do Estado*.

[3] On the outskirts of Maputo where political activists were incarcerated in the colonial time.

Madalena's throat is covered with streaks of ingrained dirt. Her hands end in nails that are overgrown and dirty, reminiscent of wretchedness and jiggers. Madalena has jiggers in her feet.

The brigade commander tries to soothe her. 'So, why are you crying, child? Aren't you happy to be going home? Don't you want to talk about what happened to you?'

Among the people surrounding the brigade commander is a woman whom Madalena knows. The commander turns to her and suggests, 'You talk to her. You women may understand each other.'

The woman is startled. She eyes Madalena and thinks, 'What does he want of the child? What could she possibly say at this moment?'

However, she asks, 'Madalena, how did you escape?'

She replies, 'It was when the soldiers attacked the big base. We were in a small base. The bandit chief ran away from the big base and came to the one we were in. The other bandits were afraid of him and hid us. There was me, Toneca and Elisa . . .'

She can't go on but it is obvious she wants to say more. The woman smiles at her and says, 'Do you know where Toneca and Elisa are?'

'No, I don't,' she replies. 'They told us to run into the bush when their chief arrived. We were running together at the beginning, but when we heard shots behind us I hid. We had agreed to escape to our homes . . . I don't know what happened to my friends afterwards.'

'But why were they afraid of their chief?' the woman asks.

'Because they were our husbands and they said they were afraid that the chief would want to keep us for himself.'

'So you had a husband? What was his name?'

Madalena begins to shake even more. She purses her lips and remains in shameful silence. She is petrified with fear.

After a while she speaks. 'There were lots. One of them was named Armando. He made me call him uncle.'

The brigade commander issues an order to the woman, 'Take the child home. Make sure she sees a doctor. She must be carrying all kinds of disease.'

The woman has one more question for Madalena:

'Were there many people at the base, apart from the bandits?'

'Yes. Men, women and children. I don't know how many. The bandits drank a lot of hooch every day, and when they were drunk, they would pick out someone to kill – with a knife, or a bayonet, or hatchet or even with a pestle.'

More tears flowed down Madalena's lean cheeks. 'And they made us watch. I know some of the people they killed. We were kidnapped at the same time.'

The brigade commander repeats his order: 'Take the child home. Don't forget to ask the doctor to examine her.'

Madalena's home is in the Maragra first neigbourhood, an area inhabited mostly by the Maconde community. These people from the plateau far away in the Cabo Delgado more than fourteen years earlier had responded to the call to defend their country and to free it from colonial rule.[4] They were arrested on the plateau in Cabo Delgado, brought to Machava prison and then sold to Maragra. Today they live freely with their families.

They reach Madalena's house. The local militia commander knocks at the door of the community secretary. He passes on the news.

Though there is no telephone or radio, almost everyone hears the news at the same time. They surge out of their houses, some bare-chested, some wrapped in blankets, the women wearing cloths on their heads to shield themselves from the intense cold cast by the dew. In the midst of them is Madalena's maternal grandmother. She is old, ages old, with wrinkles on her face, wrinkles on her arms, folds on her throat, emaciated legs seemingly unable to bear the weight even of her own thin body. On her head she wears a scarf that scarcely hides the cotton that her hair has become with the passage of time. She is crying. 'Nwananga mina! Nwananga mina u buyile! Yo nwananga . . .' ('My child! My child, you've come back! Oh, my child . . .')

And she falls on to the dew-soaked ground.

Madalena is sobbing.

Out of a hut comes a woman with one eye blinded by a cataract, and she whispers, 'Bernardo, Bernardo my beloved? When will you come back?' (Bernardo is in Maputo.) 'How shall I find you to tell you that your daughter has returned?' She embraces Madalena and weeps. Many of the women are also weeping. All of a sudden someone begins a song. A song of the people.

The woman with the blind eye whispers again, this time to Madalena, 'My child, you've come back . . .'

Someone starts to dance. Then everyone dances – except for

---

[4] The Maconde live in the northern Mozambican province of Cabo Delgado. They played a major role in the armed struggle for national independence.

Madalena's mother and grandmother. Madalena remains in the centre of the circle made by the dancers, but she doesn't dance. She sobs . . .

The militia commander and the woman who have escorted Madalena are hugged and kissed by many of those present. Someone tells Madalena, 'Don't cry any more. They will never find you again.'

ANANDA DEVI

Lakshmi's Gift

On the morning of Diwali, Shanti had woken with a prayer on her lips. Her mind was filled with thoughts of Lakshmi, and she got up, as she did every year on this day, with the certainty (produced by some quirk of her fertile imagination) that for once her prayers would be answered. That night she had dreamt that Lakshmi had appeared to her in a flash of dazzling light and, as the goddess had gazed at her long and searchingly, Shanti herself had been transformed into a bowl of light, her raised arms in flames, her long hair an immense network of stars which skimmed the confines of a sweet world, made manifest and vibrating with offerings and promises. When she awoke, her eyes bright in the early sunlight and shining with the memory of her dream, she knew the day would be propitious and that she would finally receive Lakshmi's gift after so many years of waiting patiently.

She tied her old cotton sari almost gaily, without inveighing against her fate. She was scarcely aware of her calloused hands, coarsened by work in the fields, nor the ache in her back every time she bent down. Nor did she pause to look in the tarnished mirror – to regret once more her lost beauty. On this morning, hope had washed away all dissatisfaction, smoothed away the many tribulations of her daily life. She set to work with unaccustomed vigour.

This morning, the scarlet and crimson blossom of the flamboyants and bougainvillaeas, the heavy mauve and white heads of the November-plants were as dazzling as the burning sun which beat down through the narrow window, set high in the east wall of the house. The sun was reflected in the copper and tin utensils crowding the shelves, and set up a merry play of lights and shadows. In the kitchen, flooded with steamy, murmuring heat, dozens of little cakes, white and pink, gold and brown, floated gaily in jars of syrup, while others still tossed in boiling oil over the stove and suddenly swelled up, as she deftly turned them with the big metal spoon, and they grew round and crusty, bringing a dreamy look into the eyes of the fascinated children. A heavy smell of sugar and cooking-oil filled the house, mingling with the heady aroma of crushed spices, bitter cardamom, sweet cinnamon, bitter-sweet cloves, sharp mustard . . . as Shanti set to work with her stone mortar.

The five children, with at most a year's difference in their ages, romped excitedly about the two rooms of the house. They ran and jumped and jostled each other, without bruising their muscular little bodies. Each face was one huge white-toothed grin, each voice a high-pitched trill. Sometimes they could be heard pushing one another, with the noise of furniture being overturned, the sound of broken glass, followed by an agonised silence. But that morning, Shanti, absorbed in her dreams, heard nothing, noticed nothing. The makeshift switch that she normally used so adroitly, remained in a corner, forgotten. After a moment, the games were resumed more furiously than ever. And their innocent little voices pealed out like a ring of bells.

As Shanti went joyfully about her tasks, absorbed in the Diwali preparations, she was convinced that her fortunes were about to change for the better. With every year that had passed since her marriage, a vice of bitterness and humiliation had gradually tightened around her. The endless cycle of pregnancies, confinements and all the problems of motherhood, had worn her out. Then there was the added burden of work in the fields, making her coarse and aggressive, prematurely aged. And the house, with its bare, austere interior, on whose walls no shred of fantasy hung, no breath of folly, where no secret double life, no caprice, could hide; the house that had become a prison, cramping her personality, curbing her smallest desires. A relentless routine with no place for pleasure or rejoicing. A man at her side who was no companion, but a source of conflict and hostility. Trapped by his own masculinity, evenings spent at the bar would rouse him to violence, and this would inevitably be transformed into a fit of passion, combining noise and fury, blows and screams, insults and the motions of making love.

The days leading up to Diwali were the only time when life took on some greater measure of lightness and serenity; when hope sprang up once more in Shanti's breast, and gently cradled within her, refused to be quelled, washing silently over her surroundings. This was the time when Lakshmi was believed to enter every home. The bronze form of Lakshmi, goddess of light, but also goddess of wealth, whose blessing caused riches to fall like manna on her worshippers – or so they believed. And Shanti believed this as fervently and totally as her shattered illusions and spirits, dampened by her daily life, would allow. And that day she did everything in her power to be worthy of the goddess's blessing.

The fact that in spite of all her prayers her life had remained unchanged up till now, did not alter her belief one jot. The fact that, as Diwali approached, she always found herself languishing in the same darkness which all the *diyas* lit throughout the house could not dispel, did not prevent hope springing up again in her breast the following year. This was her very own therapy; she recreated herself leaf by leaf, greening her bruised branches, freshly curling her faded petals. Once a year, she renewed herself and waited for Lakshmi's coming. If Lakshmi did not come, and the poverty remained the same with its days of scarcity and its terrible monotony, Shanti would still have obtained her elixir of strength for a whole year, at the end of which she would once more muster all the illusions of freedom around her and she would hope again.

After her dream of the previous night, she had all the more reason to allow herself to hope. A dream of Lakshmi didn't arrive out of the blue. It was *she* who chose to visit you as you slept, sometimes confirming by a smile, a word or an affectionate gesture, the glad tidings that her bounteous presence heralded. And every year Shanti who hoped for a lottery, or an opportune legacy from some deceased relative, began once more to plan a life of bourgeois comfort, fulfilling her dearest ambition. She thought electric cooker, she thought refrigerator, television, new saris and embroidered silks. She imagined her children in new clothes, weighed down under the burden of school books, pencils, satchels, all the equipment essential to make great men of them. She thought of a Diwali – the following year perhaps if her dreams came true – when the whole house would be illuminated, radiating light and gratitude. And as she reflected on all these comforts, she became more obsessed with the need for them, a need which was both an anticipated pleasure and an abstract fear of one more disappointment.

She felt herself ageing, too rapidly, too suddenly. Her long black pigtail was now shot through with a fine silver filigree and she could not face the inevitable arrival of old age, with its prospect of an existence as uniformly ugly, grey, colourless as a shroud of rain, without a single well of happiness from which to drink deeply a strong desire to live. Wherever she looked, wherever she turned, she saw the same lowering horizons, drained of colour, cloudy, heavy with certainties too long recognised, with a lucidity too bitter for rebellion or rejection of the inevitable . . .

The day had been taken up with the usual activities: preparing vegetarian dishes, meticulous spring-cleaning, washing and dressing the children. Shanti herself washed her thick hair and perfumed it in the smoke of the incense which had been burning in the house since morning. She put on a clean sari and left the house carrying a big tray of *diyas* filled with oil and wicks, ready to be lit. The children followed her, excited at the thought of the great moment drawing near, fluttering around her like so many plump little sparrows, brushing against her with their warm soft flesh.

Outside, one shaft of late sun found its way into the tiny courtyard where begonias, shasta daises and chysanthemums bloomed. Frangipani blossoms were opening their curled white petals in the setting sun and filling the air with their heady scent. Trees and foliage had all dissolved in the last glow of the sunset. The sky was shrouded in a faint trellis of clouds, mingling light and shadow, the lurid glow of the sun and the silvery gliding of the moon, the warmth of the dying day and the first cool of evening. A swarm of bengalis, perched on the branches of a huge banyan tree, suddenly set up a deafening chorus.

For a moment Shanti stood suspended between two actions, in the grip of the intense feelings that overwhelmed her. She felt she had never really looked at the things around her – as if she had been blind and her sight had just been restored at the very moment when the beauty of nature was at its most dazzling. Her head was a turmoil of ideas and thoughts. The vivid amber colour of the earth was now blended with an even more amazing blue. The air all around her was redolent with pungent aromas: the powerful green smell of mint, thyme and coriander plants, the intoxicating fragrance wafted from the gandia flower; all these treasures amassed as a result of the endless ferment deep in the bowels of the earth, which was transformed on the surface into growth and fruitfulness. With a strange detachment, almost as if under a spell, Shanti saw the disparate elements of her existence lock together to form an intricate chain. They wound around her, binding her to her obligations, and to all the allegiances that a woman forms about her in the course of her existence, while she gradually wears herself out – the better to fulfil them, the better to share the immense, inexhaustible wealth of love hidden in her innermost heart, on which she feeds endlessly.

She placed five *diyas* on the edge of a pool, in the middle of which the sacred *tulsi* plant grew, tall, broad-leaved. With silent, trembling concentration she struck a match and lit one wick. The tiny blue flame gradually flared up and shone on her first treasure: the delicate face of her eldest daughter, with huge lively eyes and an eager smile.

She lit the second lamp. Her second treasure appeared, just above the flame: her eldest son, the most loving and the best loved.

The third lamp dispelled the darkness around a cheeky, triangular, dimpled little face. Another lamp showed up a faint smile on the face of the fourth child: a delicate, sad little girl.

As she lit the last lamp, she knew she would see a thousand golden glints in the dark curls of an eighteen-month-old toddler who, for one brief moment, would look up at her with calm, trusting eyes, in which shone a fierce belief in the divine presence of his mother.

With the last lamp, Shanti herself became tall and resplendent, like the luminous creature of her dream, her hands filled with light. For the first time in her life, Lakshmi had accomplished her miracle. With her hands joined in the namaste position, as a sign of her last prayer of the day, Shanti accepted Lakshmi's gift and took it straight to her heart.

Translated by Dorothy S. Blair

SOUTHERN

AFRICA

SOUTHERN AFRICA

The Republic of South Africa is not a large country, nor is it densely populated, yet many fine writers of various cultures and ethnic groups have emerged from its 35 million inhabitants. This situation is the more surprising in that much of the majority black population is denied the leisure to write, and the educational opportunity to practise or to read standard English literature. They also lack the financial stability to produce over time a long work of art.

In 1986, Manoko Nchwe, whose work is unpublished, told interviewer Bottumelo:

> 'Women remain outside of the networks which facilitate the production of literature . . . They must be given the opportunity to express or present their works without feeling that there are few women writers around.'

Some who dared to write or speak out are in exile or banned. Amelia House, who included the Nchwe interview in her *Checklist of Black South African Women Writers* listed 19 out of 37 women writers under *Whereabouts unknown*. A further limitation frequently expressed by male and female authors is that it is impossible to write any literature that does not deal with the all-encompassing subject of racial oppression. Amelia House left South Africa for England and then America. Bessie Head left South Africa to be a 'stateless person' for many years in Botswana, because only there did she feel free to write. Even so, several women from various sectors of South African society do write moving autobiography and fiction.

Noni Jabavu began 'the modern period of South African women's writing', says Carole Boyce Davies[1]. Jabavu's first novel, *Drawn in*

---

[1] Carole Boyce Davies has written on both Jabavu and Ngcobo, and is referred to in the biographical sketches of both in *The Feminist Companion to Literature in English* (pp. 562 and 792 respectively).

Colour (1962) depicts her own Xhosa childhood. *The Ochre People* (1963) is in part autobiographical. It traces some family history (her grandfather was a journalist and her father a scholar) and shows scenes from different regional cultures in South Africa.

Ellen Kuzwayo has written her own story, *Call Me Woman* (1985) as representative of an upper-class black family who has shared frustration and persecution with many others. She wrote this autobiography, not for self-glorification, but to show the reader how many blacks have suffered, and with what fortitude they have survived. Winnie Mandela was forcibly separated from her imprisoned husband for 27 years, lived often under house arrest, and was forbidden to speak publicly. Yet she managed to dictate her autobiography, *Part of My Soul Went With Him* (1985) by telephoning parts of it abroad to England. Singer Miriam Makeba related her story to James Hall, who wrote it up as *Makeba: My Story* (1988). Ruth First, a white journalist killed by a letter bomb, wrote essays and papers criticising the apartheid system and was tried for treason. Her daughter, Shawn Slovo, wrote the story of her mother's life as a scenario for the film, *A World Apart*, produced in 1988.

Probably South Africa's best known fiction writer, Nobel Prize winner, Nadine Gordimer, has written many novels and short stories, as well as critical essays, which treat many aspects of life under apartheid. She has also helped to produce films about South Africa, such as *Maids and Madams*. She dares to remain there, despite the fact that at times her work has been banned. Novelist Miriam Tlali has also remained, although she, as a black, couldn't enter the library where her first novel, *Muriel at Metropolitan* (1975) was circulated. Gladys Thomas, denied a travel permit until 1983, won a Kwanzaa commendation for 'writing under oppressive conditions'. In 1986 she went to the church halls sheltering children whose Crossroads shanties were set ablaze, interviewed them, and published their stories in *Children of Crossroads* (1986). The next year she wrote the stories of the teenagers imprisoned in Pollsmoor, *The WynBerg Seven*. She is planning a new collection, *Women Under Apartheid*.

Even those writers who have left South Africa on exile permits, banning orders, or because of conscience, frequently continue to find their subject matter in the country of their birth. Lauretta Ngcobo left home in 1966 for London. Her 1981 novel, *Cross of Gold*, portrays the guerrilla struggle across South Africa's border. 'I wonder if it will prove to have been easier to fight the oppression of apartheid than it will ever be to set women free in our societies . . . Male domination does not "burn down".' she comments. Amelia House in her fiction includes some themes from her present Kentucky life, but she too, in poetry, short fiction, and drama continues to portray South African oppression. Farida Karodia similarly uses some Canadian settings for her recent fiction. She did revisit South Africa in 1981. Her fiction reflects the problems of variously 'labelled' ethnic groups in South Africa.

Some women manage to go to and from South Africa, and can keep current the settings for their fiction. Zoë Wicomb is presently teaching in South Africa, after many years in Great Britain with only occasional visits home. Sheila Fugard spends part of each year in Port Elizabeth, part in New York. Fugard and her playwright husband, Athol, import actors as well as stories to the United States and London.

With the recent changes, cosmetic or real, there is hope for substantial reform. Gladys Thomas danced in the streets of Capetown when Mandela was released from prison. Sheila Fugard writes[2]:

'The writing scene in South Africa is quite extraordinary. A flood of raw material by a population which was silenced for so long, a really necessary outlet. Poetry, workshops, theatre, and short stories abound, but no novels.'

Women are a part of this movement. They and their children have been shot down in the streets. More and more they are demanding the freedom to act, speak, and write.

The South African state continues to have an influence on its smaller, less powerful neighbours. Tsitsi Dangarembga gives insight into the frustrations and inhibitions teenagers feel in Zimbabwe (formerly Rhodesia) which still extends British values over local education. Bessie Head feels a partial removal from the colonial influence in Botswana, so poor and arid that it was not a prize to England nor to its stronger, richer neighbour, South Africa. She was

[2] Sheila Fugard's letter to C.H.B. is one of 25 June, 1991.

always 'restless in a distant land', however, as James Matthews saw her[3]. Sadly, Bessie Head died before she could witness any real changes in the racial tensions she so keenly felt.

[3] James Matthews in *Black Voices Shout* (Austin, Troubadour Press, 1975) included mention of her in the poem 'for those who have been'.

TSITSI DANGAREMBGA

Excerpt from *Nervous Conditions*

Babamukuru, headmaster at a mission school and uncle of Tambudzai, is the
accepted head of the extended family. A been-to, he has studied in England. He
feels that he must see that at least one member of his brother's children receives an
education, if only secondary education. Unfortunately, the son of his brother
Jeremiah, Njamo, whom he took into his home to educate, unexpectedly died, and
only nieces remained. Against precedent, Babamukuru offered to take the eldest,
fourteen-year-old Tambudzai, a promising student. She will live at the mission
and go to school with his own daughter, Nyasha. Tambudzai realises the impact
of this decision in the following episode. The rest of the novel is the story of
Tambudzai and Nyasha, their education and their dilemmas.

How can I describe the sensations that swamped me when Babamukuru started his car, with me in the front seat beside him, on the day I
left my home? It was relief, but more than that. It was more than
excitement and anticipation. What I experienced that day was a short
cut, a rerouting of everything I had ever defined as me into fast lanes
that would speedily lead me to my destination. My horizons were
saturated with me, my leaving, my going. There was no room for what
I left behind. My father, as affably, shallowly agreeable as ever, was
insignificant. My mother, my anxious mother, was no more than
another piece of surplus scenery to be maintained, of course to be
maintained, but all the same superfluous, an obstacle in the path of
my departure. As for my sisters, well, they were there. They were
watching me climb into Babamukuru's car to be whisked away to
limitless horizons. It was up to them to learn the important lesson that
circumstances were not immutable, no burden so binding that it could
not be dropped. The honour for teaching them this emancipating
lesson was mine. I claimed it all, for here I was, living proof of the
moral. There was no doubt in my mind that this was the case.

When I stepped into Babamukuru's car I was a peasant. You could see that at a glance in my tight, faded frock that immodestly defined my budding breasts, and in my broad-toed feet that had grown thick-skinned through daily contact with the ground in all weathers. You could see it from the way the keratin had reacted by thickening and, having thickened, had hardened and cracked so that the dirt ground its way in but could not be washed out. It was evident from the corrugated black callouses on my knees, the scales on my skin that were due to lack of oil, the short, dull tufts of malnourished hair. This was the person I was leaving behind. At Babamukuru's I expected to find another self, a clean, well-groomed genteel self who could not have been bred, could not have survived, on the homestead. At Babamukuru's I would have the leisure, be encouraged to consider questions that had to do with survival of the spirit, the creation of consciousness, rather than mere sustenance of the body. This new me would not be enervated by smoky kitchens that left eyes smarting and chests permanently bronchitic. This new me would not be frustrated by wood fires that either flamed so furiously that the sadza burned, or so indifferently that it became mbodza. Nor would there be trips to Nyamarira, Nyamarira which I loved to bathe in and watch cascade through the narrow outlet of the fall where we drew our water. Leaving this Nyamarira, my flowing, tumbling, musical playground, was difficult. But I could not pretend to be sorry to be leaving the water-drums whose weight compressed your neck into your spine, were heavy on the head even after you had grown used to them and were constantly in need of refilling. I was not sorry to be leaving the tedious task of coaxing Nyamarira's little tributary in and out of the vegetable beds. Of course, my emancipation from these aspects of my existence was, for the foreseeable future, temporary and not continuous, but that was not the point. The point was this: I was going to be developed in the way that Babamukuru saw fit, which in the language I understood at the time meant well. Having developed well I did not foresee that there would be reason to regress on the occasions that I returned to the homestead.

Without so much going on inside me I would have enjoyed that ride to the mission, remembering how the only other time I had crossed Nyamarira in a vehicle, rolled down my side of the Inyanga Highway and seen Chistmas Pass loom up in the distance, was when Mr Matimba took me to town to sell my green mealies. A-a-h, those green mealies! The hope of selling them had occupied my attention on that first trip, but today I was thinking of more concrete things.

There were many practical issues about my transplantation that I had to think about, all of them mixed up with each other and needing to be sorted out into discrete, manageable portions. There was great pleasure in wondering where I would sleep, since this would certainly not be in a smoky kitchen where people relaxed in the evenings so that you had to wait for everybody else to retire before you could comfortably put yourself to bed. But if not in the kitchen, then where? If Nhamo had been telling the truth, which was as likely as it was not, he had had a whole room to himself at Babamukuru's. A whole room to myself was asking for a lot, expecting too much, and besides, I was not sure that I would enjoy sleeping by myself with nobody to giggle with before falling asleep or whose presence would be comforting when dreams were disturbing. Yet it would be strenuous, disturbing too, to have to share a room with Nyasha, who was morose and taciturn, who made me feel uncomfortable because something had extinguished the sparkle in her eyes. Besides, I still disapproved of her. I thought she had no right to be so unhappy when she was Babamukuru's daughter – that was a blessing in itself. And she wore pretty clothes. She had not been obliged to adjourn her education so that now, although she was the same age as I was, she was already in Form Two. If for no other reason, her eyes should have shone vigorously with gratitude for these blessings, but she was not sensible enough to understand this. She remained ungrateful, awkward, and ill-mannered. The thought of sleeping with Anna, who was Maiguru's housegirl and had come home at the time of Nhamo's funeral to help with the chores, was much more relaxing although not without its problems. Anna could talk and talk and talk about everything and nothing. This was useful when you didn't want to concentrate on depressing things like death and grief, but what would happen when there were serious matters of permanent import like mathematics and history to think about? Still, these were minor concerns. Wherever I slept, I was sure, I would have more than one blanket to cover me. And since Babamukuru's possessions had been disciplined into retaining their newness, these blankets would be thick and fleecy enough to keep the cold out even in the worst June nights. I would not have to get up to sweep the yard and draw water before I set off for school, although on the mission it would not have mattered even if I had had to do these things, since school was close by and getting there did not mean forty minutes at a trot every morning. Nor would I, I thought, openly smiling with the pleasure of it, nor would I need to worry any more about my books becoming embellished with grime and grease-spots in their corner of the *chikuwa*, where I kept them at home. At Babamukuru's I would have a bookcase. My books would live in a bookcase. It would keep them clean. My clothes would be clean too, without fields and smoke and soot to mess them. Nor would keeping them clean entail a walk to the river, twenty minutes away, washing them on rocks, spreading them on boulders and waiting until they dried before I could go home again. I would be able to keep myself clean too, without too much trouble. According to Nhamo, there were taps right inside the house. Not only outside the kitchen like at the headmaster's house at Rutivi School, but right inside the house, where they ran hot water and cold into a tub large enough to sit in with your legs stretched straight out in front of you! And all you had to do to empty the tub was pull out a stopper and the water gurgled away into the earth through a network of pipes laid under the ground. Now, although Nhamo had not been above resorting to fantasy in order to impress, he did prefer facts when they were available. These details seemed factual enough. I could not wait to enjoy these comforts that Nhamo had described to me in patient, important detail. I could not wait to enjoy these consequences of having an education on Babamukuru's part, of being in the process of acquiring one in my case.

Nhamo had had a refrain with which he had punctuated his enthusiastic and reverent descriptions of the luxury and comfort of Babamukuru's house. 'Not even the Whites', he had used to carol in an impressionable descant, 'not even the Whites themselves could afford it!' I should have been prepared then for the splendour of that house or the mission, but I was not. Having not had the experience with which to improve my imagination, not even my brother's diligent descriptions were able to create for me a true image of my uncle's house.

The grounds were very large, as large as our yard at home. In them stood a single building, Babamukuru's house, if you did not count the outlying constructions, which turned out to be a shed, a garage and the servants' quarters. At home our yard contained many buildings which all had a specific purpose for our day to day living: the pole and *dagga* kitchen, which was about the same size as my uncle's little shed, only round; the *tsapi*, which was small, maybe half as large as Babamukuru's shed; the *hozi*, where Nhamo had slept during the holidays that he did come home; and the House, which was built of red brick, had glass windows and a corrugated iron roof. We considered the house a very fine house, not only because of the red brick, the glass windows and the corrugated iron, which made their own emphatic statements about who we were, but also because it had a living-room large enough to hold a dining-table, four matching chairs, and a sofa and two armchairs besides. It was a very fine house, because it had two bedrooms opening off from the living-room which were well furnished with a single bedstead and *koya* mattress, and wardrobes with mirrors that had once been reliable but had now grown so cloudy with age that they threatened to show you images of artful and ancient spirits when you looked into them, instead of your own face. My parents slept in one of the bedrooms, the one on the left as you entered the living-room. The bed and its mattress belonged to my father. My mother was supposed to sleep on the reed mat on the floor with her babies before they were old enough to join me in the kitchen, although she hardly ever did. Usually she fell asleep in the kitchen and could not be bothered to rouse herself to go up to the house. All the women in the family – Mother, Netsai and myself – preferred it this way, and though my father did not, there was not much he could do about it without making a scene. This he did not often have the energy to do.

The other bedroom in the house was spare. This was where Babamukuru and his family used to sleep when they came to visit before they went to England. But now that the children had grown up, Baba and Maiguru slept there alone. In the circles I had moved in until my transfer to the mission, our house on the homestead had been obviously, definitely, a fine, refined home. With that house as my standard it was not easy to grasp that the mansion standing at the top of the drive marked '14, HEADMASTER'S HOUSE' was truly my uncle's very own. Luckily the sign was there, so that by the time we were half-way up the drive I was looking forward to living in such a distinguished home. All the same, had I been writing these things at the time that they happened, there would have been many references to 'palace' and 'mansion' and 'castle' in this section. Their absence is not to say that I have forgotten what it was like. That first impression of grandeur was too exotic ever to fade, but I have learnt, in the years that have passed since then, to curb excesses and flights of fancy. The point has been made: I can now refer to my uncle's house as no more than that – a house.

It was painted white. This was one of the less beautiful aspects of that house, one of the less sensible aspects too. There seemed to be no good reason for wasting time and effort, to say nothing of paint, on painting the cheerful red brick that I had seen elsewhere on the mission as we drove up to Babamukuru's house this clinical, antiseptic white. Naturally, there was a reason. I found out from Nyasha, who knew all sorts of things, or glued together facts for herself when knowledge was lacking, that this particular house, the headmaster's house, had been built in the early days of the mission. She said that was around the turn of the nineteenth century at a time when the missionaries believed that only white houses were cool enough to be comfortably lived in. Diligently this belief was translated into action. White houses sprang up all over the mission. All those white houses must have been very uninspiring for people whose function was to inspire. Besides, natives were said to respond to colour, so after a while the missionaries began to believe that houses would not overheat, even when they were not painted white, as long as pastel shades were used. They began to paint their houses cream, pale pink, pale blue, pale green. Nyasha liked to embellish this point. 'Imagine,' she used to say, 'how *pretty* it must have looked. All those pinks and blues gleaming away among the white. It must have been so sweet, so very appealing.'

Later, much later, as late as the time that I came to the mission, there was a lot of construction going on. Houses had to be built to shelter the new crop of educated Africans that had been sown in so many Sub A and Sub B night-school classes and was now being abundantly reaped as old boys returned to the mission to contribute by becoming teachers in their turn. Possibly because there was no time for finesse, possibly because the aim was to shelter as many people as quickly as possible, these houses that accommodated the returning teachers remained dark and ruddy.

Nyasha taught me this history with a mischievous glint in her eye. I was like a vacuum then, taking in everything, storing it all in its original state for future inspection. Today I am content that this little paragraph of history as written by Nyasha makes a good story, as likely if not more so than the chapters those very same missionaries were dishing out to us in those mission schools.

At the time that I arrived at the mission, missionaries were living in white houses and in the pale painted houses, but not in the red brick ones. My uncle was the only African living in a white house. We were all very proud of this fact. No, that is not quite right. We were all proud, except Nyasha, who had an egalitarian nature and had taken seriously the lessons about oppression and discrimination that she had learnt first-hand in England.

As the car slowed down to turn into the drive, the pace of my life increased. I packed a lot of living into the few minutes that it took to creep up the drive to the garage. First was the elation from realising that the elegant house ahead of me was indeed my uncle's. Then there was a disappointment. There was a building almost as long as the house if not as high, so that it could very well have been a little house itself and I thought I had made a mistake. I thought I was not going to live in a mansion after all and my spirits went plunging down. But even then there were plenty of things to be happy about. The smooth, stoneless drive ran between squat, robust conifers on one side and a blaze of canna lilies burning scarlet and amber on the other. Plants like that had belonged to the cities. They had belonged to the pages of my language reader, to the yards of Ben and Betty's uncle in town. Now, having seen it for myself because of my Babamukuru's kindness, I too could think of planting things for merrier reasons than the chore of keeping breath in the body. I wrote it down in my head: I would ask Maiguru for some bulbs and plant a bed of those gay lilies on the homestead. In front of the house. Our home would answer well to being cheered up by such lively flowers. Bright and cheery, they had been planted for joy. What a strange idea that was. It was a liberation, the first of many that followed from my transition to the mission.

Then I discovered that Nhamo had not been lying. Babamukuru was indeed a man of consequence however you measured him. The old building that had disappointed me turned out to be a garage. It was built to shelter cars, not people! And this garage sheltered two cars. Not one, but two cars. Nhamo's chorus sang in my head and now it sounded ominous. Its phrases told me something I did not want to know, that my Babamukuru was not the person I had thought he was. He was wealthier than I had thought possible. He was educated beyond books. And he had done it alone. He had pushed up from under the weight of the white man with no strong relative to help him. How had he done it? Having done it, what had he become? A deep valley cracked open. There was no bridge; at the bottom, spiked crags as sharp as spears. I felt separated forever from my uncle.

It all became very depressing and confusing. At first I had been disappointed because I thought the garage was Babamukuru's house. Now I was worried because it wasn't. For the first time I caught sight of endings to my flight from the homestead that were not all happy. I scolded myself severely for having dared this far in the first place. Hadn't I known, I asked myself, that Babamukuru was a big-hearted man? That didn't make me anything special. Or even deserving. I didn't have anything to do with my uncle's kindness. He would have taken in any poor, needy relative, and to prove it I was only here because my brother had died.

Had I really thought, I continued callously, that these other-worldly relations of mine could live with anyone as ignorant and dirty as myself? I, who was so ignorant that I had not been able to read the signs in their clothes which dared not deteriorate or grow too tight in spite of their well-fleshed bodies, or in the accents of their speech, which were poised and smooth and dropped like foreign gemstones from their tongues. All these signs stated very matter-of-factly that we were not of a kind. I deserved to suffer, I threatened myself, for not having been too proud to see that Babamukuru could only be so charitable to our branch of the family because we were so low. He was kind because of the difference.

With a sigh I slid into a swamp of self-pity. My finely tuned survival system set off its alarm at once, warning me to avoid that trap, but I was lost. I could see no path of escape except the one that led back to the homestead. But that, I knew, would do me no good because I was burning up with wanting to escape from there. I did make an effort to improve my state of mind. I scolded myself strongly for not appreciating Babamukuru's concern for my family and me. I tried to call up my courage by imagining the fine grades I would make, which was what mattered, why I had come to the mission in the first place. I must have been much more frightened by the strangeness and awesomeness of my new position than I knew, because none of these tactics worked. I climbed out of the car much less hopefully than I had climbed into it, and followed Babamukuru uneasily as he walked towards the house.

A huge, hairy hound appeared in front of me from nowhere. It leapt out of thin air and scared me to death. Its black lips wrinkled up to show piercing incisors spiking out of gums that were even blacker than its lips. Its ears flattened themselves so far back on its head that its eyes stretched upwards in a demonic squint. Its sudden appearance made it seem all the more sinister. I could not help it. I yelped, which annoyed the beast and set it barking to summon its pink-eyed companion. The albino hound was even more unsettling. Everything about it was either pink or white. So pink were its gums that it took very little for my unhappy mind to conjure up blood and have it seep through the animal's skin to stain its pale teeth red. I was in a bad state or else I would have noticed the chains that bound them to their kennel and the fence that enclosed them in their pen. To me they were loose, ferocious guardians of the gates to this kingdom, this kingdom that I should not have been entering. Their lust for my blood was justified: they knew I did not belong.

Anna came to my rescue. 'If they were loose,' she called cheerfully, coming round the back of the house to greet me, 'they would have chewed you to pieces by now. Welcome, Tambu, welcome. It's good to see you again. That's why they are tied, these dogs. They aren't dogs to play about with, these.'

Tied . . . Tied . . . Ah, yes, they were tied! Perspective restored itself. I saw the chains and the fence. My knees calcified again, speech returned. I laughed nervously and tried to tell Anna how silly I had been not to realise that I was safe, but one did not need to do much talking when Anna was around. 'What about luggage? Where is it?' she chattered on. 'But sometimes they aren't tied – just think! – because they go off and we can't find them. When that happens, ha-a! you don't catch me outside, not even to hang the laundry. But it's good you have come. I've been thinking of you. Enter, enter,' she invited pleasantly, holding the back door open for me.

I was not half-way through the door before Nyasha was on me with a big hug, which I understood, and a kiss on both cheeks, which I did not. She was excited to see me, she was pleased she said. I was surprised to see her in such high spirits, pleasantly surprised, since this was not the cousin I had been steeling myself to meet. Believing my words, I hugged her back and told her that I too had been looking forward to her company.

Nyasha had a lot to say, during which time Anna disappeared to tell Maiguru that I had arrived. Nyasha was baking a cake, she said, for her brother, who was going back to his boarding school next day. The cake was ready to go into the oven, the weather was hot: the cake would rise in the mixing-bowl and flop in the baking-tin if it was not put to bake immediately. Anna would show me where to go. Nyasha disappeared back into the kitchen, taking with her some of the security that had settled on me with her warm welcome. I grew disapproving again of my cousin's bad manners and hoped that she would not carry on like that, because in the few minutes of our conversation I had seen that here at the mission at least I might have my old friend back.

She was very busy, dextrously greasing and flouring a cake tin and pouring in the batter. Not wanting to impose I busied myself with inspecting the kitchen. It looked very sophisticated to me at the time. But looking back, I remember that the cooker had only three plates, none of which was a ring; that the kettle was not electric; that the refrigerator was a bulky paraffin-powered affair. The linoleum was old, its blue and white pattern fading to patches of red where the paint had worn off and patches of black where feet had scuffed up the old flooring at its seams and water had dripped from hands and vegetables and crockery to create a stubborn black scum. The kitchen window was not curtained; a pane of glass was missing. This missing pane caused many problems because through the hole a draught blew, mischievously lowering temperatures in the oven so that buns and cakes were never quite light unless you could close the kitchen door and stop anybody from opening it, blocking the draught in its path. The broken window, the draught and its consequences were particularly annoying to Maiguru.

'It surprises me!' she used to mutter whenever she battled with oven temperatures. 'You'd think people would find time to fix windows in their own homes. Yet they don't. Ts! It surprises me.'

Later, as experience sharpened my perception of such things, I saw too that the colours were not co-ordinated. The green and pink walls – it was the fashion to have one wall a different colour from the others – contrasted harshly with each other and with the lino. It pleased me, though, to see that the kitchen was clean. What dirt that could be removed from the lino was removed regularly by thorough scrubbing with a strong ammonia cleaner, which was efficient but chapped your hands much more roughly than ash dissolved in water from Nyamarira ever did. The enamel of the cooker and the plastic of the fridge, although not shining, were white, and the kitchen sink gleamed greyly. This lack of brilliance was due, I discovered years later when television came to the mission, to the use of scouring powders which, though they sterilised 99 per cent of a household, were harsh and scratched fine surfaces. When I found this out, I realised that Maiguru, who had watched televison in England, must have known about the dulling effects of these scourers and about the brilliance that could be achieved by using the more gentle alternatives. By that time I knew something about budgets as well, notably their inelasticity. It dawned on me then that Maiguru's dull sink was not a consequence of slovenliness, as the advertisers would have had us believe, but a necessity.

Anna came back with the news that Maiguru was resting. She would be with me in the time that it took to get out of bed and dressed. She would show me to the living-room, where I was to wait for my aunt.

Hoping that it was not illness that had put my aunt in bed at that time of the day, I followed Anna to the living-room, where I made myself comfortable on the sofa. It was impossible not to notice that this sofa was twice as long and deep and soft as the one in the house at home. I took stock of my surroundings, noting the type, texture and shape of the furniture, its colours and its arrangement. My education had already begun, and it was with a pragmatic eye that I surveyed Maiguru's sitting-room: I would own a home like this one day; I would need to know how to furnish it.

Since I had entered my uncle's house through the back door, and so had moved up a gradient of glamour from the kitchen, through the dining-room to the living-room, I did not benefit from the full impact of the elegance of that living-room, with its fitted carpet of deep, green pile, tastefully mottled with brown and gold, and chosen to match the pale green walls (one slightly lighter than the other three according to the fashion). The heavy gold curtains flowing voluptuously to the floor, the four-piece lounge suite upholstered in glowing brown velvet, the lamps with their tasselled shades, the sleek bookcases full of leather-bound and hard-covered volumes of erudition, lost a little, but only a very little, of their effect.

Had I entered from the driveway, through the verandah and the front door, as visitors whom it was necessary to impress would enter, the taste and muted elegance of that room would have taken my breath away. At it was, having seen the kitchen, and the dining-room, which was much smarter than the kitchen, with shiny new linoleum covering every square inch of floor and so expertly laid that the seams between the strips were practically invisible, I was a little better prepared for what came next. This was not altogether a bad thing, because the full force of that opulent living-room would have been too much for me. I remember feeling slightly intimidated by the dining-room, with its large, oval table spacious enough to seat eight people taking up the centre of the room. That table, its shape and size, had a lot of say about the amount, the calorie content, the complement of vitamins and minerals, the relative proportions of fat, carbohydrate and protein of the food that would be consumed at it. No one who ate from such a table could fail to grow fat and healthy. Pushed up against a window, and there were several windows flanked by plain, sensible sun-filters and sombre, blue cotton curtains, was a display cabinet. Glossy and dark as the table, it displayed on greenish glass shelves the daintiest, most delicate china I had ever seen – fine, translucent cups and saucers, teapots and jugs and bowls, all covered in roses. Pink on white, gold on white, red on white. Roses. Old English, Tea, Old Country. Roses. These tea-sets looked so delicate it was obvious they would disintegrate the minute you so much as poured the tea into a cup or weighted a plate down with a bun. No wonder they had been shut away. I fervently hoped I would not be expected to eat or drink from them. I was relieved to find out in due course that everyone was a bit afraid of those charmingly expensive and fragile tea-sets, so they were only ever admired and shown off to guests.

If I was daunted by Maiguru's dainty porcelain cups, the living-room, as I have said, would have finished me off had I not been inoculated by the gradient I have talked of, although calling it a glamour gradient is not really the right way to describe it. This increase in comfort from kitchen to living-room was a common feature of all the teachers' houses at the mission. It had more to do with means and priorities than taste. Babamukuru's taste was excellent, so that where he could afford to indulge it, the results were striking. The opulence of his living-room was very strong stuff, overwhelming to someone who had first crawled and then toddled and finally walked over dung floors. Comfortable it was, but overwhelming nevertheless. Some strategy had to be devised to prevent all this splendour from distracting me in the way that my brother had been distracted. Usually in such dire straits I used my thinking strategy. I was very proud of my thinking strategy. It was meant to put me above the irrational levels of my character and enable me to proceed from pure, rational premises. Today, though, it did not work.

Every corner of Babamukuru's house – every shiny surface, every soft contour and fold – whispered its own insistent message of comfort and ease and rest so tantalisingly, so seductively, that to pay any attention to it, to think about it at all, would have been my downfall. The only alternative was to ignore it. I remained as aloof and unimpressed as possible.

This was not easy, because my aunt look a long time to come from her bedroom. I put this interval to good use in building up my defences. I had only to think of my mother, with Netsai and Rambanai superimposed in the background, to remember why and how I had come to be at the mission. And having seen how easily it could happen, I judged my brother less harshly. Instead, I became more aware of how necessary it was to remain steadfast. Then, to make sure that I was not being soft and sentimental in revising my opinion of Nhamo, I had to survey my surroundings again to see whether they really were potent enough to have had such a devastating effect on him, thus exposing myself again to all the possible consequences. I triumphed. I was not seduced.

You might think that there was no real danger. You might think that, after all, these were only rooms decorated with the sort of accessories that the local interpretations of British interior decor magazines were describing as standard, and nothing threatening in that. But really the situation was not so simple. Although I was vague at the time and could not have described my circumstances so aptly, the real situation was this: Babamukuru was God, therefore I had arrived in Heaven. I was in danger of becoming an angel, or at the very least a saint, and forgetting how ordinary humans existed – from minute to minute and from hand to mouth.

BESSIE HEAD

Woman from America

This woman from America married a man of our village and left her country to come and live with him here. She descended on us like an avalanche. People are divided into two camps: those who feel a fascinated love and those who fear a new thing.

Some people keep hoping she will go away one day, but already her big strong stride has worn the pathways of the village flat. She is everywhere about because she is a woman, resolved and unshakable in herself. To make matters worse or more disturbing she comes from the west side of America, somewhere near California. I gather from her conversation that people from the West are stranger than most people.

People of the West of America must be the most oddly beautiful people in the world; at least this woman from the West is the most oddly beautiful person I have ever seen. Every cross-current of the earth seems to have stopped in her and blended into an amazing harmony. She has a big dash of Africa, a dash of Germany, some Cherokee and heaven knows what else. Her feet are big and her body is as tall and straight and strong as a mountain tree. Her neck curves up high and her thick black hair cascades down her back like a wild and tormented stream. I cannot understand her eyes though, except that they are big, black, and startled like those of a wild free buck racing against the wind. Often they cloud over with a deep, intense, brooding look.

It takes a great deal of courage to become friends with a woman like that. Like everyone here, I am timid and subdued. Authority, everything can subdue me; not because I like it that way but because authority carries the weight of an age pressing down on life. It is terrible then to associate with a person who can shout authority down. Her shouting matches with authority are the terror and sensation of the village. It has come down to this. Either the woman is unreasonable or authority is unreasonable, and everyone in his heart would like to admit that authority is unreasonable. In reality, the rule is: If authority does not like you, then you are the outcast and humanity associates with you at their peril. So try always to be on the right side of authority, for the sake of peace, and please avoid the outcast. I do not say it will be like this forever. The whole world is crashing and interchanging itself and even remote bush villages in Africa are not to be left out!

It was inevitable though that this woman and I should be friends. I have an overwhelming curiosity that I cannot keep within bounds. I passed by the house for almost a month, but one cannot crash in on people. Then one day a dog they own had puppies, and my small son chased one of the puppies into the yard and I chased after him. Then one of the puppies became his and there had to be discussions about the puppy, the desert heat, and the state of the world and as a result of curiosity an avalanche of wealth has descended on my life. My small hut-house is full of short notes written in a wide sprawling hand. I have kept them all because they are a statement of human generosity and the wild carefree laugh of a woman who is as busy as women the world over about things women always entangle themselves in – a man, a home . . . Like this . . .

'Have you an onion to spare? It's very quiet here this morning and I'm all fagged out from sweeping and cleaning the yard, shaking blankets, cooking, fetching water, bathing children, and there's still the floor inside to sweep and dishes to wash . . . it's endless!'

Sometimes too, conversations get all tangled up and the African night creeps all about and the candles are not lit and the conversation gets more entangled, intense; and the children fall asleep on the floor dazed by it all.

She is a new kind of American or even maybe will be a new kind of African. There isn't anyone here who does not admire her. To come from a world of chicken, hamburgers, TV, escalators, and whatnot to a village mud hut and a life so tough, where the most you can afford to eat is ground millet and boiled meat. Sometimes you cannot afford to eat at all. Always you have to trudge miles for a bucket of water and carry it home on your head. And to do all this with loud, ringing, sprawling laughter?

Black people in America care about Africa, and she has come here on her own as an expression of that love and concern. Through her, too, one is filled with wonder for a country that breeds individuals about whom, without and within, rushes the wind of freedom. I have to make myself clear, though. She is a different person who has taken by force what America will not give black people.

The woman from America loves both Africa and America, independently. She can take what she wants from both and say, 'Dammit'. It is a most strenuous and difficult thing to do.

JEAN MARQUARD

Regina's Baby

In the night there is rain, loud and hard, a charge of energy in the outside dark, perforating the thirsty garden. I love the rain; it is a curtain shutting me off from the world. I lie in bed not moving, hardly breathing, so that I can shift the burden of consciousness over and let in the pleasant thoughts. Fantasies of privacy encapsulate me in a shelter legitimised by the rain. My favourite dreams of winter take shape: log fires, deep armchairs drawn up, a love nest. Ghosts outside. Rain on the window panes, creaking branches, the friendly commotion of family suppers, steaming mugs . . . the pungency of a felt content. Glowing faces, sweet smelling after-bath children in flannel pyjamas, comfortable dogs snoring on the hearth . . . slow, quiet, inward evenings with the cold locked outside.

The winter never existed. The winter conjured by novels and pictures.

The telephone punctures my images, Johan is asleep. Probably he has a hangover. The party last night, like most parties, went on too long. After dinner over liqueurs there was a second wind – the build-up of that counterfeit animation which is an essential part of proper party behaviour. Discussion was shrill and vigorous, bent on ignoring small underground tremors of animosity and boredom. We all knew each other so well, without ever feeling enriched by that knowledge. You felt that if you had not met the individual, then at least you knew the type. Issues were raised. Abortion. Euthanasia. Censorship. A sort of verbal karate to try and make these interesting.

Johan is asleep and there is no sound from the children's room. Reluctantly I get up to answer the phone. Rain on the roof, gutters belching water. Trees outside toss in a blur of wind and wet. The Pieter Grobbelaar Hospital is on the line. A crisp woman's voice dispensing words like pills. One of the nurses. Do we employ a servant by the name of R. Joseph? A blank moment. I am unaccustomed – a momentary slip – to the appendage of a surname.

Politics too. Sequential pontification; first World Affairs, then the Continent, then the Country. Like those modern French films in which documentary flashes and news-reels in the background fill in what is important while Mr and Mrs Everyman carry on significantly meaningless lives in the foreground. Declamatory triumph. Clever talk. Predictable formulae and prophecies produced, limp-eared rabbits, tired, from the conjurer's hat. Party games.

'Regina? Yes we do. Would you like to speak to her?'

'No, I would rather speak to you Mrs Jackson, if you wouldn't mind.'

The voice has adopted the stance of disapproval – the firm, no-nonsense accents of a majestic, all-encompassing authority. Regina's child had been admitted to the hospital last week. 'Yes, I know the child. A little girl. My maid often talks about her. I know she has been in hospital several times for observation.'

•

The Blacks are seen to be (in the near future) inviolate and isolate in their (ultimate and inevitable) realisation of Black Power. Somehow *we* are doomed and irrelevant. (In Rhodesia) there will be a blood-bath pretty soon now.

•

'The baby died this morning. Well, Mrs Jackson . . . The doctors, I might tell you are puzzled by this death – the child seemed to be quite all right – in fact we were thinking of discharging her in a day or two.'

•

Each guest, imprisoned in the ritual of discussion, has something to say and says it in the clamorous accents of conviction; yet beneath the noisy babble of voices, the inebriated, fatigued sincerity, there seems to be nothing – nothing recognisable that is – in the way of an accepted and acknowledged background of assumptions.

•

'The death was quite unexpected.'

•

For after all, if you were, as you believed, decent and humane, capable above all of standing up for your beliefs, then how on earth were you to define yourself in the framework of your country's values, in the confusion of ambiguities and compromises and evasions you were forced to live by? Vehemently you expressed an image of yourself, but your emotions were fed only by the thin gruel, the unsustaining trickle of personal animosity and the nervous irritation engendered by boredom.

•

'But how dreadful!' Regina had worshipped the child.
'Now the problem is that your girl will want to come over here to see the child and we must ask you to forbid this, Mrs Jackson. We want to hold the body for a few days so that we can do an autopsy.'
'An autopsy? Will that help . . .?'

•

'Ian Vermaak is a bloody hypocrite.'
'I hate it when they talk politics. It gets you nowhere.'
'Fine for Ian Vermaak to talk about handing it all over.' (Johan drives aggressively as if the car is his enemy.) 'He's got a nice little pile stashed away in Switzerland and you can be bloody sure he'll get the rest of it out in time too.' I learn to say nothing. I learn to ignore the small irregularities in the pattern, the breaks in the rhythm of compatibility. Compatibility with Johan. My life is like my knitting. Even, monotonous, sometimes one notices a small mistake. A perfectionist would start unravelling but the eye can be trained not to see. In all things the habit of evasion is easily acquired. My life is like that. I put it away and start again, just where I left off.

•

'We *must* ask you to make your girl understand that she is *not* to come over here. You *must* please explain to her that she *will* have her funeral, but she *must* wait for a few days.'

•

'And I suppose it will bloody rain tomorrow,' said Johan before going to sleep, 'and wash out our foursome.'

•

I go into the bedroom and, without waking Johan, I carefully step into my slippers and slip on my warm camelhair dressing-gown. I even comb my hair, looking at myself in the mirror – a smooth, becalmed face, in which the signals of anxiety are almost ready to go on – and then I go carefully down in the passage to the back. I feel self-conscious. I have a nervous, not entirely unpleasant sensation, as if I am about to appear on stage or enter a crowded room where all eyes are beamed on me. I do not want to feel this way. I am on my way to Regina's room to break tragic news – I want to feel something other than the adventure of hollow fright – some warm fellow-feeling of grief and pain. But there it is: the familiar, nagging barrier of disengagement, arresting the natural flow of feeling. Then, as I have taught myself, I rationalise. After all, I am *fond* of Regina who has been a servant in the house for fifteen years; after all, I have children of my own and naturally, but naturally, I am fond of those children. If one of *them* were suddenly to die Regina would feel the anguish I don't feel now.

But walking a careful tight-rope to the maid's room, hearing the steady release of rain, I can tap the source of nothing but an alarmed, dry-eyed incredulity, aimed as much at myself, my dying heart, as at the brand-new shocking fact of the child's death.

Regina's baby had been unexpected, but when it arrived she was pleased. 'A beautiful girl, Madam,' she said when she came back. 'She's got such pretty hair! Such a fresh child, Madam!' She seemed no longer to care about the extra trouble and expense.

The baby lived in the kitchen, snuggling contentedly on Regina's back while she did the housework. She put it down to sleep in a cardboard box under the window and when the weather turned she moved the box nearer the stove. I said, 'You can have the old cot in the garage – and see if Thomas can't mend Bertie's old high chair.'

The baby had a circle of toffee-coloured hair that caught the light and a pretty, creamy complexion. I saw very little of the baby but the children made a fuss; picking it up and playing with it when they came in from school. They gave it their old toys which were claimed and discarded with a confident belief in the natural right to possession that is common in babies. Sometimes I would hear the baby's fat, extravagant laughter behind the closed kitchen door. It seemed to be a lively little character and Regina glowed with pleasure almost permanently in those days. Her other children were grown-up, virtually, and had gone off somewhere or other to earn money. Regina, not much past thirty, thought of this child as the daughter of her old age. The father was not mentioned. 'I suppose you don't know which one he is,' I said to Regina.

When the child was a year old and just beginning to toddle it was taken from my kitchen to be looked after in the location by one of Regina's numerous relatives. That was its final exit as far as I was concerned and now, after two years, I had almost forgotten its existence – remembered it only through occasional references made by Regina.

The baby had been periodically ill; it had been taken to the hospital several times, latterly for observation. Mysteriously, now, it was dead.

Regina took the news badly. She screamed when I told her. She made brutal sounds. She tore her hair, bit her hands, punishing herself. She even grovelled on the floor, twisting and wrenching her body like an animal in its death agony. This is terrible. I stand aside, watching. I am alarmed. I have never been close to such uncontrolled behaviour. When Billie was killed in the car accident Mummy was beside herself with grief, naturally, but it was a stately, poised emotion – nothing like this. Really, I can't cope with this; emotion, turmoil, confrontation, Johan, all this. I want the rain, like a pent-up breath expelled, to come down outside with me inside – inside my house and my head like a snail.

'Now Regina, now Regina,' I said, giving her shoulders a little, sharp shake – which is what Mummy would have done. Regina is a tiny woman, child-shaped. When I felt her frail shoulders collapse slowly and lightly under my fingers like a house of cards my throat suddenly closed up. I have not, thank God, forgotten how to feel pain. The shoulders capitulated so quietly and completely, without rebellion; the little woman sat subdued on the bed, surrendered to my mother's controlled severity, falsely resurrected in me. She was shuddering, but only involuntarily and only because these terrible massive sobs had to pass out of her body. Her face was swollen, grossly misshapen from weeping. I wanted to hold her tight and love her tight but how could I when she was repulsive, covered in tears and stuff from her nose. I said, 'Now Regina, I want you to sit very quietly here. I am going to fetch you some handkerchiefs and a cup of tea. I will be right back. I won't forsake you.' She was such a child, you see. I let go of her and now I am outside myself, I watch myself again.

There is no sound in the house. Incredibly the family is still asleep. How innocent Johan looks, sleeping . . . almost as if one might wake him up and tell him what is happening . . . I pull open a drawer and grab a handful of his pastel-coloured silk handkerchiefs. How soft they feel. They were bought in Rome; the monogram beautifully embroidered in the corner, two curly J's very close together, snug under the roof of a single bold head stroke. Oh, we were happy in Rome. We were tourists then, we felt free . . .

Regina insisted on going to the hospital. She drank the tea, pushed the wet handkerchiefs into the pocket of her overall and, although still silently crying, she was quite calm and quite adamant. She was stubborn. Her mouth closed stubbornly. She would have to go to the hospital to see her child. What could I do? I sat on the edge of Regina's narrow bed – the coir mattress felt scratchy. The narrow room with its tiny window set high above eye-level (they feel safer with a smaller window and they don't really care for views you know, the builder had said) reminded me of the obscure, fretful loneliness of a dormitory cubicle at boarding school. Life thus narrowed down by outside dictation relieves you of responsibility. At school we ignored our ugly cubicles – you pretended you were someone else, somewhere else.

It is hard to believe that the tiny, isolated Regina has been a mother.

Yet the cubicles at school were impersonal, odourless, virginally bland. They carried the message of an essential abdication. In Regina's room is an aura of intense, furtive life, the vivid smell of personal activity.

The room is carefully neat, a doiley on the scrubbed table, a clutch of flowers in a cracked vase – a rather pathetic collection – hibiscus browning at the edges, two geranium twigs, a couple of yellow daisies. Why didn't Regina pick the good flowers? . . . the garden was blooming, wasting almost. A framed snapshot (O God, the child is in it), a faded Valentine card with a red heart pierced by a pink arrow.

But this is only the surface. There is another kind of life in the room, a smokiness of corporate energy; the evidence, dense but invisible, of bodies other than Regina's tiny frame. She has women friends but she also has men in here. I wonder about that. Johan would be furious (although I would never tell him), he would be furious and I too, yes definitely, I sense something not quite pleasant – something threatening. It seems not quite tasteful and it seems not quite safe for my family that Regina should have concourse with men in this tiny capsule of a room. I remember once in the summer I came in and found Regina entertaining two men and a woman. The men had been holding their hats in their hands and talking in low murmurs, very discreet, but I was frightened. They were drinking tea in enamel mugs. Their black, patient eyes had looked up with the familiar expression of ironic servitude; polite, pleading, suspicious; but coiled up in the depths of the men's eyes a fine, steely, just discernible point of contempt – like a snake's tongue – that flicks and just might dart out to poison you. One could not complain about visitors – after all, it had been broad daylight – yet I felt irritated and almost wished Regina would dispense with a private life or confine it, at least, to her days off.

Regina got her way in the end.

'If you promise not to make a fuss when we get there.'

'Yes, Madam.'

'You do understand about the – well – the body. That they have to keep her for a short while.'

'Yes, Madam. I promise, Madam.'

Regina sat in the car in silence with one of Johan's handkerchiefs pressed to her mouth. Down in the valley umbrellas had popped open like mushrooms. Under them people hurried into cars and buildings. The church bells of the Methodist church played a recorded medley – Rock of Ages, Abide with Me, What a Friend we have in Jesus.

We hurried down the vast, blank, ether-smelling corridors of the hospital – past starched soft-shoed nurses, past the crowded out-patients' waiting room (I averted my eyes in case there was visible blood).

'But lady, I did tell you *not* to bring her.' The owner of the crisp voice is a stout unattractive nurse with a heavy, large-pored face. Regina cowered in a corner, clutching the handkerchief, looking all but effaced in her over-sized black jacket with the sagging pockets.

'I really had no choice,' I said firmly in Mummy's voice, beginning to be annoyed. 'After all, she has a perfect right to see her own child.

She has given me her word that she will behave perfectly. All she asks is to see her child.'

'Mmmm,' says the nurse grimly. 'That's what they all say. As soon as she sees the child there will be screaming and carrying on. You'll see.' She is cross, tight-lipped, an unattractive person. 'Well then, come with me, my girl,' she says grimly. 'You'd better come too, Mrs Jackson.'

We follow the nurse, I put my arm around Regina's shoulders. I will not desert her. It is we two against the nurse. 'You won't let me down will you, Regina?'

'No, Madam.'

•

The baby is in a small covered cot in a private ante-room. From a nearby ward comes the blurred hum of female voices. Brisk footsteps in rubber-soled shoes squeak down the corridors. The nurse gives me a look, then she lifts the sheet and folds it neatly back, exposing the face of a delicate, fair child – almost blonde. Tears swell in my throat when I look at the little peaked face, so unchildlike in its expression of chill solemnity. There are fine blue shadows like bruises on either side of the round unformed nose. Sand-coloured eyelashes curl on the pale cheeks, the fine baby hair lies damply on the pillow. This tiny drop of life has drained quietly, unobtrusively away. I think suddenly of desolation – of the sea ebbing back, of empty, luminous shells cast up on the beach. I stare at the small shut face – it seems almost transparent – I have seen death before. Billie was death closed in a box, something shattered we were not allowed to see. But this child's face will be impressed on my memory for ever. I want to bow my head in a reverent silence so that my memory might be stamped by the occasion, stamped with its indelible signature. But Regina flings herself at the cot and howls. She keens, she struggles like a wild animal, she claws and she kicks so that the nurse and I have to grab her arms, our combined strength hardly sufficing to hold her down. We have to drag her down the corridor away from the little cot. An awful, humiliating episode, which I shall edit from my memory. But the nurse suddenly reveals a crude, practical sort of compassion, a crack in her armour. She covers Regina's head and ears with two large, reddish hands and pushes the weeping face hard down as if thus it might find the softness of a female bosom under the uniform. Regina is half smothered and she stops crying. The nurse comforts her in a loud scolding voice and gives her a sedative to drink. Now it is over and I must take her home.

●

The rain has stopped. A hard sun was already soaking up puddles and drying the tarmac. I was tense; I had never been into the location – I wished the whole wretched episode were ended and that I could return to Johan and breakfast with the children. I was made estranged and nervous by the throngs of coloured people in the bumpy pot-holed location streets. In a vacant lot a man was juggling an empty beer bottle on the palm of his hand. His fly was open. He couldn't have been drunk on a Sunday, but he staggered about in a manner half clownish, half despairing. People stood in the doorways of their squalid little houses, staring at the big car. I had to drive slowly to avoid jagged holes in the road, skirting deep puddles of muddy water. Here it took the sun some time to complete its mopping up operation. In places the water that had dammed up at the edges of the road overflowed and rushed across our path, bearing its load of township rubbish. Soggy newspapers stuck to fences, blown there by the previous night's wind. The slow journey down the narrow gravel road became a kind of procession as if we were visiting royalty (of dubious popularity). Children ran behind the car, jeering and laughing. I felt myself ripped out of time, hurled into that squalid and picturesque past conjured up by nineteenth-century illustrators – the world of Charles Dickens's London or maybe Hogarth – not my world at all.

When we reached Regina's cottage, members of her family came tumbling out of the door and suddenly, as they clamoured around the car doors, pandemonium broke loose. No word had been spoken, apparently, yet the news was out, spreading ubiquitously like rain over the street. Women lifted their aprons and wailed aloud. Regina was half lifted, half dragged from the car and borne into the house on a giant wave of sympathy, her renewed cries of grief mingling with those of her neighbours. I was forgotten, ignored. All around me, pressing close, moving towards the car and away like a tide were the wailing, weeping women. This noisy community of pain from which I, who thought of grief as a private, a dignified, ultimately a character-building emotion, was irrevocably excluded, bewildered and frightened me. I experienced vague terrors, the falling away from safety, the clay-footed inability to escape that accompanies nightmare. Some terrible unspecified thing might happen – riots, rape, racial reification, violence. I sat tight and unmoving behind the wheel while the people milled about. But nobody thought of blaming me or of harming me. They were grateful to me for bringing Regina home. Beneath the ritual of shared grief, like a gift in a wrapping, was genuine concern for Regina, true fellowship. Real wet tears rolled copiously down the faces of the women – half of them (I am dazed thinking of it) must be strangers to Regina – while they crowded about my side of the car.

'Madam, when did the baby die? Where is the baby, Madam, Madam, where is the baby?'

I did answer questions, you know, I explained why the child's body was being held at the hospital. Nevertheless, they continued, stupidly, the same things asked, until I realised dimly that they, the questioners, were indifferent to the surface logic of my answers. I could not still their questioning any more than I could quieten their distress; neither by persuading them by what authority the hospital could hold the baby's body nor by repeating that the baby was dead.

I drove out of the location and, once on the tarmac, sped home through the now bright, sunny morning. Surrounded as I had been, breathed on by so much open pain, I felt tremulous and weak, as though I had caught the term of a contagious grief. I wished the rain would drop its comforting curtain around me again.

When I got home there was a clattering of cutlery and children's voices from the kitchen.

'They are getting their own breakfast,' says Johan accusingly. Suddenly I am in the real world again.

'Regina's baby died. I took her home.'

Johan is dressed in golfing slacks and a red T-shirt. His hold-all is open on the chest of drawers. Neatly he lays out a change of clothes for me to pack. Socks, underpants, a warm cotton-knit shirt, his grey sweater.

'Where the hell are all my handkerchiefs?' He hunts diligently through his drawers.

'Oh, Johan, I can't play golf to-day. Not now.'

'Why not? It's cleared up. Why shouldn't we play?'

I turn my face to the wall. I do not want to cry unless there is someone to comfort me. I think of the nurse. She would have been someone to offer solace.

'I gave the handkerchiefs to Regina. To wipe her face. Her child died.'

'Listen, did you have to give her *all* the handkerchiefs? All the *silk* handkerchiefs? Wasn't cotton good enough?'

Johan's exasperation, the children beginning to fight in the kitchen, the sunlight in harsh white squares on the floor.

'Could someone please for Christ's sake go out there and discipline those bloody children,' says Johan, as if to himself, and flinging a golfing glove on to the bed he stalks out. He turns back at the door and says, 'You realise of course that those handkerchiefs will not be seen again in this house. I hope Regina appreciates the value of the gift, although I doubt it. I reckon the equivalent in cash would have meant more.'

The familiar ache of loneliness, incompletion. I look at the neat twin beds, mine and Johan's, which seem forlorn in their emptiness, the starched white sheets crumpled only in the used spaces where our bodies had curled in sleep such a short while ago. Might as well be coffins. Everything is spoiled. Everything has gone wrong. The rain has stopped. In my life there will be golf and unpleasantness . . . I put my head in the pillow and cry – quietly and privately and desperately. My grief is a silent, dignified, poised emotion. It allows me to resume my life again later, just as before.

ZOË WICOMB

Bowl Like Hole

Origins trouble the voyager much, those roots that have sipped the
waters of another continent . . .

it is solitude that mutilates,
the night bulb that reveals ash on my sleeve.

ARTHUR NORTJE

Don't travel beyond
Acton at noon in the intimate summer light
of England

ARTHUR NORTJE

In writing the history of unfashionable families one is apt to fall into
a tone of emphasis which is very far from being the tone of good
society, where principles and beliefs are not only of an extremely
moderate kind, but are always presupposed, no subjects being
eligible but such as can be touched with a light and graceful irony.

The Mill on the Floss, GEORGE ELIOT

At first Mr Weedon came like any white man in a motor car, enquiring
about sheep or goats or servants.

A vehicle swerving meteor-bright across the veld signalled a break
in the school day as rows of children scuttled out to hide behind the
corner, their fingers plugged into their nostrils with wonder and
admiration. They examined the tracks of the car or craned their necks
in turn to catch a glimpse of the visitor even though all white men
looked exactly the same. Others exploited the break to find circuitous
routes to the bank of squat ghanna bushes where they emptied their
bowels and bladders. On such occasions they did not examine each
other's genitals. They peered through the scant foliage to admire the

shiny vehicle from a safe distance. They brushed against the bushes, competing to see, so that the shrivelled little leaf-balls twisted and showered into dust. From this vantage point they would sit, pants down, for the entire visit while the visitor conducted his business from the magnificence of his car.

At an early age I discovered the advantage of curling up motionless in moments of confusion, a position which in further education I found to be foetal. On these topsy-turvy days I crept at great risk of being spotted to the kitchen which jutted out at a near ninety degrees of mud-brick wall from the school building. Under the narrow rectangular table I lay very still. The flutter inside subsided the instant I drew my knees up and became part of the arrangement of objects, shared in the solidity of the table and the cast-iron buckets full of water lined up on it. I could depend on Mamma being too absorbed by the event to notice me. Or if she did, she would not shout while the car squinted at the kitchen door.

So under the kitchen table I invariably found myself when vehicles arrived. And at first Mr Weedon arrived like any other white man enquiring about sheep or goats or servants.

As the time between sunrises and sunsets began to arrange itself into weeks and months and seasons, Mr Weedon's arrivals became regular. Something to do with the tax year, at the end of March, Mamma explained. The children still ran out to whisper and admire from a distance, and I with a new knowledge of geography still crept under the kitchen table, but with the buckets of water was now swept along on the earth's elliptical journey around the sun.

Mr Weedon spoke not one word of Afrikaans. For people who were born in England the g's and r's of the language were impossible, barbaric.

'A gentleman, a true Englishman,' Mamma said as she handed Father his best hat. For the Mercedes could be seen miles away, a shining disc spun in a cloud of dust. A week or so after the autumn equinox he arrived. He did not blow a horn like the uncouth Boers from the dorp. There was no horn in the back seat. Neither did he roll down a window to rest a forearm on the door. Perhaps the chrome was too hot even in autumn and he did not wish to scorch the blond hairs on his arm. With the help of the person who occupied the driver's seat, Mr Weedon's door was opened, and despite a light skirmish between the two men, he landed squarely on both feet. The cloud of dust produced by the car and the minor struggle subsided. Soo Mr Weedon puffed deeply on a thick cigar, producing a cloud of smoke. Mr Weedon loved clouds. Which may explain why his eyes roved about as he spoke, often to rest ponderously on a fleecy cloud above.

'A true gentleman,' Mamma whispered to herself from the kitchen window as he shook hands with Father, 'these Boers could learn a few things from him.'

'Well and how are you, how's the wife?' The English r's slid along without the vibration of tongue against palate. Mamma's asthma mentioned, he explained how his wife suffered with hers. And Cape Town so damp in winter she was forced to spend a hideous season in the Bahamas. Father tutted sympathetically. He would hate to spend several days away from home, let alone months.

'Yes,' said Mr Weedon, braiding his lapel with delicate fingers. How frail we all are . . . an uncertain world . . . even health cannot be bought . . . we must all march past as Death the Leveller makes his claim, and he looked up at a floating cloud in support of his theory of transience.

Father too held his chin slightly to the left, his goitre lifted as he scanned the sky. Possibly to avoid the cigar smoke, for he supported the school of thought that doubted whether God intended man to smoke; why else had he not provided him with a chimney?

Mr Weedon dropped his cigar and rubbed his palms together, which indicated that he was ready for the discussion held annually in the schoolroom. Father smiled, 'Certainly,' and tapped the black ledger already tucked under his arm. He rushed to open the door and another cloud of dust ensued as the man who opened doors tried to oust him. Everyone mercifully kept their balance and the man retreated sourly to lean against his Mercedes.

'Good Heavens,' whispered Mamma, 'he's picking his nose.' Was she talking to me? Even in the topsy-turviness of the day I dared not say anything, ask who or where. Only the previous day I had been viciously dragged by the hair from under the table with threats of thrashings if ever I was found there again. It was not worth the risk. Fortunately she went on. 'I wouldn't be surprised if he were Coloured, from Cape Town I suppose, a play-white . . . one can never tell with Capetonians. Or perhaps a registered Coloured. Mr Weedon being a civilised man might not mind a brown person driving his car.'

So she knew that I was there, must have known all along, for I had been careful not to move. I turned my head towards the window and through the iron crossbars of the table saw in her two great buttocks the opposing worlds she occupied. The humiliation of the previous day still smarted; she was not to be trusted and I pursed my lips in disgust when she sat down, occupying her two worlds so fully.

'Oom Klaas Dirkse has been off work again. You must take him an egg and a mug of milk, and no playing on the way.'

A brief silence, then she carried on, 'And I've warned you not to speak Afrikaans to the children. They ought to understand English and it won't hurt them to try. Your father and I managed and we all have to put up with things we don't understand. Anyway, those Dirkse children have lice; you're not to play with them.'

As if the Dirkse children would want to play with me. Kaatjie Dirkse may lower her head and draw up her thin shoulders, but her plaited horns would stand erect and quiver their contempt.

Oh how Mamma spoiled things. The space under the table grew into the vast open veld so that I pressed against the wall and bored my chin into clasped knees. Outside the shiny Capetonian leaned against his car; only Kaatjie Dirkse would have dared to slink past him with a single sullen glare. The murmur from the schoolroom rose and fell and I was glad, very glad, that Kaatjie's horns crawled with lice.

'Stay there, you're not to hang over the lower door and gawp,' Mamma hissed unnecessarily. She heard the shuffling towards the school door and, finding her hands empty, reached for the parts of our new milk separator. These she started to assemble, tentatively clicking the parts into place, then confidently, as if her fingertips drew strength from the magic machine. Its scarecrow arms flung resolutely apart, the assembled contraption waited for the milk that it would drive through the aluminium maze and so frighten into separation. I watched her pour the calf's milk into the bowl and turn the handle viciously to drown the sound of the men's shuffling conversation outside. Out of the left arm the startled thin bluish milk spurted, and seconds later yellow cream trickled confidently from the right.

'That's Flossie's milk. She's not had any today,' I accused.

'We'll milk again tonight. There'll be more tonight,' and her eyes begged as if she were addressing the cow herself, as if her life depended on the change of routine.

Father did not report back to the kitchen. He was shown to the front seat of the car in order to accompany Mr Weedon to the gypsum mine on the edge of the settlement. Mr Weedon's cigar smoke wrapped itself in blue bands around Father's neck. He coughed and marvelled at the modesty of the man who preferred to sit alone in the back seat of his own car.

Children tumbled out from behind the schoolroom or the ghanna bushes to stare at the departing vehicle. Little ones recited the CA 3654 of the number plate and carried the transported look throughout the day. The older boys freed their nostrils and with hands plunged in their pockets suggested by a new swaggering gait that it was not so wonderful a spectacle after all. How could it be if their schoolmaster was carried away in the Mercedes? But it was, because Father was the only person for miles who knew enough English, who could interpret. And Mr Weedon had a deep fear of appearing foolish. What if he told a joke and the men continued to look at him blankly, or if they with enamelled faces said something irreverent or just something not very nice? How they would laugh later at his blank or smiling face. For Mr Weedon understood more than he admitted, and was not above the occasional pretence.

With Father by his side Mr Weedon said the foreign Good Afternoon to the miners, followed by a compliment on how well they looked, their naked torsos glistening with sweat, rivalling only the glory of the pink desert rose that they heaved out of the earth. Distanced by the translation, the winged words fluttered; he was moved to a poetic comparison. A maddening rhythm as the picks swung with a bulge of biceps in unison, up, cutting the air, the blades striking the sunbeams in one long stroke of lightning; then down the dark torsos fell, and a crash of thunder as the blades struck the earth, baring her bosom of rosy gypsum. Mr Weedon, so overcome, was forced to look away, at a cloud that raced across the sky with such apparent panting that in all decency he had to avert his eyes once again.

And so midst all that making of poetry, two prosaic mounds rose on either side of the deepening pit. One of these would ultimately blend in with the landscape; fine dust cones would spin off it in the afternoons just as they spun off the hills that had always been there. There was no telling, unless one kicked ruthlessly and fixed an expert eye on the tell-tale tiredness of the stone, that this hill was born last year and that had always been. The other mound of gypsum was heaved by the same glistening torsos on to lorries that arrived at the end of the week. These hobbled over gravel roads to the siding at Moedverloor from where the transformed plaster of paris was carried away.

Mr Weedon turned a lump of jagged gypsum in the sun so that its crystal peaks shimmered like a thousand stars in the dead stone.

'For my daughter,' he said, 'a sample of nature's bounty. She collects rocks, just loves the simple things in life. It's nature, the simple things,' he said to Father, who could not decide whether to translate or not, 'the simple things that bring the greatest joy. Oh Sylvia would love our Brakwater, such stark beauty,' and his gaze shifted . . . 'the men are doing a marvellous job' . . . as his eyes settled on a rippled chest thrown back.

'These man-made mountains and the bowls they once fitted into, beautiful and very useful for catching the rain, don't you think?'

So he had no idea that it never rained more than the surface of the earth could hold, enough to keep the dust at rest for a day or so. Father decided not to translate.

'Tell them that I'm very happy with things,' and he turned, clicking his fingers at the man who opened doors. An intricate system of signals thus triggered itself off. The boot of the car flew open, a cardboard box appeared, and after a particularly united blow at the rock the men laid down their picks and waited in semaphoric obedience. Mr Weedon smiled. Then they stepped forward holding out their hands to receive the green and white packet of Cavalla cigarettes that the smiling man dealt out. Descants of 'Dankie Meneer' and he flushed with pleasure for he had asked many times before not to be called Baas as the Boers insisted on being called. This time not one of the men made a mistake or even stuttered over the words. A day to be remembered, as he reviewed the sinewed arms outstretched, synchronised with simple words of thanks and the happy contingent of the kind angle of sun so that a bead of sweat could not gather at his brow and at a critical moment bounce on to the green and white Cavalla packet, or, and here he clenched his teeth, trail along the powdered arm of a miner who would look away in disgust.

'I don't smoke thank you, sir,' Father seemed very tall as his rigid arm held out the box. Mr Weedon's musings on harmony splintered to the dissonance of Father's words, so that he stared vacantly at the box of one hundred Cavallas held at him between thumb and index finger. Where in God's name was the man who opened doors?

Was the wind changing direction? Moisture seeped on to his brow and little mercurial drops rolled together until a shining bead gathered dead centre then slid perpendicularly to the tip of his nose where it waited. Mr Weedon brushed the back of his hand across the lower half of his face, rubbed the left jaw in an improvised itch and said, 'Well we must be off.' The box of cigarettes had somehow landed in his free arm.

The men waited, leaning on their picks, and with the purr of the engine shouted a musical Goodbye Sir in Afrikaans, words which Mr Weedon fortunately knew the meaning of. The wheels swung, a cigar moved across the back window and a cloud of dust swallowed all. The men screwed their eyes and tried to follow the vehicle. When it finally disappeared over the ridge they took up their picks once more.

'Here he co-omes,' the children crooned, as they do about all vehicles flashing in the distance. I ran to meet Father who would be dropped just above the school. From behind a bush I watched the Mercedes move on. A cloud of dust shaped itself into a festive trail following the car. A dozen brackhounds, spaced at intervals along the road and barking theatrically, ran in the manner of a relay race alongside the vehicle until the next dog took over.

I trotted to keep up with Father's long stride, my hand locked in his. His eyes like the miners' were red-rimmed in his powdered face. He handed me a lump of gypsum which I turned about in the sun until its crystal peaks shimmered like a thousand stars in the dead stone.

'That was quick,' Mamma said. Obscure words of praise that would invite him to give a full account.

'Funny,' Father replied, 'Mr Weedon said that the mine was like a bowl in the earth. Bowl like hole, not bowl like howl. Do you think that's right?'

She frowned. She had been so sure. She said, 'Of course, he's English, he ought to know.'

Then, unexpectedly, interrupting Father as he gave details of the visit, she turned on me. 'And don't you think you'll get away with it, sitting under the table like a tame Griqua.'

But revenge did not hold her attention. A wry smile fluttered about her lips. She muttered. 'Fowl, howl, scowl and not bowl.' She would check the pronunciation of every word she had taken for granted.

I knew that unlike the rest of us it would take her no time at all to say bowl like hole, smoothly, without stuttering.

SHEILA FUGARD

Lace

'The baai', the familiar name for Port Elizabeth, a dry industrial town beside the Indian Ocean. I did not always live there, but came from the Karoo. An even dryer world, with whirlwinds that pitched on the horizon, and tumbled bushes along the veld.

I am old now, and feel that I have seen it all. It's a changing South Africa for most people, but for me, it stays the same. I am a woman past seventy, Hester de Jong. Once everyone uttered my name, and my picture appeared in the newspapers, but now I am forgotten.

Here in 'the baai', I take the road to Uitenhage. I pause beside shacks, where Xhosa youths, naked with threadbare grey blankets, undergo tribal circumcision. I understand, even though I am not one of them, because I too underwent a strange journey. It was as if I sank beneath the earth, and crawled along narrow, twisted passages, that were dark and suffocating. Fellow survivors, I recognise that they like myself have bridged the chasm between the familiar and the unspeakable.

Now, all is changed, the past is behind me. I sit in a tea-shop and buy biltong and honey. I am like everyone else, a citizen of the new South Africa. At least, it feels like that to me. Nobody cares about an old woman, whose husband and son are dead. I envy women, like myself, who are old too, and live in cottages by the sea. They have come home, and chosen a place to rest. Dare I do the same . . .

The crime . . . though I hate the word . . . happened because of lace. Lace is my word for beauty . . . love . . . and hope. I speak the word lace, and everything else is clear, even sublime. It is the Saviour, more powerful even than Christ, with his all-embracing love. I held lace, and felt complete, even more so than in the arms of my husband, Karel, or with my young son, Tomas. It was not that I did not love them. I did and most devotedly. It was just that I was claimed long ago as a child by lace. My mother wore a lace collar, which allowed her head to emerge like a swan from the water. When at school, as a small girl, I first learnt embroidery, and then was ravished by lace. I did not think that marriage would deprive me of that passion.

The Karoo is a place of contest. The mountains are great, while man struggles, is often alone, and also deaf. Yes, deaf in the land-locked Karoo world of stone, and light. Deaf to the voice within, that warning that comes from one's own terror. The still voice that shrieks . . . be careful . . . take care . . . watch out. In the Karoo, you hear nothing. You see only the faces of others . . . Karel and the child . . . the demand for love . . . and more love . . . until it's all taken. When the winter is cold, the house freezes, and trees lopped by heavy snow. The sky is a dark frenzy of cloud, with the sun so askew that it mimics the moon on a path of fright. It never seems to end. June is a year . . . July creeping age . . . August, the cruellest month, death itself. How else to describe the Karoo winter?

Perhaps, if I had been thirty rather than twenty-nine, things might have been different. I would have been mature enough to know that winter ends. The cruel month of August, the one with the mantel of death, was no time for playing charades. When my son, Tomas, fell ill, it was not a game, but grim reality. Despite winter, we struggled to save him up in that cold house. We stumbled across the chessboard of our lives, and rammed each other, a battling white knight, and his black queen.

There was sacrifice, terrible sacrifice. Karel refused me money for lace, the fabric of my soul was in shreds. It was as if winter cast a cruel spell over Karel, whose every word was a rebuke. Love turned to drought, a dry bitter resentment. Our faces resembled those grey stones of the Karoo.

Tomas was taken by winter, a child whom neither love nor medicine could have saved. When he died, I became mute and deaf to all reason. Even the koppies with their blind faces of immutable stone, turned against me. They had no advice, no criticism. They were empty like the pale body of my five-year-old son, who was like the carapace of a Karoo insect.

I thought it would never stop, the terror within. A whistling, lurching grief that shuddered and shook me in my dreams, only to become a piercing echo through the long hard days. I felt caught in a prison, a vacuum between sky and the Karoo floor of sand and stone.

A place that was devoid of meaning, a crazy space, for it was like my mind.

I held Karel responsible for our misfortune. This husband, who had been changed by winter's spell. He'd become tight-fisted, and when I could no longer tolerate his excuses about the drought, failed crops, and lost livestock, he lied and said that our money was gone. Yet, I knew that there were pennies in his purse, and even saw his fingers clenched round a roll of notes. He hid money in all sorts of strange places. His tobacco bowl, inside the lining of his hat, even in his slippers. I went through his clothes every day. Pushed my fingers into the lining of his jacket, and even pulled out a note. Then, I knew that he was evil, and wanted to deprive me not ony of my son, but also beauty. That was why he had refused to allow me to buy thread for lace.

August, that cruel month, lingered on like death itself. It was then that I began to stalk him in my dreams. I laid traps for him, so that he fell through the kitchen floor, and landed in the fiery pit of hell. I saw him alone on a koppie, where a lynx waited to tear him apart. Such dreams invaded reality. I found that there were days when the wind blew, so that I screamed and bit his hand. The red blood flowed like a rivulet of pain that was shared by us both.

Then came the moment, when we almost reclaimed one another. I was surprised by the faces of the first spring flowers. Then, I saw that Karel was carrying a lamb that had been lost in the veld. The innocence in both our hearts was revealed. Karel's face was suddenly young like the time when we were first married. I almost believed that it was our son, Thomas, who lay in his arms rather than the lamb. I rushed over to him, out of breath, and with a smile of greeting, and great longing. We embraced, as if we were again lovers, and Karel's body was warm, and giving. It all ended, when he looked at me, and said, 'Hester, we are leaving. Tomorrow, we will drive to Pretoria. There is a psychiatrist there, who can help you. Then, our life will be better. We will be together like in the past.'

I was too shocked by his words to fight back. The next day, I simply got into the car. We drove along the gravel road that lead across the Karoo, and past those deformed hills, with the bodies of stone. We passed streams, where echoes rose up and told me that I too would soon be dead. I suddenly remembered that it was 1940, and there was a great war going on in the world. People were dying, soldiers as well as women and children, were being bombed in the great cities of Europe.

In the Free State, just outside Bloemfontein, we stopped on the side of the road for tea. I had not come unprepared. The knife had been in my thoughts for a long time. It had arrived there during the month after Tomas's death. When the image of the carapace of the locust left my mind, the knife slipped in like an absent friend that had returned. I found the real knife in the kitchen, sharp, for it had cut up a springbuck, which Karel had shot in the autumn. I remembered the sad eyes of the dead springbuck, and its shining pure horns. Tomas had not looked as beautiful as that springbuck. He became only a carapace. I knew that was because he did not possess a pelt, but only a terrible thin skin of pain and terror like myself.

On that windy, dust-filled day, where we perched like miserable birds, and drank our tea, I understood. We were, all of us simply redundant. If we slipped off the earth, it would make no difference at all. Grass would still grow . . . rocks would stand . . . creatures would find sustenance. We were useless, and gave nothing back but our tears that were not even effective like rain. Tears saved nothing . . . solved nothing . . . only buried others.

Karel stood with his back to me, and looked out across that tear-stained landscape, where everything had died. People no longer loved one another. Worst of all was the loss of beauty. I cried out softly . . . lace . . . lace . . . lace. I will find you again. Then, I lifted the knife, and repeatedly stabbed Karel in the back. He fell dead at my feet, a man that had been felled by the woman, who was his wife, and finally became his death.

I crawled along the road, as if I searched for a place that was not death. It was rather some other form of life . . . even if it meant going back to being a reptile . . . an eagle . . . or the lynx of the veld. Some other kind of life that was preferable to this human shape that brought with it a host of problems that were impossible to solve. I felt overwhelmed. It was as if the worst possible Karoo storm that had brooded on the horizon finally broke overhead in a cloudburst.

After the trial, layers of ignorance of myself and the world peeled off like different skins, as if I was a snake. Twenty years is a long time to sit in a mental hospital, and relive the past. Twenty years to imagine oneself as the locust within the carapace . . . the buck within the pelt . . . the sea within the shell . . . the sky about the moon . . . the tongue and soul of Karel . . . the blue-eyed innocence of Tomas . . . and finally the enveloping power of lace . . . in my dreams always . . . the white beauty of pure lace.

It ended. I was released on the recommendation of the state psychiatrist. I was considered normal . . . recovered . . . and rehabilitated.

It was then that I came to 'the baai', this city of Port Elizabeth, beside the Indian Ocean. I was fifty years old, and worked a little, and then there was the pension. I had lived a full, even a devastating life, and in old age, seek my rest. I had seen the many skins fall from my body, and recognised myself as a woman, with a past, and a single passion for lace. I have sustained that passion, and know that it makes the mind supple, and prepares the soul for the great freedom.

FARIDA KARODIA

Cardboard Mansions

'Chotoo! Eh Chotoo!'

'*Ja*, Dadi-Ma?' the boy cried from the far side of the yard.

'Don't *ja* Dadi-Ma, me! Come here!' the old woman called from the *stoep*. Leaning over the low abutment wall, she craned to peer around the corner but her view was obstructed by a pile of rubbish. She stepped back knocking over the chipped enamel pail which was normally kept beside her bed at night. The empty pail rolled out of reach, clattering against the wall.

She waited for the boy, pulling the end of the faded green cotton sari over her head. Her wide, flat heels hung over the back of the blue rubber thongs almost two sizes smaller than her feet.

Dadi-Ma looked much older than her seventy-three years. She was a tall, heavily-built woman with slow, tired movements. Her dark brown eyes were set deep in a face scored and marked with age and hardship. The gap in the front of her mouth was relieved only by three stumps of rotted teeth, bloodily stained by betel-nut.

In her youth she had been much admired for her beauty, with her dark lustrous eyes like those of a young doe. But there was no one left to remember her as she'd been then. Sonny, the youngest of her sons, and her grandson, Chotoo, were the only surviving members of her family. Three of her sons and her husband, like so many of the men who had toiled in the sugar-cane fields, had all died of tuberculosis.

And now the only ones left to her were her grandchild, Chotoo, and her friend Ratnadevi. Dadi-Ma in her old age was left to gaze upon the world with the patient endurance of the old water buffalo they had once owned in India.

The boy, Chotoo, took a long time coming. His grandmother waited, her broad, varicose-veined feet and legs planted astride. A rip in her sari revealed a discoloured slip, unadorned and frayed. Her dark eyes stared out from under thick brows, slowly gathering in impatience.

'Chotoo!' she called again and sat down on the step to wait.

•

The row of shanties were all connected. At one time they had served as a shed, but an enterprising landlord had used sheets of corrugated iron to divide the shed into stalls which he rented to the poor. All the dividing walls stopped at least twelve inches short of the ceiling.

On Saturday nights when Frank Chetty beat his wife, Nirmala, her cries swirled over the heads of the other tenants. Some ignored them. Others were just grateful that they were not in Nirmala's shoes. Dadi-Ma's daughter-in-law, Neela, had once remarked to their neighbour, Urmila, that no matter what Sonny was guilty of, this was one thing that he had not yet stooped to.

'Just you wait and see,' Urmila said. 'It'll happen when Sonny loses his job.'

But even when Sonny lost his job he never raised a hand to his wife. Chotoo, however, was not so lucky and in his short life had been slapped many times, often for no apparent reason. Despite this, Dadi-Ma's pride in her son remained undiminished. She could hold up her head and say that he had never lifted a hand to his wife or his mother.

It had come as a terrible blow to Dadi-Ma when Neela had died in childbirth three years ago, leaving Sonny with the boy, Chotoo. But Sonny was hardly ever around and everything had fallen on her shoulders. Somehow they managed. Even when Sonny lost his job they still managed. Dadi-Ma used many of the ideas she had picked up from Ratnadevi who had a real knack for making do.

But eventually Sonny had fallen in with a bad crowd and everything seemed to come apart. Now there was a new element in their struggle; one that caused Dadi-Ma a great deal of anxiety. As Sonny was jobless, there was not a penny coming in any more, yet all weekend long Sonny smoked *dagga*. Sometimes he drew the reefers through a broken bottle-neck making himself so crazy that he'd end up running amok with a knife. At times like these Dadi-Ma and Chotoo had to hide from him until the effects of the *dagga* wore off.

Without means to pay the rent there was constant friction between himself and the landlord. Sonny, desperate and irritable, pleaded with the landlord until they reached a state of open hostility. The tenants were all drawn into this conflict, all except Dadi-Ma. She alone remained aloof and detached. Sitting on the concrete step in front of their room, she listened in silence to the two men arguing when the landlord came to collect the rent. Sonny's response was always wild and abusive. Although she was afraid that he would harm the landlord, she remained impassive.

The landlord, Mr Naidoo, grew to resent the old woman. He thought that her silence was a way of showing contempt for him. Who was she to judge him, a man of means and property? He often wondered as he drove off in his Mercedes why it was that she never said anything. What thoughts crossed her mind as she sat there implacable as a stone Buddha? In the end he grew to hate the old woman.

Then one day the inevitable happened: Sonny got into a drunken brawl and stabbed someone. He was arrested, sentenced and thrown into jail. Mr Naidoo saw his opportunity to evict the old woman, but he hesitated fearing censure from the other tenants, some of whom had contributed to help Dadi-Ma with her rent. He knew, though, that this situation could not continue indefinitely. Those who had supported her were themselves experiencing difficulty. So he bided his time.

It happened that a few months later the old woman fell so far behind with her rent that the others could no longer assist her. Now at last Mr Naidoo could exercise his rights; he gave Dadi-Ma her notice.

She was devastated. She had tried so hard to keep the roof over their heads. There was nothing for her to do now but pack their few possessions. They would have to move, but where to? she fretted. Dadi-Ma's concern was more for her grandson than for herself. She did not have many more years left, but what would happen to this boy who was only starting out in life?

•

'What took you so long, hey?' Dadi-Ma demanded, feigning severity when the boy finally joined her.

He shrugged, his hands thrust deep in his pockets, emulating the cockiness of the older boys who hung out in the alley. She tousled his hair and he sat down on the step beside her, pressing close to her side where he felt safe and secure.

For a time they sat like this in silence, the boy content with this closeness while his grandmother brooded about the past and the problems which were driving them into the unknown. Her mind moved slowly and ponderously, like an ox picking its way over the stones, lingering on the good times.

Lately her thoughts had started returning to those happy years; to Ratnadevi and Stanger. The two women had shared a friendship that went back a long way. They had arrived on the same boat from India to marry two indentured labourers on the sugar-cane fields in Natal. They had lived in the same compound, as close as sisters, sharing in each other's joys and tragedies.

'Why you like the *skollies*?' the old woman asked the boy, adjusting the sari over her head. 'They no good.'

'Why you say that Dadi-Ma?' he asked. His enormous brown eyes turned up to her questioningly.

He was so young, she thought, how could he understand that she wanted him to make something of his life? How could he understand that if he didn't try, this was all he had to look forward to?

'Because they bad. They smoke *dagga*. You best go to school so you can be something hey?' she said in her broken English.

'We don't do nothing wrong Dadi-Ma, we just sit out there bullshitting.'

The old woman shook her head wearily.

'They say old man Naidoo going to throw us out. Where we going to go Dadi-Ma?'

Dadi-Ma felt a deep attachment to her grandson. She had been drawn to him from the moment he was born. It had been Dadi-Ma who took care of him right from that first day, not his mother who was too tired and sickly to care. From Chotoo, came the only warmth and caring that life still apportioned to her. All that the boy had known of love and tenderness came from her; not from his mother, whom he could not remember. It was a bond that neither had words for. The only expression Dadi-Ma ever gave her grandson of her feelings, was a rare and awkward pat on his cheek, or the tousling of his hair with her arthritic fingers.

The boy, undernourished and small for his age, with eyes as large and expressive as hers had once been, was conscious of his grandmother's love. The others, like his parents, had deserted him. But not her. She was the fulcrum in his fragile existence.

'I was thinking Chotoo, maybe you and me, we go to Stanger. It will be a good place for us. This place is no good,' she muttered.

'Where is Stanger, Dadi-Ma?' he asked, his voice catching in breathless excitement.

'It's not so far away.'

'How will we go . . . by car, by train?' he asked, in his shrill little voice.

She nodded, smiling down at him. 'We go by train.'

Dadi-Ma had saved some money for just such an emergency. The money, fifty rands, was what she had amassed in her long lifetime. Money that she had artfully secreted. Many times the money had gone for some other emergency but somehow she had always managed to replace it. Sometimes it had been slow to accumulate; money from the sale of a few pieces of gold jewellery brought with her from India, a few cents here and there from what she could scrimp out of the money Sonny had given her to buy food and clothes in the good old days when he still had a job.

These savings were all that stood between them and destitution now. The previous night she had removed the money from its hiding place beneath the linoleum under her bed, and in the dim light of the lamp she had counted it carefully, stacking the small coins in even piles, smoothing out the crumpled notes. Then she had returned it to the hiding place for safe keeping.

After a while Chotoo started fidgeting and wriggled out from under her arm.

'You don't tell nobody,' Dadi-Ma warned him. 'If old man Naidoo find out he make big trouble for us.'

Chotoo nodded. Despite his age, he understood. 'Can I go and play now, Dadi-Ma?'

'*Ja*, you go and play, but you remember what I tell you.'

'I won't tell nobody, Dadi-Ma.'

She nodded and he sauntered off to the side of the house where the *dagga* smokers hung out. She watched him go, legs thin and scaly, the knobbly knees protruding just below his short trousers, his feet rough and thickened from going barefoot.

The tenement somehow always reminded Dadi-Ma of the quarters they had once occupied on the sugar-cane plantation. There she and her husband had lived in a barracks with dozens of other workers, separated from the rest by paper-thin walls, or frayed curtains. In summer the windowless barracks were like ovens and then when the rains came it was like the monsoons in India, lasting for weeks and turning the compound into a quagmire.

Further north along the east coast, was the town of Stanger where Ratnadevi had eventually moved after her husband died. His death had released Ratnadevi and her family from the contract which had bound them to the plantation. When Dadi-Ma's own husband had died and Sonny had run off to the city, Dadi-Ma had also moved to Stanger to live with Ratnadevi.

She remembered every detail so clearly. The wooden shack set back from the road amidst a clump of mango, banana and litchi trees. There had been an abundance of everything on that small piece of property, even the birds flocked to feed off the ripening fruit. It was indeed a wonderful sight and one that Dadi-Ma had cherished since that time.

She had never been happier than during those days with Ratnadevi in that old shack in Stanger. The two of them had managed by taking in laundry from the white people, most of whom were English-speaking. They also used to weave baskets which they sold in the local community, or peddled in the market place where Ratnadevi had a hawker's barrow.

The house was at the end of a gravel road. It was the last house on the street with a large corner lot where parts of an old picket-fence still stood. On windy nights they could hear the pickets clattering and rattling against each other. Each sound had its own particular significance and was like music to Dadi-Ma's ears. Some nights when it was very quiet she imagined she could hear the strains of a flute, the same poignant sounds made by Manu, the confectioner in her village in India, when he sat on the front step of his hut playing to the night.

From one of the big trees in the front yard hung a swing carved from an old tyre. There had been enough room for a large garden and the eggs produced by the hens were taken to the market each day. Dadi-Ma learnt a great deal about survival from the years she had spent there.

Then to interrupt this happiness, something unexpected had happened which irreversibly altered the tempo of her life. Sonny, who had married and moved to Port Elizabeth, sent for her. He was her son; her only son, how could she have refused him? Without the slightest hesitation, Dadi-Ma packed her few belongings and went to live with her son and Neela, her daughter-in-law. Neela, she found, was a frail and sickly girl who was unable to withstand the rigours of married life. Dadi-Ma took care of them all.

Several years went by and to Dadi-Ma's dismay her daughter-in-law, Neela, had still not produced a child. For reasons that Dadi-Ma did not understand the young girl could not carry a single pregnancy to its full term, miscarrying each after only four months.

It was a difficult life but Dadi-Ma never complained, even though she hated city life, and constantly longed for Stanger and for Ratnadevi. The years passed and memories of those happy years began to dim. Eventually she stopped thinking about them. For fifteen years she lived with Sonny and his wife, taking care of them, and suffering constant abuse at the hands of Neela who grew resentful of her role in the house. Then one day, five years ago, Neela gave birth to Chotoo and it was as though Dadi-Ma had finally found fulfilment.

•

Now, ever since the landlord had given them notice, her thoughts returned again to that little house at the end of the road with the swing in the front yard. She could see the trees and hear the plank verandah and fence creaking in the wind.

Dadi-Ma remained on the step, dreaming. There was a stench of urine and human excrement in the air which came from a blocked sewer. They were accustomed to the stench which mingled with the rancid smell of old *ghee* and curry.

In a way Dadi-Ma was relieved that they were leaving. It was too difficult to raise a boy in this environment. He needed to run free, to breathe air unpolluted by smoke and odours of decay. Dadi-Ma's thoughts drifted back to the long low line of hills in the north, to mango and litchi trees laden with fruit. She remembered how she and Ratnadevi had sat out on the verandah, identifying the gaily coloured birds as they swooped down into the trees.

She and Ratnadevi had spent so much of their time in the backyard, doing the wash, kneading and scrubbing the heavy linen against the fluted surface of the washboard. In their spare time they sat beneath the tree, weaving baskets. Sometimes they chatted about their life in India, or life on the plantation; other times they worked in easy companionable silence.

Chotoo returned to his grandmother's side, wanting to know more about this place called Stanger. She was smiling to herself now as she thought of how she and Ratnadevi would once again sit out in the yard. She remembered the long washing line and the sputtering sizzle as Ratnadevi deftly spat against the iron. She remembered the smell of lye and freshly ironed laundry.

They could weave baskets again. As if following her thoughts, her fingers, now stiff with age and arthritis, fell awkwardly into the familiar movements of weaving. The boy seeing this, pressed closer to her side. She looked down upon him sombrely and drew his head against her chest. She began to talk to him of the life she had once known. The boy listened and with her words felt a new sense of adventure.

That night Dadi-Ma bundled together their few possessions. Her plan was to leave under cover of darkness since she did not have the money to pay the landlord the rent that was owing.

They caught the train for Durban early the next morning. For Chotoo the adventure had begun. Through most of the journey he was awake, his nose flattened against the window. In the second-class coach, they shared their compartment with two other women, who chatted amiably with his grandmother while he remained at her side.

When they arrived in Durban, he grabbed a handful of his grandmother's sari, and hung on while she carried the bundle of belongings on her head. In the street outside the station they got into the bus for Stanger.

It was a long drive and they passed fields of sugar-cane. Dadi-Ma pointed out many things to him, drawing his attention to this or to that. He stood against the seat, his nose once again pressed to the window, lurching against her as the bus bumped and swayed. They stopped often to offload passengers on the road and it was afternoon before they arrived at their destination.

Dadi-Ma became excited as they approached the town. She asked the woman across the aisle about the bus stop. The woman told her that the bus went all the way to the market. Dadi-Ma was pleased. She knew her way from there.

They entered the town and Dadi-Ma looked around for familiar landmarks, but things had changed. The market was no longer where she had remembered it to be. It had been moved to a new location. Dadi-Ma was puzzled. She spoke to the woman again, asking where the old market was, but the woman shrugged, saying she didn't know. She did not live here, only visited occasionally.

'Ask the woman over there,' she said.

Dadi-Ma got up from her seat and Chotoo followed her, clutching the end of her sari. In her anxiety she was impatient with him. 'Stay there,' she snapped.

Chotoo's eyes grew large and mournful and she was sorry that she had spoken sharply. She touched his cheek and explained that she would be back in a moment, that she was merely going to speak to the woman over there, near the front of the bus. She told him to remain in the seat so that no one could take it.

Chotoo understood and hung back.

Dadi-Ma spoke to this other woman for several minutes. Chotoo watched her and sensed her unease.

'What is it, Dadi-Ma?' he asked when she returned.

'We will have to walk a long distance,' she told him.

'Why?' he asked.

'So many questions!' she exclaimed. Then she said, 'The market-place where the bus stops, is no longer where I thought it would be, they have moved it.'

The boy did not say anything; he sensed in her a new anxiety that bewildered him.

When they got off the bus at the market-place, the woman Dadi-Ma had talked to in the front of the bus, asked why they wanted to get to that particular street.

'It is where my friend Ratnadevi lives,' she said.

'Your friend lives there?' the woman asked, surprised.

'Yes, she has a small house with big trees.'

The woman fell silent. Then she shrugged her shoulders. Perhaps this friend was a servant in one of the big houses out there, she concluded.

Dadi-Ma smiled and thanked the woman.

The woman repeated her instructions telling them to go to the end of the wide road and then to turn to the left and continue on for five more streets to where there was a big store. At that point they were to turn right and walk for several blocks until they reached the area of big houses and mansions. There they were to turn right again to the street Dadi-Ma was enquiring about. 'But there is no small house there like the one you have described,' the woman said.

'From there I will know my way,' Dadi-Ma assured her. She thanked the woman, hoisted the bundle on to her head, and waited for Chotoo to get a good grip on her sari. Then she left. Her feet in the old *champals* flip-flopped as she walked away. The other woman watched them going.

Dadi-Ma and Chotoo walked a long way that day, stopping often to rest. Chotoo was tired and dragged on her sari and she had to urge him on with quiet words of encouragement. She talked about the trees and the birds, nurturing the anticipation which lightened his step. At the end of the road, they stopped. She took down the bundle from her head and carefully unwrapped it. Packed amongst their belongings was a bottle of water. She handed it to Chotoo who took a long drink, then after taking a sip herself, she screwed the cap back on and returned the bundle to her head.

They turned left and continued on. She recognised some of the landmarks, her heart lurching excitedly as she pointed these out to the boy. Then they turned right and suddenly nothing seemed familiar any more.

Nevertheless they pressed on, following the woman's directions. They walked all the way to the end of the street in silence. On both sides of the street were large houses surrounded by walls and fences. The open field she remembered was no longer there. Her legs automatically propelled her forward. The pain that had racked her limbs through the past few days now gave way to fear which turned her legs to jelly.

They had made the last right turn and supposedly this was the street where she had once lived. Her dark eyes looked out upon an area that was unrecognisable. Slowly and wearily they made their way to the end of the street, but Ratnadevi's house was no longer there, neither were the trees and the groves of bamboo. She took the bundle from her head. The boy raised his eyes to look at her. In her face he saw the bewilderment.

Dadi-Ma was tired now, her legs could no longer hold her weight and she sat down on the curb, drawing the boy down beside her.

'What's wrong Dadi-Ma? Where is Ratnadevi's house?'

Dadi-Ma's fingers moved, weaving an invisible basket.

'Dadi-Ma?' he said in a small voice.

'Hush Chotoo. Don't worry. We'll rest a bit and then we'll find Ratnadevi's house.'

Chotoo drew close to his grandmother, resting his head on her lap for he was tired and sleepy.

•

The woman must have made a mistake, she thought. Ratnadevi's house was probably at the end of some other street and she would find it. A small house with a plank verandah and many trees with birds. Chotoo would be able to climb trees and pick fruit to his heart's content and sometimes he'd help them to pick bamboo for baskets.

A servant who had seen them sitting there, came out of one of the houses. 'Why are you sitting here?' she asked.

Dadi-Ma described the house she was searching for.

'Yes, I remember that one,' the woman said. 'The house was torn down a long time ago.'

'What happened to the people who once lived here?' Dadi-Ma asked.

The woman shrugged and shook her head.

Dadi-Ma sat back, the pain that had nagged her all day numbing her arms, suddenly swelled in her chest. The woman noticed the way Dadi-Ma's colour had changed.

'Are you all right, Auntie?' she asked.

Dadi-Ma compressed her lips and nodded. She did not want to alarm Chotoo. Did not want him to be afraid. She struggled to get up, the woman helping her to her feet.

But Chotoo saw the expression on his grandmother's face and for the first time in his life he felt insecure and uncertain about the future; felt a dreadful apprehension of being wrenched from the only human being he had ever loved.

'Dadi-Ma, Dadi-Ma,' he sobbed.

'It's all right Chotoo, it's all right.'

But he knew that it wasn't all right, that it would never be all right again.

NORTHERN

AFRICA

NORTHERN AFRICA

Despite North African cultural and religious constraints on women, a few women writers have already achieved wide recognition for the excellence and power of their work. Since they write mainly in French or in Arabic, however, they have been little known in Britain or America until quite recently. Some have won recognition in Europe; some have gained regard also at international colloquia. They are viewed as significant interpreters of their own cultures and of women's place therein. Some have already 'made a difference' through their lives and their work. They are very individual contributors to our own time.

Egyptian Nawal El Saadawi has been acknowledged world-wide as a leading feminist through her campaign against female circumcision and excision in the many countries, African as well as Middle-Eastern, where such practices obtain. At times imprisoned in Egypt, her writings banned, she has found a hearing in United Nations conferences, during the International Women's Year and then the Decade for Women. Nonetheless, although she has written seven novels and several collections of short stories, as well as studies of women's role and women's work in the Muslim World, her work has began to appear in English translation only in the last few years.

Recognition of El Saadawi and Andrée Chedid as Egyptian artists by African literature scholars has been further limited by the ambiguity of definitions of that field. Should African literature be considered to be predominantly black? Should only the Maghreb be included from Northern Africa? Is Egypt so ancient and so venerable that its literature must be considered a thing apart? El Saadawi does not think so. 'Egypt is Africa and I wonder how some people think that Egypt is outside Africa. The term Middle East is a political colonial term (Middle: relative to whom?). Also the division between black and white Africa is a colonial division. We are one continent.'[1]

[1] El Saadawi's letter to C.H.B was dated 11 March 1990.

Andrée Chedid exploits her own Egyptian background (ancient and modern) in much of her fiction. She does not believe in barriers of time and circumstance. She lives in France by choice; she is not exiled. Rather, she finds links and bridges between women and a common humanity. She deplores bigotry, violence, war, wherever they occur. Her immense *œuvre* in many genres has won her prizes from many lands. She autographs books with a peace symbol.

Gisèle Halimi of Tunisia is widely known in Europe and North Africa as a defence lawyer, but less recognised as a writer. She has argued cases for the oppressed – for 'slave' migrant labour, for torture victims – often risking her life to establish their civil rights. She is a strong feminist and has written, worked and marched with Simone de Beauvoir. Both walked in 1971 in Paris for abortion rights for women. Halimi's charming autobiography provokes astonishment. Why haven't we known of her before?

Assia Djebar of Algeria started writing and won French acclaim for her first four novels when she was just in her twenties. Moving back and forth between France and Algeria, she portrays to the western reader the quandaries many Muslim women face. Djebar is increasingly conscious of the 'journey within' they must take to find self-worth, those who are sequestered, behind the veil. Her latest work, *Quartet*, is being translated almost as soon as it appears in French.

Another Algerian, Leïla Sebbar, has written several novels and short stories portraying the Algerian immigrant workers in France, and the special underworld they create there. Neither literate nor francophone nor Christian, they accommodate as best they may to the French culture surrounding them. In our global society today with its enormous demographic movements, the statistics regarding rural-urban, national and international migrant labour, political and economic refugee migrations, are impressive. But statistics alone cannot produce the empathy and understanding that Sebbar arouses by her fictional portrayal of these migrant women.

Of course these five writers are outstanding, unique. But if the reader previously unfamiliar with their work cannot quite take in the force of their messages, other writers are appearing who do substantiate their positions. Does El Sadaawi overemphasise the trauma of excision? Read Lebanese Evelyne Accad's *l'excisée* or Egyptian Laila Said's autobiography, *Bridges in Time*. Is Assia Djebar unduly harsh in picturing restraints on North African women? Consider Moroccan

Fatima Mernissi's *Beyond the Veil: Male-Female Dynamics in Modern Muslim Society*. Read the short stories of Alifa Rifaat, who may not condemn the system, but who still conveys the shallowness and impoverishment of women's ordinary lives in Egypt. Does Leïla Sebbar exaggerate the confusion and exploitation of the Algerian workers, men and women? Read the accounts of actual trials in the French courts where Gisèle Halimi defended immigrant rights, and was hounded for so doing.

Can women provide any different answers to our world chaos? Are war, oppression, violence always to be an inevitable part of the human condition? Read Andrée Chedid's poetry, plays, or fiction, or Evelyne Accad's study *Sexuality and War* and take heart. These articulate women share a hope, if not a promise, that a new world order of equality and empathy could exist, based not on might, coercion and violence, but on mutual respect and understanding. Women writers write feelingly of these desires.

NAWAL EL SAADAWI

She was the Weaker

Only the middle finger of his right hand. No other finger would do. The little finger was longer than it should be, the thumb fatter. The nail of the index finger was dead; it had not grown after being squashed by a hoe. And the nail was important, maybe more important than the finger itself, for it was the nail that would open the way. He had implored his mother to be allowed to use something else, something harder, like the tip of a bamboo stick. But his mother poked him in the shoulder with her strong fingers and he rolled on to the ground, unable to spit but only to lick the earth with his tongue as he watched his mother's large feet steadily advancing, her lofty muscular body shaking the earth, her long hard fingers around the hoe, lifting it high as though it were a dry stick of corn, then bringing it down onto the earth to split it open like a watermelon.

As strong as an ox. On her head she carried loads heavier than an ass. She kneaded troughs of dough, swept, cooked, hoed, carried children and gave birth, yet nothing about her grew tired or weary. But although she was his mother, who had created him from her flesh, from whose blood he had drunk, she had kept the strength for herself. He had inherited nothing from her but ugliness and weakness.

This violent urge to cling to his mother, to put his head on her breast and inhale the smell of her body was not love. He wanted to merge with her once more so that she could give birth to him anew with stronger muscles. He wanted to inhale some strength from her breath. When he kissed her, he didn't want to kiss but to bite her and eat her muscular flesh piece by piece. But he could not do it. All he could do was hide his head in her lap and hate her. Sometimes he would cry, sometimes he would run away. Once he stole away from the field at the end of the day and, with the hem of his *galabia*[1] between

---

[1] Long loose robe commonly worn by Egyptian men and women.

his teeth, he kept on running until he came to a place he did not know. Darkness surrounded him on all sides and he heard the distant howl of a wolf and turned on his heels and ran back home. And once he stole a five piastre piece from his mother's bag and took the Delta train to a village whose name he did not know. He began walking along its streets until his stomach rumbled and the soles of his feet burned. So he bought a ticket and took the train back to his village. Another time he stole a ten piastre piece and secretly went to the barber-surgeon. He stood before him panting.

'Speak up, lad. What d'you want?'

He tried to dislodge his dry tongue from the roof of his mouth, hiding his hands in his *galabia*.

'My fingers . . .'

'What's wrong with them?'

'They won't hold a hoe like my mother's do.'

The man jabbed him in the shoulder.

'Shame on you, boy. Go and get your mother to feed you a pound of meat and you'll grow as strong as a horse.'

He cried in his mother's ample lap until she bought him a piece of meat which he gobbled up. He drank and burped, feeling a pleasant warmth run through his fingers. He clenched them and stretched them, bent them and spread them, happy in his new-found power. But feeling his eyelids heavy, he closed his eyes and fell into a deep sleep. When he awoke two days later, he ran outside feeling that the remains of the meat had slipped away from inside him, together with the new-found power.

But there had to be a solution. In his head there was a brain at work. He was the cleverest man in the village. He read the newspapers to them, wrote letters for them, solved their problems, delivered the Friday sermon when the *Imam*[2] was away. But his brain and intelligence would not excuse him. For them, a real man meant having a strong body even if he had the mind of a mule.

His brain worked but his muscles were slack. Time passed. The fateful day was approaching and nothing he tried was of any avail. He locked the door of the back hall and exercised his muscles. He clenched his fingers, bent them and spread them and cracked them. Every night

[2] Muslim prayer leader.

he exercised. At times his fingers clenched into a fist, at other times they would contort and then fall slack . . .

The day arrived. He watched his mother sweep and clean the hall before dawn and stack up wooden benches in front of the house. He pretended to be asleep or to be dead, but his mother poked him in the shoulder with those fingers of hers and he jumped to his feet. Groups of people began to fill the courtyard of the house; men carrying sticks, playing and dancing, women wearing gaily coloured robes, singing and ululating, throwing at him things which stung the nape of his neck. He was nailed to the ground by new slippers of yellow leather which chafed his feet. Around his neck was a new *kuffiya*[3] at which he tugged with cramped fingers and with which he would have strangled himself had his muscles not been as soft as dough. His legs did not move but were pushed from behind, from the left, from the right, making him sway as though he were dancing with the dancers and reeling with the reelers . . . until he found himself at the threshold of the hall. Raising his head, he saw before him a curious thing, a thing the top half of which was covered in a large red shawl, the lower half, two thin bare legs, beside each leg a woman, grasping them with sturdy arms from which coarse veins bulged out.

He remained standing at the threshold, his eyes dazzled, his mouth trying to open to scream. But nothing emerged from between his lips except saliva which ran, warm and smooth, from the corner of his mouth, like the tail of a harmless snake . . .

He felt powerful fingers, like those of his mother, push him in the shoulder and sit him down. He felt somehow relieved with his buttocks on the washed damp ground. He remained seated, his eyes closed, semi-conscious. But another thrust in his shoulder made him open his eyes to find himself face to face with the parted legs. He turned his face away and from the corner of his eye noticed a crowd of men and women behind him assembled in the courtyard, playing drums and flutes, dancing and standing waiting. Their eyes were wide open, eagerly and anxiously watching the door of the hall. No, he would not provide them with a scandal. He was not stupid. He was the cleverest man in the village . . . he read the newspapers and wrote letters for them, delivered the sermon when the *Imam* was away. He had to come

---

[3] Head-dress worn by Egyptian men.

out to them with his head held high, as all village men did, including the stupid boy who stammered and dribbled . . .

He stretched out his right hand and pushed his finger forward between the legs. But his arm trembled, violently shaking the finger which fell dangling like the tail of a dead puppy . . .

He did not stop. He kept trying and struggling. Copious sweat ran down the creases of his face and poured into his mouth; he licked it with his tongue, glancing furtively at the two women sitting beside him. Each of them was bearing down on a leg, faces turned away towards the wall, too polite to look at such a scene, or indifferent to something they'd seen many times, or declining to make themselves into inspectors of the virility of a man at his wedding ceremony, or embarrassed or apprehensive, or something. What was important was that they did not see him.

Cautiously, he turned his eyes towards the door to find a section of the crowd standing and watching. From the corner of his eye, he noticed the old man, the father of the bride, standing at the door, his eyes darting back and forth from the door of the hall to the people's faces, anxious and fearful.

He rubbed his fingers confidently. No one knew the truth. The two women had seen nothing except the wall and the one it *did* concern was absorbed in worrying about his own honour . . .

No one knew the truth . . . except her. Her? Who? He did not know her, had never seen her, had seen neither her face nor her eyes nor even a single hair of her head. Now was the first time he was seeing her and he did not see a bride, did not see a person, but only a large red shawl at the end of which were two parted legs like those of a paralysed cow. But there she was in front of him, exposing his impotence. She stood up like a snare to entrap his weakness and failure and he hated her just as he hated his mother. He would have liked to tear her to shreds with his teeth or pour acid on her to burn her.

The hatred endowed him with wit and pride. He spat on the ground in displeasure and sucked his lips in contempt. He steeled himself, got up slowly from his place and turned towards the door, his head high, the handkerchief low. Striding slowly and surely towards the old man, he threw him a glance of superiority, then tossed the handkerchief in his face. It was as clean as before, as washed as before. Not one drop of red blood had stained it.

The eyes of the bride's father dropped in shame. His shoulders crumpled until his head was on his chest. Men surrounded him from all sides to comfort and support him, then they all turned to the door of the hall, at the ready . . .

The bride appeared at the threshold, her small head under the red shawl hanging in dejection, burning and accusing looks thrown at her from all sides . . .

ASSIA DJEBAR

Three Cloistered Girls

Three girls live cloistered in an airy house in the middle of the tiny Sahel village, surrounded by vast vineyards, where I come to spend my spring and summer holidays. My stay there, shut up with these three sisters, is my 'visit to the country'. I am ten, then eleven, then twelve . . .

All through the summer I play with the youngest of these girls who is a year or two older than me. We spend hours together on the swing at the bottom of the orchard near the farmyard. Now and then we break off from our games to peep through the hedge at the village women shouting from the neighbouring smallholdings. At dusk the farm gate opens to let in a flock of goats. I learn to milk the most docile ones. Then I drink from the skin bottle, whose tarry smell makes me rather nauseous. Not being allowed to wander in the dusty lanes of the village is no hardship to me.

The house is large. There are many cool shady rooms filled with mattresses piled up on the floor, and hung with Saharan tapestries woven in the past by the then mistress of the house – a relative by marriage of my mother, who herself comes from the nearby town.

I never go into the end room: a senile old relative of the family squats there in permanent darkness. Sometimes the youngest sister and I venture as far as the doorway, petrified by the sound of her cracked voice, now moaning, now uttering vague accusations, denouncing imaginary plots. What hidden drama do we touch on, resurrected, revived by the ravings of the old crone in her second childhood, violently denouncing some past persecution in a voice that paralyses us? We do not know the magical formulas, the passages from the Quran, that the grown-ups recite aloud to exorcise these outbursts.

The presence of this ancient, with one foot already in the grave, ensures that the other women of the household never miss one of their daily prayers. They gather in the largest room, next to the kitchen or pantry; one of them sews or embroiders, while another squats on the floor, busily sorting chickpeas or lentils, spread out on white cloths. Suddenly five or six slight figures, their veils covering their heads and shoulders, silently straighten up, keeping their eyes lowered. Frail phantoms, both strengthened and weakened by the propitiatory liturgy, they prostrate themselves several times in unison . . . Sometimes my mother forms part of this group of pious women, making their obeisances, brushing the cold floor tiles with their lips.

We little girls take refuge beneath the medlar trees. To shut out the old woman mumbling to herself, the others' fervent whisperings. We go to count the pigeons in the loft or savour the smell of carobs in the shed, and of the hay trampled under the mare's hooves when she was let out into the fields. We compete to see who can swing highest. Oh! the exhilaration of swinging rhythmically, now high, now low, up over the house and the village! To soar with our legs higher than our heads, till the sounds of the animals and women are all swallowed up behind us.

In a gap in my memory, I suddenly recall one torrid, interminable summer. The raving old crone must have died the previous winter. There are fewer women in the family around: that same season there have been a great number of circumcisions and marriages in the nearby town – so many new brides to be comforted, congratulated, consoled by the band of frustrated females accompanying them . . . I find the girls of the hamlet practically alone.

In the little farmyard, in spite of the carobs and the pigeons in the loft, I wish I were back at school; I miss the companionship of the other boarders, I describe the basketball games to the three country girls. I must be now about twelve or thirteen. I seem older; probably because I'm too tall, too thin. The eldest of the sisters keeps on bringing up the occasion when I first attended a gathering in the town and I was wearing the veil, and one of the city ladies came buzzing round me like a bee.

'Her son must have fallen in love with your silhouette and your eyes! You'll soon be hearing news of your first proposal!'

I stamp my feet in childish anger exacerbated by an ambiguous unease. I sulk for days on end, refusing to speak to the eldest sister.

During that same summer, the youngest sister and I manage to open the bookcase belonging to the absent brother, which up till then had always been kept locked. He works as an interpreter in the Sahara, which seems to us as far away as America. In one month we read all the novels pushed away indiscriminately: Paul Bourget, Colette, Agatha Christie. We discover an album of erotic photographs and an envelope containing picture postcards of bare-breasted Ouled-Naïl girls, loaded with jewels. This brother was extremely strict and before this we were in daily terror of his unpredictable temper; and now we are suddenly aware of his uncomfortable presence during those dim siesta hours. We discreetly close the bookcase as the women rise for their afternoon prayers. We feel we have trespassed into some forbidden territory; we feel we have aged.

•

That summer the girls let me into their secret. A strange and weighty, unexpected matter. I never spoke of it to any other woman in the family, old or young. I had given my solemn promise and I kept it scrupulously. These girls, though confined to their house, were writing; were writing letters; letters to men; to men in the four corners of the world; of the Arab world, naturally.

And letters came back from far and wide: letters from Iraq, Syria, Lebanon, Lybia, Tunisia, from Arab students in Paris or London. Letters sent by pen-pals chosen from adverts appearing in a women's magazine with a wide circulation at the time in the harems. With every number the subscriber received a pattern for a dress or a housegown that even an illiterate woman could follow.

These sisters were the only Muslim girls in their little village to have attended primary school. Their father – a robust, pious countryman, who was the most expert market-gardener in the area – could neither read nor write French. Every year he had to rely on one or other of his daughters to see that the invoices which he had to send to his accountant were correct.

The postman, the son of a local artisan, must have wondered at all these letters from such distant places landing up at his post-office, which no one had ever heard of till then. Nevertheless, he never breathed a word: 'The three daughters of the Sheikh!' He had never set eyes on these girls who must have seemed like princesses to him! ... The backs of the envelopes bore fancy names borrowed from Eastern film-stars, giving the impression that the senders were women. He was not deceived. He must have mused over the girls' sweethearts, 'suitors' he probably thought. He knew that the girls never left the house, except when their father drove them himself in a barouche to the smartest Turkish bath in the nearby town ... The continual arrival of these letters, from every corner of the world, must have weighed upon his mind, feeding some secret frustration!

The only thing I can recall about these letters is their proliferation and the number of different places they came from. When the youngest sister and I spent our evenings together, we no longer discussed the novels we had read during the long afternoons, but the audacity needed to carry on this clandestine correspondence. We conjured up the terrible dangers they were exposed to. There had been numerous cases in our towns of fathers or brothers taking the law into their own hands for less than this; the blood of an unmarried daughter or sister shed for a letter slipped surreptitiously into a hand, for a word whispered behind shuttered windows, for some slanderous accusation ... A secret spirit of subversion had now seeped into the house, and we happy-go-lucky children were casually watching it spread.

The eldest sister, who had a reputation for being very high-and-mighty and never finding any of her official suitors good enough for her, had started this correspondence as a joke. One day, while the women in the next room were starting their prayers again, she had read the following advertisement from the magazine aloud to her sisters:

'"Tunisian, aged twenty-two, blue eyes, fond of Farid el-Attrash, seeks girl pen-pal in Arab country, romantically inclined." ... Suppose I replied to him?'

I never knew what she wrote to the first, the second or the third correspondent: did she write of her uneventful everyday life, or of her dreams, or of the books she read? Perhaps she invented adventures for herself. I never asked her. I was simply dismayed to discover how quickly she found herself saddled with a dozen distant pen-pals. The youngest sister had almost as many. But the middle one – the one who had been silently, meticulously preparing her wedding trousseau for years; the second sister, the prettiest, the gentlest, the most docile – continued to protest that she would never, ever write to a stranger. If she did so, it would indicate that she was prepared to fall in love with him. And she preferred to wait, to get on with her sewing and embroidery, ready in due course to 'love' the eventual fiancé.

And I, at thirteen – perhaps this time it was during the winter holidays – I would listen, during these evenings we spent together, to the youngest of these marriageable girls describing the arguments they had had about what to write in their letters. The eldest sister sent her many pen-pals the words of Egyptian or Lebanese songs, photographs of Arab actresses or film-stars. The youngest maintained a sibyline silence about the contents of her own letters . . .

Everything is a jumble in my memories of this last visit: the novels in the brother's forbidden bookcase and the mysterious letters that arrived by the dozen. We amused ourselves imagining what the postman must be thinking – his curiosity and bewilderment. Moreover he must have felt vexed that he himself could never hope to win the hand of any of these village princesses!

The youngest sister and I continued our whispered confidences. In the periods when sleep crept over me I imagined written words whirling furtively around, about to twine invisible snares around our adolescent bodies, lying side by side across the antique family bed. The same bed in whose hollow the ancient crone used to give vent in her delirium to a corrosive litany of grievances, harping blasphemously on long-forgotten wrongs.

I was afraid and I admitted it. I was certain a light would blaze down from the ceiling and reveal our sin – for I included myself in this terrible guilty secret!

The youngest sister went on whispering spasmodically. She was in the grip of her own determined will, while the night thickened around us and all living things had long fallen asleep.

'I'll never, never let them marry me off to a stranger who, in one night, will have the right to touch me! That's why I write all those letters! One day, someone will come to this dead-and-alive hole to take me away: my father and brother won't know him, but he won't be a stranger to me!'

Every night the vehement voice would utter the same childish vow. I had the premonition that in the sleepy, unsuspecting hamlet, an unprecedented women's battle was brewing beneath the surface.

ASSIA DJEBAR

My Father Writes to My Mother

Whenever my mother spoke of my father, she, in common with all the women in her town, simply used the personal pronoun in Arabic corresponding to 'him'. Thus, every time she used a verb in the third person singular which didn't have a noun subject, she was naturally referring to her husband. This form of speech was characteristic of every married woman, from fifteen to sixty, with the proviso that in later years, if the husband had undertaken the pilgrimage to Mecca, he could be given the title of 'Hajj'.

Everybody, children and adults, especially girls and women, since all important conversations took place among the womenfolk, learnt very quickly to adapt to this rule whereby a husband and wife must never be referred to by name.

After she had been married for a few years, my mother gradually learnt a little French. She was able to exchange a few halting words with the wives of my father's colleagues who had, for the most part, come from France and, like us, lived with their families in the little block of flats set aside for the village teachers.

I don't know exactly when my mother began to say, '*My husband* has come, *my husband* has gone out . . . I'll ask *my husband*,' etc. Although my mother did make rapid progress in the language, in spite of taking it up fairly late in life, I can still hear the evident awkwardness in her voice betrayed by her laboured phraseology, her slow and deliberate enunciation at that time. Nevertheless, I can sense how much it cost her modesty to refer to my father directly in this way.

It was as if a floodgate had opened within her, perhaps in her relationship with her husband. Years later, during the summers we spent in her native town, when chatting in Arabic with her sisters or cousins, my mother would refer to him quite naturally by his first name, even with a touch of superiority. What a daring innovation! Yes, quite unhesitatingly – I was going to say, unequivocally – in any case, without any of the usual euphemisms and verbal circumlocutions. When her aunts and elderly female relations were present, she would once more use the traditional formalities, out of respect for them; such freedom of language would have appeared insolent and incongruous to the ears of the pious old ladies.

Years went by. As my mother's ability to speak French improved, while I was still a child of no more than twelve, I came to realise an irrefutable fact: namely that, in the face of all these womenfolk, my parents formed a couple. One thing was an even greater source of pride in me: when my mother referred to any of the day-to-day incidents of our village life – which in our city relatives' eyes was very backward – the tall figure of my father – my childhood hero – seemed to pop up in the midst of all these women engaged in idle chit-chat on the age-old patios to which they were confined.

My father, no one except my father; none of the other women ever saw fit to refer to their menfolk, their masters who spent the day outside the house and returned home in the evening, taciturn, with eyes on the ground. These nameless uncles, cousins, relatives by marriage, were for us an unidentifiable collection of individuals to all of whom their spouses alluded impartially in the masculine gender.

With the exception of my father . . . My mother, with lowered eyes, would calmly pronounce his name 'Tahar' – which, I learned very early, meant 'The Pure' – and even when a suspicion of a smile flickered across the other women's faces or they looked half ill at ease, half indulgent, I thought that a rare distinction lit up my mother's face.

These harem conversations ran their imperceptible course: my ears only caught those phrases which singled my mother out above the rest. Because she always made a point of bringing my father's name into these exchanges, he became for me still purer than his given name betokened.

•

One day something occurred which was a portent that their relationship would never be the same again – a commonplace enough event in any other society, but which was unusual to say the least with us: in the course of an exceptionally long journey away from home (to a neighbouring province, I think), my father wrote to my mother – yes, to my mother!

He sent her a postcard, with a short greeting written diagonally across it in his large, legible handwriting, something like 'Best wishes from this distant region' or possibly, 'I am having a good journey and getting to know an unfamiliar region' etc. and he signed it simply with his first name. I am sure that, at the time, he himself would not have dared add any more intimate formula above his signature, such as 'I am thinking of you', or even less, 'Yours affectionately'. But, on the half of the card reserved for the address of the recipient, he had written 'Madame' followed by his own surname, with the possible addition – but here I'm not sure – of 'and children', that is to say we three, of whom I, then about ten years old, was the eldest . . .

The radical change in customs was apparent for all to see: my father had quite brazenly written his wife's name, in his own handwriting, on a postcard which was going to travel from one town to another, which was going to be exposed to so many masculine eyes, including eventually our village postman – a Muslim postman to boot – and, what is more, he had dared to refer to her in the western manner as 'Madame So-and-So . . .', whereas, no local man, poor or rich, ever referred to his wife and children in any other way than by the vague periphrasis: 'the household'.

So, my father had 'written' to my mother. When she visited her family she mentioned this postcard, in the simplest possible words and tone of voice, to be sure. She was about to describe her husband's four or five days' absence from the village, explaining the practical problems this had posed: my father having to order the provisions just before he left, so that the shopkeepers could deliver them every morning; she was going to explain how hard it was for a city woman to be isolated in a village with very young children and cut off in this way . . . But the other women had interrupted, exclaiming, in the face of this new reality, this almost incredible detail:

'He wrote to you, *to you?*'

'He wrote his wife's name and the postman must have read it? Shame! . . .'

'He could at least have addressed the card to his son, for the principle of the thing, even if his son is only seven or eight!'

My mother did not reply. She was probably pleased, flattered even, but she said nothing. Perhaps she was suddenly ill at ease, or blushing from embarrassment; yes, her husband had written to her, in person! ... The eldest child, the only one who might have been able to read the card, was her daughter: so, daughter or wife, where was the difference as far as the addressee was concerned?

'I must remind you that I've learned to read French now!'

This postcard was, in fact, a most daring manifestation of affection. Her modesty suffered at that very moment that she spoke of it. Yet, it came second to her pride as a wife, which was secretly flattered.

●

The murmured exchanges of these segregated women struck a faint chord with me, as a little girl with observing eyes. And so, for the first time, I seem to have some intuition of the possible happiness, the mystery in the union of a man and a woman.

My father had dared 'to write' to my mother. Both of them referred to each other by name, which was tantamount to declaring openly their love for each other, my father by writing to her, my mother by quoting my father henceforward without false shame in all her conversations.

GISÈLE HALIMI

God on Probation

When I was a child I looked on death as immobility, then as the obliteration of people I loved. Twice already death had transformed my universe, thinned out my landscape, taking my little brother André from me, then a few years later my paternal grandfather Babah.

When death struck elsewhere it scarcely worried me, its other victims did not really exist, they inhabited another planet, out of sight, where my voice could not reach. As I neither loved nor hated them, I was not aware that they too would die and, if they did, it was nobody's business but their own and those who loved them.

The deaths of my grandfather and my little brother had split my universe in two; one part was the world of light, shapes, sounds, the other that of absence.

The former had taken on a curious turn since death became part of my childhood. The sun drew out strange shadows, the sand, albeit smooth, was pitted with holes.

I would stand silently, alone in front of the mirror, as long as my sister and brothers did not burst into the bedroom I shared with them.

There was this one mirror, streaked with verdigris, set in the door of the old wardrobe – what Fortunée insisted on calling a 'mirror-wardrobe'. I would stand in front of it and move both my heads slightly: my real head did not much care for the one in the reflection. I would lean slowly forward until I was touching – as if to look right through it. I shut one eye to look at myself. Through the open eye I could see quite clearly. The world minus Babah and André.

André, so small that death could not have known what to do with him once he had been cast into the huge empty sack. On the dark side, where my eye was hidden by the palm of my hand, I could see them both. Not together, I think; he was such a tiny kid and grandfather, with his short thick beard, was so old.

'What do you expect?' mother said. 'Everyone dies sooner or later.'

'And you? And Papa?'

Was the closed eye side to become still more populated and the light on the other side be still more distorted?

'Stop asking questions. God decides.'

So God was death?

I didn't know much about God at that time. He seemed to have been undecided about taking grandfather off with him for good. Although dead, Babah had stirred as though he were coming back to the open-eye side, among my living people. Lying on the ground, naked – so I was told (I didn't like that) – covered with a red, green and yellow striped *foutah*, he reminded me of a life-sized statue over which the owners had thrown a pretty dust cover for protection. Absolute immobility – I can certify to that. I had prayed, wept, entreated this God, though I didn't know what he was up to and I suspected him of having a bone to pick with me. I don't think I liked him and I didn't like begging for anything. My reputation on this score was established at an early age and followed me at every confrontation, every dogged refusal to give way. 'A "problem" child,' they sighed, 'but to behave like that with God, really!'

'God can reduce you instantly to a heap of ashes,' my mother threatened, worried by such presumption.

This prospect, which at the time I took for gospel truth, far from helping matters, made me more defiant than ever. My dealings with the Eternal very quickly smacked of contention.

But suppose I began to pray again that day, just for once, half closing my eyes as I'd seen my grandfather do; suppose I kissed the *mezuzah* insatiably, once, thrice, ten times – who knows if he might not allow himself to be won over? In concrete terms, God Elohim had been responsible for my young brother André's disappearance, and today he was after Babah. His power left me at a loss, I felt I was personally under attack. André had not been given back to us; Babah was lying there on the tiled floor, covered with the *foutah*, ready to be carried away for ever.

I stared at the body, without moving. I grew stiff all over. In the next room the family and the hired mourners were fulfilling their various duties. The latter clustered around a *canoun* – a terracotta charcoal stove – full of ashes. They scooped these up by the handful and sprinkled them over the rest of the company, pausing from time to time to beat their breasts with their clenched fists. Then, with one accord, they broke into a spontaneous chorus of prolonged ululations which rose up to heaven from the depths of their souls. Some of them sat on the ground cross-legged and swung their loosened hair around their heads. I watched them, crouching in my corner. Terror-struck. I flattened myself even more against the wall to hide from their turned-up eyes, of which only the whites were visible. I stared at the multicoloured sheet and held my breath to stop myself from blinking. Just suppose grandfather began to move when I wasn't looking . . .

Alone with him, just the two of us. Babah, laid out naked on the floor by God; me, huddled there, with throbbing temples.

•

I remembered how he used to laugh with his toothless mouth at our French, a language which he could neither understand nor speak; but the incongruous sound delighted him. On every occasion, without rhyme or reason, he loved to bring out the word 'uncivilised'. It was his way of expressing his astonishment or protest at anything he found peculiar.

'You start school at eight in the morning? Uncivilised!' If my garters left a mark on my legs, 'Uncivilised!', and he gently massaged my calves. Whenever an argument around him became acrimonious, he would shake his Turkish fez, repeat 'Uncivilised, uncivilised!' in his harsh accent and drag me off for a walk under the orange trees.

Babah loved the orange trees. He endowed them with every virtue. The leaves? An incomparable scent. He would pick a few, rub them between his hands and say, 'Just smell that!' as he poked his nose into his damp palms. 'It'll help you breathe!' The flowers? As beautiful as they were beneficial. From the delicate mother-of-pearl buds one obtained *maazar*, orange-flower water, with its essential properties. No tension, no anger could resist it. It could cure insomnia, heal discord. *Maazar* soothed body and mind, restored their harmony. A few drops in the *kaoua*, the ubiquitous Turkish coffee, and the beverage's harmful properties were overcome, so that it only did one good. My grandparents often gave me a lump of sugar soaked in orange-flower water. 'Instead of forcing you to drink milk,' Babah said, 'your mother ought to give you *maazar*.' Adding, a fraction contemptuously, 'They won't teach you that at the French school.'

•

Aching and stiff all over and the world around me growing dim. The previous day I had been fairly polite to God. 'Please, be kind, give Babah back to us!' I think I had even promised to kiss the *mezuzah* every morning and never again to commit the sin of buying anything on Saturdays, not even sweets.

And suddenly one of the stripes – a yellow one – is askew. Then the striped pattern of the shroud begins to buckle, to float, the lines curl, swell, criss-cross as when a film is set at the wrong speed. The miracle! A quiver under the sheet. However much I sniff and, using my school pinafore, wipe away my tears that form a screen between me and the resurrection, I still can't manage to see clearly. Everything is distorted, gradually the white sheet shrouding the mirror in the old wardrobe – according to the Sephardic funeral custom – creases and the closed wooden shutters begin to lurch.

I shouted over and over, 'He's moving, he's moving, Babah's moving!' The optical illusion – my tears and staring – was all it needed to upset the apple-cart. Grandfather was stirring. First his feet, then his head. He was not dead! Sure, they'd all see for themselves.

I think my head began to swim as I tried to extract myself from the corner where I was hiding, and to approach my beloved ghost, and I had to be carried out of the room.

The ghost of my grandfather did not return.

I was sent to the country with the rest of the children until the psalm-singing, the ceremonial and the funeral were all over.

I spent the first evening of this exile settling my account with God. He had pretended to grant my prayers, only to let me down. Artfully.

Final decision deferred, pending further inquiries.

•

Fortunée drummed into us that as God decided everything, the good results we obtained for tests or exams were more dependent on the Eternal One's goodwill than on our work or intelligence. To win divine grace boys must pray. Girls – not initiated into Hebrew and merely quasi-domestic auxiliaries as far as religion was concerned – must simply abstain from sin. And all must regularly kiss the *mezuzah*. Harder and several times when there was a class test.

Quite soon, possibly when I was about ten and just starting at the Lycée Armand-Fallières, this arrangement struck me as rather fishy. It was probably at that time that my maternal grandfather explained to me that women couldn't bind the *tephilim* round their arms during morning prayers, because they were impure. Moreover, a woman's function was not to pray but to serve the man, so that he can pray.

'*Blessed be the Eternal, who did not make me a woman.*'

Thus did every faithful Jew begin his prayer and his day.

'And the women, what do they say?'

At this question my grandfather nodded towards the kitchen where my grandmother had disappeared. 'A sainted woman, but she doesn't have to pray.'

To tell the truth, if she had wanted to do so, she would simply have replied, '*Blessed be the Eternal, who has made me according to his wishes.*'

I found this role that God assigned to us very tame. And besides, why should being born a woman be life's booby prize, a sort of transgression for which one must pay, a fault to be atoned for? However much my mother vaunted the importance of being the one who sets out the objects for worship in the home and brings the man water for his ritual ablutions as soon as he wakes and makes sure the children don't commit any sins, I still couldn't help thinking God was very off-hand towards us women. He clearly gave us very short shrift.

When I accompanied the men of the family to the synagogue, I had to go up to the balcony, like the rest of the women. From there we could look down in silent wonder to the 'stalls' where the males – men and boys – gathered round the Byzantine riches of the Tablets of the Law and enjoyed the privilege of speaking directly to God.

'Probably a man, too,' I muttered one day, intending my mother to hear.

•

This segregation weighed on me and fuelled my quarrel with the Lord. As I left for school I kissed the *mezuzah* more and more grudgingly. One morning mother called me back on the stairs. I'd forgotten – or rather I didn't feel like asking God's blessing any more before the French test.

The idea germinated in my mind of putting this power to the trial. 'Today I shall know. I'll see the experiment through, I'll not kiss it today. Courage!'

I pick up my satchel, button up my blue school pinafore and walk right past the *mezuzah* with my chin in the air. The little metal case challenges me, knowing it has the commandments on its side. 'God can reduce you to ashes in a second'. I am pursued by Fortunée's voice and the prospect of the Apocalypse. What a din! I turn a deaf ear, I shiver. What if this defiance were to bring about my annihilation? I go on down the stairs, still shivering; I turn round, the *mezuzah* is not at my heels. I run panting to school – this God is capable of anything, he can swoop down like a thunderbolt on to my double squared page.

'Describe a Christmas which you particularly remember.'

I begin; I remember what I have never experienced, what I would like to experience: to be like those who always win, who make the decisions, who have fine houses, books, who travel. I remember the snow which covers with its unreal flakes the pictures in books I have read. Snow I have never seen, but I remember. And I remember that village in the Alps, in France – never seen France; I write, describing the peasants in their brightly-coloured costumes, the sound of their clogs – yet what silence in the snow! I don't want to omit any detail of my scenario, the Christmas in my head: people are singing, they go into a room where logs crackle gaily in the fireplace – a fire is always jolly! Why? Fire also kills; it killed André. The Christmas tree is there, I can see it, huge, essential, bending beneath the weight of the presents in their gay wrappings, the fairy lights twinkle, the children laugh with glee, I write, I write, I don't stop writing, I must hurry to beat God to it.

Does God even know that every Christmas – 'It's a holiday for the *Roumis*, not for us,' our parents drum into us – I have it in for him for excluding us from this land of childhood?

I've almost finished, I add FRENCH COMPOSITION in capitals and copy out the title.

What cheek, I've just fabricated a Christmas! But no, I've described what I feel, what I've seen in my dreams, in my books. It's as true as my non-existent Christmas. God and his guardianship have disappeared. I've fled from the *mezuzah*, and – height of provocation – I express my resentment at being forced to belong to a religion which excludes Christmas.

You've had it, Gisèle!

I stick to my guns and write the word END. On the fifth page of my exercise I have drawn a picture of all my family in their Sunday best, young and old, gathered round the Christmas tree, clogs in the fireplace, the excitement of the presents criss-crossing my lines, the soft whiteness of the snow covering the classroom.

I look round, God is not there, he has not put in an appearance during my flight. But you don't lose anything by waiting. Your marks for the composition? They'll certainly be terrible. Gisèle, always first in French? Out of the question, the *mezuzah* will have its revenge.

Come the day when the marks and the places are read out, I can already hear the teacher saying severely, 'Whatever came over you, Gisèle, this is bad, very bad!' Fortunée is right, I'm turned into a heap of ashes. Shame, dismay, fear, if I'm no longer amongst the top girls, if I have to stay down, I shall lose my scholarship at the *lycée*, that's the way it is.

'First, with 14 marks, Gisèle . . .' the teacher announces. Adding, with a scarcely disguised sigh of pleasure, 'As usual!'

That's it, God has lost. The power that my family ascribes to him does not exist, he neither rewards nor punishes, his *mezuzah* is null and void. It and all the other baubles, *tephilim*, ritual candlesticks, to the scrap-heap . . . God himself, I remand on bail. On account of his being a second-rater. Perhaps he does exist, but he's rather undesirable. In any case, he should stop bothering us. I've just settled the matter.

Since that day, by subterfuge for the most part, by humouring him as one does a formidable tyrant, I have avoided all these minor observances and once and for all have distinguished superstition from belief. At fifteen or sixteen I entertained a vague idea, a fear more than a belief, that a God or someone or something was necessary. But I did not count this problem among my existential preoccupations. My experiment had confirmed my doubts, my path and God's did not cross. Let him go in peace, I'd manage without him and he'd find a way of rampaging somewhere else without poking his nose into my business.

From that moment I gained a sort of confidence in my studies, in my family relationships, in my games. My parents lamented, 'She blasphemes, the insolent girl!'

I had just won my first share of freedom.

Translated by Dorothy S. Blair

LEĪLA SEBBAR

The Stone Bench

She is the last one.

The mesh-like baskets of red plastic are stacked across from her, almost up to the ceiling. A larger washing place in the city doesn't exist. Thirty monumental red or white machines with glass portholes – she hasn't even counted them, but her neighbour used that figure when explaining where the most modern laundromat in the city was. Without writing down the address or making a map, she remembered easily that it was in the centre of town – you go past the elementary school, the square, and the open space beyond the filling station. It always glows with a reddish light, the colour of its machines. It is magnificent, the neighbour repeats, as though it is festival time, and it sparkles all night long. Once when coming back late from the cinema with her sister – it must have been one or two o'clock in the morning – they had remarked that it didn't practise any shabby economy with electricity. Her sister also likes the laundromat – she has a machine of her own, but it's old, she has no husband, and to repair it would cost too much. When it doesn't work – and that's becoming more and more frequent – she telephones and the two of them go to the laundromat with their bundles of laundry, the two of them together, to spend the afternoon.

She, the neighbour – her husband has left her, leaving her and the children without money to support them. He disappeared and despite legal suits and searches he has not been found. He's perhaps in America and one day will tell her to come with the children and join him. What will she say? When he left, the washing machine broke down and she has never replaced it. She prefers to go to the laundromat where she chatters with her sister, the women who are there, and sometimes with single men. They talk – and that was how she found a man – but it didn't last. He wouldn't accept the children, and he left.

In the laundromat the light is white – not like the signboard of vivid

red letters which draw your attention. Inside, everything is white –
except for certain red machines and the baskets. The tiled floor, the
ceiling, the stone bench across from the machines for waiting clients,
like a long sofa running the length of the room, but without cushions –
all are white. It is a bit like a hospital, but not its smell, which is a
mixture of dirty linen – often moist – and scented detergent. The steam
has its own smell, so do the clothes from the machines: piles of clothing
pressed into cubes like the carcasses of cars at the car dump which
have been reduced into compact masses to make room for more
wrecked cars brought in.

She is always the last one.

When all is done, the clothes are clean and almost dry – in winter
she can't spread them on the narrow balcony or on the windowledges
to dry: they would freeze. In the laundromat it is warm and she can
stay as long as she likes – it stays open late.

Seated on the stone bench, she has met women like herself who
don't speak the local language. They come with neighbours who speak
their own language or with neighbours from two countries who can
switch from one language to the other. Then they can talk. She has
learnt that women who look like her come from the mountains or from
the hill country or from islands far away across the sea. She can't say
their names rightly – she hears them often enough, but she doesn't
remember the names of the countries so far away, nor of the cities
where the women lived before, which they have spoken about to their
neighbours who translated. She has learnt that the cities are the largest
in these former lands, though their washing places are smaller than
the one here, where they meet up with one another towards the end of
the afternoon. The names of the cities get all blurred in her mind, but
not the women, their gestures, their laughter, their clothing.

She knows if they come from the mountains, or from an island across
the seas, from the high plateaus, or from the bush. They don't handle
their laundry the way other women do. Women who have always lived
in the cities put everything into the machines, indiscriminately. They,
too, have children of course: trousers, underclothing, blouses, socks,
shirts, sweaters – they pile all these in front of the half-open door of
the machine, just as she does. But the under things, those that she
washes herself in a basin at home with her own soap – those intimate
things which shouldn't be seen anywhere but at home, nor washed
anywhere but in a special bowl – the panties, the brassières, the

petticoats, the socks, the stockings, the tights, the handkerchiefs, and the nightgowns: that kind of laundry these foreign women don't hide at all. The city women spread it out before the eyes of people who are strangers to their homes. What if someone was going to take some of it? And what if someone they'd never ever seen should take it to cast a spell? To do harm? City women don't understand such things – they don't distrust others. She would have liked to warn them not to take the under things out but let them remain in the bottom of the bag by themselves, so they wouldn't be in the bright white light of the laundromat in full view of other women, neighbours, also men – sometimes men were there and even if they didn't look, they *knew* what the women of *their* village never allowed to be seen, unlike the immodest women *here*. In the laundromat there are men from cities who are not surprised to see the personal laundry of women, to see before their very eyes – on the white tiled floor, private things which women wear *under* their slacks, their shirts, or their pullovers – things worn pressed next to the skin itself – which are now soiled! And certainly in city shops men have a full, clear view of the large counter surfaces and trays where women's clothing is cast pell-mell (clothing which they paw through in the sales and dispute about). And if it isn't in trays, it is hung up, exposed like outer clothing. Sometimes a woman even chooses a piece of underwear in cooperation with a man who accompanies her! A black piece or a white piece. She speaks to him and he gives her his advice – they examine it together!

But *there* on the tiles, underwear, brassières which have been worn the night before, dirty at the seams, under the arms when they are inside out – spots on the panties, a mixture of old colours, right side or wrong side, it's all the same to them. They don't realise that the men seated on the stone bench notice in spite of everything. The women act out of habit – just as if they were at home. They don't know these men – who also come from cities. The men aren't disturbed by what harm might happen one day because of the women's lack of prudence. Such clothing, women like *her* (and others whom she meets at the laundromat who are not city women, but women from the mountains, the plateaus, and the hills), such clothing – they hide it; they don't let it lie about just anywhere, even at home; they are vigilant: hairs, clipped nails, flaked bits of skin – everything which has been part of one's body – the soilings of underclothing – *they* let none of that be left about even in their bedrooms. But then at the laundromat, in front of the machines each one empties her pile of clothing from which those things stick out which others should not see – above all, not single men, strangers, even those not born in a city, even men from the same faraway villages. She doesn't recognise them, she doesn't look at them, but she *knows* that even if they turn their heads and if they lower their glances they see everything.

She stays there, the last one. That gives some comfort.

She returns home with her bags of clean clothes. She will spread the damp laundry out in the kitchen that night, and in the washroom for several days after. She irons these damp clothes, inhaling the vapour with its scent of the laundromat. Once she was unable to stay to be the last one, as she usually was. A man whom she had not noticed at first amongst the other men present that day on the length of the stone bench, decided not to leave the laundromat ahead of her. The women, her friends, neighbours, all left, one group after another. Some young men who were talking among themselves followed the women, but he – whom she had not seen washing any clothes – was still there, a bag at his feet, seated, not budging. She knew he was a man from her country, even without hearing him speak. He had been by himself from the beginning, his hands crossed over his lap, looking straight ahead. The shop's employees were leaving. The owner stacked the last of the red baskets and disappeared through the door at the back of the laundromat.

She has folded and ordered the laundry in her bags; her scarf has slipped and she readjusts it round her cheeks. The man must have seen her hair! It extended several centimetres below the corner of the scarf at her back. Without turning, she has again covered her glistening black hair (she washed it the night before in her bath), pushing behind her ears the curls which might escape from under her scarf and she knots the scarf more tightly under her chin, before picking up her bags and placing them on the stone bench at a distance from the man. Just when she is about to sit down, the man stands up and seeming less large suddenly moves toward her. He is wearing an imitation astrakan cap. The owner has put out the lights in the back room. The man stops in front of her. She is petrified. She has not lowered her head, she looks at him – he also looks at her – without saying a word. She hears the owner coming down the hall, the red lights twinkling outside. The laundromat is going to close. She rises suddenly, brushes against the man and escapes, running. She has forgotten her bags of laundry.

Next morning she sends her daughter to get them. Since that night she has not seen the man again. He must have left town.

Now she can once again be the last one to leave.

She used to go regularly to the river with the women from the great house and with her own neighbours, early in the morning in summer when the weather was quite hot. They would all leave home with basins full of laundry balanced on their heads. Little girls who as yet were not helpers would run ahead on the dirt road to the path which led down to the rocky shore, causing their little brothers (who could hardly walk and whom they had to carry on their backs) to cry out. At the shore they abandoned the brothers and played at the edge of the stream in the reddish earth. The little ones continued to cry and waited for the arrival of their mothers, who threatened the little girls, making them dry their brothers' tears before lifting the tots up on to their hips or astride their backs. Each woman had her rock, her place, and her bushes. They went into the clear water, at times up to mid-thigh, skirts raised and held at the waist by a woollen sash.

Washday was women's day at the river, for pieces of laundry which one could not wash at home as they were too large; one had to beat them with a stout stick before spreading them out upon the bushes in the sunlight. The children sprayed them with lemon or ashes and then the mothers rinsed them again in the stream of water. Sometimes something would escape and follow the current – even as far as the next pool where the girls would recapture it, clamouring. The women were alone; men do not come to the river on women's day, and on hunting days, they make a detour around the area. The children go into the water naked, little boys and girls. The younger women bathe in the shelter of hidden rocks, soaping each other, rinsing their hair. They eat alongside the stream (the little girls may have gone to get the food), they chatter while the washing (which they keep in sight) dries on bush and rock. The mothers put the littlest children down on dry clothing for a nap in the shade, before resuming the work which lasts until evening.

At the laundromat, changing from one language to another, the women tell each other about the river, the cascade, the pool, the fast stream, the dams and locks made of stones which the children go looking for along the river's edge. Gestures accompany their words, and where words are inadequate, the sounds and the songs tell everything as if all were the same story from the Caribbean to the

Black Sea, from the Dead Sea to the African Mediterranean. In the cities where women don't hide their intimate washing at the laundromat, where *are* the rivers? Some women say they *have* seen large rivers in the cities themselves, even wider than the boulevards. These are called *fleuves*, great rivers, but here you can only walk along the concrete paths which border them – or sometimes sit upon stone benches to look at them. No one touches it, the water of the big rivers in the big cities; it really doesn't flow. Who would ever go into it with legs and bottoms bare? Who would wash her face in it, her hair? The water isn't even clear. She has gone with her children to walk along this city's river. The children throw rocks in it to make splashes, to make it move. They yearn for their river, its cascades, its wild pools, the fast-flowing stream of their early childhood – the river which *ran* and made your skin soft, the clothing, white. She used to say they would go back. They are grown up now. Now they know only the dirty water of the *fleuve*. They hear their mother say time and again that that water is not the water for washing clothes. In the laundromat she sees the water through the convex glass porthole, white with bubbles, then grey, almost black. Finally it becomes colourless, drawn into the clothing which turns, creased, tangled, pounded in the drum. You can't tell what is being washed; trousers, a shirt, a napkin. She scarcely touches the household laundry, only before the machine starts, to sort it, or when the machine has finished to fold it. She washes the intimate clothing by hand for a long while in her home washbasin, when the children are asleep, and their father as well. She does not lean over the washbasins in the bathroom as the other women do as they stand up. From time to time, pressing a hand on their lower back, they bear down on the place where they ache and straighten up, letting out a long painful sign before wiping their brows, their faces lifted to the mirror. They look at themselves. It is night. Perhaps they too have a river, a childhood beside a pool bordered with rocks, cries of alarm from the edge of the river as it carries off a doll's dress or the little brother's windmill, when they see its red wings turn, and hear the child cry. He wants to go after the windmill spinning away; his sister holds him back. She takes him on her back and gallops towards the windmill, which is caught farther on in long eucalyptus leaves. A wing is broken. The child seizes the windmill, runs towards the river, throws it on the other side of the dam made of eucalyptus leaves. He watches it disappear, frozen with the menacing looks of his older sister . . .

No one will come into the bathroom; she has no need to lock the door. She sits on the soft shag rug which she keeps for doing the laundry. She hides it in the hall cupboard. If she left it out to be trampled on by the children, she would have to dispose of it, dirty and wet. She could do nothing but throw it away as she had to do the first time when, neglectfully, she forgot and left one in front of the tub. When she spends the day at home, she wears long bloomers under her skirt – the *saroal* – which her sister sends her every year that she does not return to her own country with the children. In between her legs she places two basins, one square one of red plastic into which she puts the washed clothes; the other, a round enamelled one (bought at a Tuesday market, a Chinese one, less expensive than the red plastic one) with red, green and pink peonies on the bottom which can be seen when the bowl is empty. In this one she lets her washing soak a bit before rubbing it slowly several times with household soap. For her laundry, she doesn't like toilet soap which smells like eau-de-Cologne or like apples. With her back against the wall where she sits, she washes the clothes for a long time, piece by piece, and she sings. One night she didn't hear the sound of dishes in the kitchen; her husband came in because of the light – he thought she was still with the children. Sometimes she falls asleep in the children's room while consoling one who has called for her in his sleep and who is crying after a nightmare. The husband pushed open the door and looked at her surprised. She didn't have time to pull her skirt down over the Chinese basin. He was preparing the morning coffee. She was unaware that it was four o'clock.

'You are singing and forgetting everything,' the husband said.

'Yes, I'm singing, but I'm not forgetting – not the children, not the house. Don't be upset . . . Anyhow, at least I know that I haven't forgotten the songs. I get worried – sometimes it happens that I can't remember the words, that I can't seem to find the words again, and I try like crazy. Finally, when I stop trying to remember and I happen to sing in the bathroom or at the laundromat with the other women, the words are there – I haven't forgotten them after all. I'm not forgetting you . . . don't worry . . . I'm always mindful of the children. I'll sleep during the day. I'll take a siesta today, I guess.' The husband said that *he* doesn't take siestas.

She is the last one in the laundromat.

The owner says she is going to close up. She turns out the last luminous panel of lights above the machines, after having checked that the automatic coin boxes are empty. She calls out in her native tongue more briskly this evening, 'I'm closing. You must leave . . . Why are you staying there like that?'

The woman hasn't budged. The owner, who has turned the door light off, turns it on again; the woman seated on the stone bench is dimly lit. The owner walks over to her between large, grey plastic sacks. (Her husband works in city administration; quite regularly he gives her large, new-folded garbage sacks in a transparent envelope.)

Just when she gets close to the seated woman, through the window of the laundromat, the owner sees a large man in a black coat, a flat cap of imitation astrakan on his head.

'What does he want, that one? I've no money on me, fortunately,' the owner says in a low voice, stopping in front of the seated woman.

The seated woman weeps.

The owner leans over her, speaks softly to her, a few simple words which the woman can understand, and points to the man on the other side of the window. He hasn't moved. As she gets up the woman replies 'yes' with a nod of her head to a question the owner poses to her. The owner helps her carry the bags of laundry to the door. Before turning off the lights, the owner watches the man and the woman who walk away together. It is the man who carries the bags.

Days follow days – the woman has not returned to the laundromat. The owner has seen the neighbours, but never the woman who used to stay behind, the last one to leave, she who wept one night on the bench of stone.

Translator's note: *The title itself 'Le sofa en pierre', like many passages in the story, poses a question for the translator. The desire to be literal and accurate must often yield to the desire to the render the inner story (the mood, the fears, the shifting focus of the woman's attention) in the comparable English idiom and rhythm. This is a poignant story, after all; and it is a subtle picture of a sensitive person who never could be fully at ease in an alien land.*

D. K. Bruner

ANDRÉE CHEDID

Death in Slow Motion

The young woman felt the point of impact of the bullet in her back. A brief, sharp pain. She continued walking as if nothing had happened; but the illusion did not last. Around her: uprooted trees, the street torn up, charred and gaping rectangles of buildings, proved clearly that the fighting had been violent; and the truce, once more, precarious. M. had just been hit by a sudden blast of which she was not the target; her wound was quite real.

She didn't wish to know more. The pain had left her; what counted at that moment, more than her very life, was to reach the place where someone was waiting for her; at the head of the bridge, in the angle of the parapet.

The clear light illuminated a deserted environment, shone upon her face, clothed her thirty-year-old body. It would move forward, her body; she would force it to move. She *will* use all her strength, she *will* hold on. She *will* get through the quarter of an hour which separates her from the meeting.

The street wavers, darkens; all at once the air thickens and the sky is shrouded over. An infinite slowness governs the motions of M., her sensations weaken. Only the pressing desire to arrive in sight of the bridge still stabs her.

Pushing her hands, her arms straight before her, she looks to each of them in turn, to draw forward her body which has grown heavy, her legs which are stuffed with cotton-wool. The anguish in case she does not arrive in time is eating into her more savagely than the bullet.

Where and why fix the boundaries of this place? A succession of names come to mind. In the mud of rice fields, on the asphalt of cities, imprisoned in a crowd which is destroyed or dying in solitude, the massacred ones, the refugees, those shot or tortured converge at once into this place, into someone. Into this living woman, wounded to death. Violences pile upon each other, horror overlying horror, bloody faces, faces drained of blood, a haemorrhage of men . . . What does the place matter? Everywhere humanity is involved, and the pageant is without end. In each body struck down all bodies groan and founder, blown by blind forces, into the same hell.

M. has counted too much upon her own strength; now seeking help around her, her eyes find nothing. She drags herself towards the wall; her hands grope, they cling to its roughness. She struggles again, persists, her head and shoulders drawing themselves upwards, but her feeble knees buckle, dropping her to the ground.

M. calls. Her voice catches in her throat, merely inflames her temples, becomes a murmur brushing her lips and then dies out. For a second time a smarting pang pierces her body from one point to another. A warm flow seeps between her shoulder blades, making her shirt sticky.

Now the young woman stops resisting her body, but tries rather to go along with it. Avoiding sudden movements, she accompanies her flesh, its whirling, its rotation; she does not struggle against the shaking head or the waving arms which raise themselves up, beat at the air, or even grasp for support. Husbanding her breath in the hope of surviving until the coming of a passer-by to whom she can entrust the message, M. lets herself be manoeuvred, without losing herself from view.

Twisted, she twists again, is bent over, pivots slowly, as in the movies, through the length of a heavy fall, until she gradually lands on the pavement where she finds herself huddled in the foetal position.

Her cheek to the ground, her eyes watching, clinging desperately to the remaining glimmers of awareness, the young woman panics at the disappearance of the sunlight behind a thin cloud. But, quickly again, the sun reappears. She experiences a real comfort in that. Not far away, a window creaks. The smell of coffee reaches her.

M. drives away the memories which flow over her in waves; she does not want anything to exist but the present moment, nothing other than the portion of the future which she is still seeking to save. Taking infinite precautions, she succeeds in drawing a coloured postcard from her pocket, and a stub of pencil. The end is near, so near, but to live on a bit was still possible wasn't it? Death overhangs her tiny territory which, minute by minute, is shrinking. She sees once more – with its large brownish wings – the kite which planes endlessly above the buildings of her native city before swooping down majestically on a morsel of food placed upon the ledge of a balcony.

On her left, some distance away, a *port-cochère* has just been opened. Before venturing into the street, an old couple carefully observe the roofs on which sharpshooters are often positioned. The man carries a suitcase crudely tied with twine. Once outside they straighten up and hold hands. M. drinks them in with her eyes, takes refuge between the two palms so gently joined; she poses, like the old woman, her head upon the chest of her companion, receives the same kiss upon her hair . . .

From the depth of her silence, M. cries out towards them and desperately seeks to draw their attention. Why did she put on this grey dress which blends in so with the stony ground?

Neither of them notices her. They speak in hushed voices to each other; then they start off in the opposite direction.

Just as she goes forward, the old woman turns one last time towards her abandoned lodgings. There, down there, she makes out a body stretched on the pavement.

'Stop. Look.' Quickly they turn back. Supporting each other, they cross the road as quickly as their legs will allow.

The old man kneels down, examines the wounded woman, realises that the situation is grave, fatal. Suddenly, overcome with indignation, with 'Why?', his eyes fill with anger and with tears; while the woman cries out, knocks upon doors, tries to arouse the neighbours. No response. Most of the buildings are empty, their inhabitants have fled to the country. After the recent sporadic gunfire the rest of the population goes into hiding, fearing that the fighting is going to begin again.

With an unexpected effort M. raises her hand, with trembling fingers offers a card. The man takes the picture, looks at it, turns it over; the back is covered with writing in brown ink.

'I can't see well. You read it.'

Drawing her silver-rimmed glasses from the case suspended around her neck, the old woman reads aloud. The face of the young woman appears to relax.

'I'll go.'

'Alone?'

'You can see very well that we can't just leave her alone.'

He agrees. Tucking in her elbows, going as fast as she can, she runs up the middle of the street, exposed on all sides to hostile fire, impetuous as always! He watches her, growing smaller as he watches, and he follows her with his eyes, anxious at heart. He sees her again . . .

But this time it is in the past. She is the same age as the young woman dying. To rejoin him from the other side of the boulevard, she hurls herself into the crowd, she runs towards him, she appears bigger, charging between the vehicles, cheeks flushed . . . her hair flying wildly, reckless as always!

Seated upon the parapet at the turn of the bridge, he was just putting his foot on the ground. The evening before he had discovered the address of the young woman and knew that she would have received his card. The city, he was thinking, had been granted peace once again, and M. was punctuality itself. The waiting had been too unbearably long; surely she would not be coming.

From a distance, because of the same blue sweater he was wearing in the photo, the old woman recognised him. Waving the card in her extended hand she tried to make a sign to him; then a loaded bus honked so stridently behind her that she jumped on to the pavement to let it pass; it grazed her slightly and continued on its way.

A moment later, she saw the young man grasp an arm extended from the vehicle. Hooking himself on, he leapt on to the running-board and was swallowed up in its interior . . . The old woman shouted in vain, the rumbling of the machine smothering her words. In a few seconds, the bus vanished behind a cloak of dust.

Crushed, she leant back against the parapet, let several minutes pass before reading and rereading the message on the card. With each word a shred of her own youth was torn from her. Shuddering at the thought that he who was going away, without knowing anything at all, could have been her own companion, she had but one intention: to get back to her man at once. Swiftly, she again took the road against the traffic, muttering to herself by heart the words on the card:

Destruction, horror and hate have gripped the faces of everyone. In whom, in what can we believe from now on? Since daily I live with death all seems mad, useless – except true love. We love each other, M., whatever may have taken place. I shall wait for you the day after tomorrow at one in the afternoon at the turn of the great bridge, as at our first meeting (six years ago). A friend will bring you this word. I will be certain that you have received it. If you do not come, it is because all will have been definitely broken off.

Just below, the young woman had written in wavering letters in pencil: 'I was coming . . .'

The old woman kneeled down, put her arm around the shoulders of her husband, told him of the failed meeting, adding: 'One day, we must, we *must* find him again.' In turn, in a low voice, the old man whispered that a passer-by had gone in search of an ambulance; but he had known from the very start there was no hope of saving the young woman.

The young woman no longer moved and hardly breathed at all. The old woman bent over her, swept the wan cheek with her warm breath, brushed the temple with her lips. Then she drew back the hair, freed the ear and, taking care with each syllable, carefully poured out one word after the other.

'He was waiting for you at the turn of the great bridge. I have seen him, little one. I have spoken to him.'

A sigh from M. urged her to go on. 'He is on his way. He is coming.'

Raising her face towards the old man she met his glance of comradeship. Soon he took the relay: 'He is at the end of the street and he is coming towards us. I recognise his blue sweater.'

The old woman echoed, 'There he is!'

'He approaches . . .'

Their voices came together. Waves flowed through the veins of the young woman, spread throughout her frame, a surge of joy broke through her features; from her breast there arose a sigh greater than the seas.

A giddiness of joy and distress, of despair and of calm overtook the old couple. The absurdity and the meaning of things intermingled in their minds. Their hands sought each other, to form but a single hand.

A single hand which placed itself like a cloak of tenderness over the young motionless hand. That hand which was not yet completely chilled.

Translated from the French by David Bruner

NOTES ON CONTRIBUTORS

ACHOLONU, CATHERINE OBIANUJU Born in Orlu, Imo State of Nigeria in 1951, she is the eldest child in the family of Chief Lazarus Olumba. She attended Holy Rosary Primary School in Orlu and Holy Rosary Secondary School in Ihioma. She was in Nigeria during the civil war, and based a play on it, *Into the Heart of Biafra*.

After the war Acholonu left Nigeria in 1973 to study abroad. She received both her MA and PhD in English and African Literature from the University of Dusseldorf in West Germany. She married Dr Acholonu, son of the Orlu traditional ruler, and has four children. She teaches in the Department of English at Alvan Ikoku College of Education in Owerri. Acholonu spent 1990-91 as visiting professor at Manhattanville College in Purchase, N.Y.

She has written poems, plays, scholarly articles, and some children's literature in English and in Igbo. She is the editor of the *AFA Journal of Creative Writing*. Her poetic drama, *Trial of the Beautiful Ones*, incorporating dance, ritual, and spectacle, is based on the Igbo Ogbanje myth. In its production in 1984 she played the part of Ezenwanui, the mermaid queen.

Acholonu has done extensive field work in Nigeria, conducting oral interviews with various informants to trace the actual place of origin and family line of Equiano, the eighteenth-century slave autobiographer. In her study, *The Igbo Roots of Olaudah Equiano*, she used oral histories and linguistic evidence to trace Equiano's background. She is also interested in the history of the women in her region, particularly the lineage of Amazons in her maternal line. She plans that her novel, *Letters to God*, will be the first volume in a series of novels on this theme. 'African feminism is perceived by me as MOTHERISM,' she states. Her story 'Mother was a Great Man' is based on the character and life of her grandmother, Oyidiya.

OKOYE, IFEOMA was born in Umunachi, rather than state her birthday, she says she is 'ageless.' She was educated in Nigeria at St

Amonica's Teachers' College at Ogbunike and received an honours BA in 1977 at the University of Nigeria in Nsukka. She teaches at the Institute of Management and Technology in Enugu. She spent 1986–7 at Aston University in Birmingham, England. She is married and has five children.

Okoye's interest in education has led her to write books and texts for children. In 1978 she won the Macmillan Children's Literature prize for *Village Boy*. Her first novel, *Behind the Clouds*, 1982, won a prize at the National Festival of Arts and Culture. Her second novel, *Men Without Ears*, won the Nigerian Author's Prize for Best Fiction of 1984. Her novels disclose many problems of contemporary Nigeria: a wife's responsibility to bear children, corruption in government, business practices exploiting workers and clients, extravagant expectations for funeral costs, etc. She even exposes the trafficking in human organs obtained from ritual, cult killings. She says of her work that she hopes to 'if I can, through my writing, bring about the upliftment of the oppressed, the underprivileged, and those discriminated against, whether male or female.'[1]

Although well established as a writer of children's books and of novels, until now she had not written any short stories: 'I've not tried my hand at writing short stories and now that you have drawn my attention to it, I would like to make an attempt.' A year later she sent 'The Pay-packet' with the comment 'I needed some courage to venture into a new field.'

In 'The Pay-packet', Okoye exposes not only the trauma of the battered woman, but also problems as traditional economic practices shackle women despite their education and career status.

ALKALI, ZAYNAB A Muslim of Borno State origin, she was born and brought up in a Christian village in Congora State. She still remembers vividly listening to the old village women and their accounts of traditional beliefs and the 'disasters' of civilisation. Alkali received her education in Nigeria, graduating from Bayero University in Kano with a BA in English in 1973. In 1979 she took her MA in African Literature. She teaches at the University of Maiduguri, where her husband is Vice-Chancellor. They have six children.

Alkali comes from a creative family: 'My mother sings. My maternal grandmother was a composer/singer, and my maternal grandfather was

---

[1] Quotations are taken from correspondence with C.H.B.

a drummer.'[1] Her grandmother told stories to the children in the evenings. Early on, Alkali was impressed with local proverbs and traditional mannerisms and speech patterns. She finds writing in English necessary for a wider audience, but also 'agonizing' as she fears losing idioms and meanings by converting dialogue from Babur and Hausa to English. She is encouraging her children to write, and two daughters have already written stories and produced school plays. When Adeola James asked Alkali in her letter-interview published in *In Their Own Voices: African Women Writers Talk* (1990), how she fits writing into her busy life, she answered with just one word, 'Snugly'.

Alkali's first novel, *The Stillborn*, appeared in 1984 and won immediate acclaim and the Nigerian Authors' Prose Prize for 1985. She found that, 'I have earned a great responsibility of setting the pace for younger writers, as the first woman novelist in Northern Nigeria.' She feels that women are not so much resented as ignored: 'In African literature women are not even adequately presented'. She is not a protest writer as such, but finds traditional 'wounds' and 'thorns' of civilisation natural themes for her fiction. She finds also: 'A lot of material to write on which concerns the woman: Bride-child and its consequences, forced marriages, polygamy, extended families, etc.'

Her second novel, *The Virtuous Woman*, 1986, is directed particularly toward teenagers and their confusions about education and romantic love. Her short stories often concern family affairs and differing views between family members, not just generational gaps and culture clashes. The family scenes she sketches are often funny, with children's rebellious schemes to outwit parental supervision, grandparents' squabbles for domination – the strong, the weak, the devious, the loving – all portrayed with warmth and humour.

AMARÍLIS, ORLANDA Born on 9 October 1924, on the island of Santiago into a family of writers. Her father began a Portuguese-Creole dictionary on which he worked for many years. Orlanda received her primary and secondary school training in Mindelo on St Vincent Island. She completed her study for her Magisterio Primario in Goa, where she spent six years. Later in Lisbon she went on to further study.

In 1946 she married Manuel Ferreira, a writer. He had been a soldier in the Portuguese army during the Second World War. While they lived in Cape Verde they helped to found the review *Certeza* in 1944 and

[1] The quotations come from Adeola James' letter-interview with Alkali, published in *In Their Own Voices: African Women Writers Talk* (1990), and from letters and an interview in Iowa City in July 1989 with the Bruners.

Orlanda contributed short stories to the publication. Both she and her husband were active in promoting lusophone literature in the islands.

They travelled widely on professional and cultural missions, to Nigeria, Canada and the USA. They spent six years in Goa where Manuel directed the newspaper *O Heraldo*. They spent two years in Angola where he taught secondary school in Luanda. Finally they settled in Lisbon, and Manuel established the chair of Lusophone African Literature there. They have been active in meetings on Culture and Literature of Cape Verde (1986), the Portuguese Movement against Apartheid, the Portuguese Movement for Peace, and the Portuguese Association of Writers.

Orlanda's fiction has appeared in many magazines and anthologies. She has published three collections of her own short stories: *Cais do Sodré té Salamansa* (1974), *Ilhéu dos pássaros* (1983), and *A gasa los mastros* (1989). *Facécias e Peripécias* is a collection of stories for children. 'Where the Sea Ends' is included in a Pen Club anthology for 1991. Maria Ellen says of her fiction: 'Writing in a style close to colloquial language, Orlanda Amarilis explores the day-to-day events in the life of emigrants, their surprise and their disappointments.'

MAÏGA KA, ROKHAYATOU AMINATA Born in St Louis, Senegal, in 1940, she received her diploma in English and American Literature at the University of Dakar in 1967, and taught English from 1967–75. She is married to journalist and playwright Abdou Anta Ka.

She has travelled widely and since 1978 has been a technical counsellor in the Ministry of Education. After a long involvement in women's issues and the status of women at local and national level, she is currently the editor-in-chief of the National Movement of Socialist Women's newspaper. She counted novelist Miriama Bâ, an outspoken advocate for changes in women's role, among her friends.

In 1985 Maïga Ka published a volume, *'La voie du salut' suivi de 'Le miroir de la vie'* (Présence Africaine, Paris). The first of the short stories, 'The Way of Salvation,' covers the lives of two women, a mother, Rokhaya, and her daughter, Rabiatou. Throughout, Ka shows Senegal in a state of transition. Change seems to occur without real progress for women, even those of higher caste who enjoy city life. At fourteen, Rokhaya, a traditional village girl, is married to a modern outsider, a young Sudanese doctor. He is educated in western medicine and comes to her village to inoculate the well population and to treat the victims of a smallpox epidemic. Despite the reluctance of Rokhaya's father to let her marry outside her own group, the doctor, Baba Kounta, by an unworthy subterfuge, wins and takes Rokhaya back to his own city of Tandia. With childlike devotion and unquestioning observance of her wifely role, Rokhaya finds some contentment. But the daughter, Rabaitou, though educated and privileged, attempts to lead a 'liberated' life, with tragic results.

Maïga Ka says of her own work. 'My main themes are polygamy, caste and education . . . a criticism of our society . . . The short stories are very dramatic and gloomy. I did it on purpose to show that African women are most of the time victims who do not react enough to their fates and are toys between the hands of men.'[1]

AYODA, EVELYN AWOUR Born in Kenya in 1956, she now lives with her American husband and child in Urbana, Illinois. She has a varied cross-cultural education and practical experience in many areas. Having attended Kenya High School, Loreto Convent Msongari and Kianda College for Teachers and Business Training, she spent four years of further study in Europe. She received a BA at Sussex University in England, and then studied in Paris for part of her International Relations and French specialisation. She speaks five languages (Luo, English, French, Kiswahili, and Spanish) and acted as a bilingual translator at the Triennial Conference of the International Council of Women in Nairobi in 1979. She is particularly interested in both anglophone and francophone African Literature. For over five years she served as Office Manager for the CREDU, a French centre in Nairobi established to encourage co-operation between universities in France and in ten eastern African countries. She is working towards her PhD in Comparative Literature at the University of Illinois.

Ayoda has won prizes for essays and letters and has published short stories in the East African magazine, *Drum*. She has appeared regularly on the Voice of Kenya. In 1991 she went to Tanzania to do a series of interviews with fellow woman writer, Penina Muhando.

Ayoda says of her stories, 'What particularly concerns me is the condition and situation of the women in Kenyan society. In short, they are given little respect, their work is devalued, and they are abused physically and mentally . . . despite the fact that they are a productive, active and essential part of the society and economy. Within the patriarchal society . . . the woman's present condition is maintained first by the men, and then by the women who have internalised patriarchal

---

[1] The quotation is taken from correspondence with C.H.B., 1990, when Ka was a participant in the International Writing Programme at Iowa City.

views on women and, sometimes inadvertently, act as agents of male suppression . . . My stories may not bring about a social revolution, but they may lead a few people to question certain accepted practices.'[1]

LANNOY, VIOLET DIAS Born in Quelimane in 1925, she spent most of her childhood in the capital of Mozambique, Laurenço Marques, where her father was stationed in the Portguese administration. She was eleven when the family moved to Goa, then to Bombay, partly for the educational opportunities available there for their three children. Violet was an outstanding student, and won scholarships to secondary school and college. She attained a BA in 1947, and went on to postgraduate teacher training. Educational practice and policy were always important to her, and feature in all her writing.

Influenced by Gandhian principles, she rejoiced at India's independence. She worked directly with Gandhi, and married Behram Warden, a Parsi disciple of Gandhi. Together they worked for peace, and lived in poverty until Behram's death.

After Gandhi's assassination, Violet went to Portuguese-colonised Goa, her ancestral home, to teach and to study for her MA. She also worked for Goan independence, but this limited her academic freedom. She went to London on scholarship to University College, where she obtained her MA.

Following a move to Paris, she met photographer Richard Lannoy in 1954. They joined a circle of intellectual humanists, national and international, including Richard Wright and James Baldwin. She married Lannoy, and they worked together, shared many social concerns, and travelled together in India (1956) and in Africa. She formed the habit of writing through the night, actually damaging her health by ignoring medical advice to slow her pace of work. Ever a teacher, she formed many international bonds between people of differing ideologies and religions. For herself, she refused allegiance to any dogma.

Violet kept journals, but not until she was thirty did she consider writing fiction. During her three years in India and the year spent teaching in London, she worked on her novel *Pears from a Willow Tree*, set in a school with exceptional children. She sent it to Richard Wright, who offered to champion it, but died suddenly shortly afterwards. For ten years she and Lannoy were headquartered in Paris in 'a cold-water, fifth-floor, walk-up flat – a laughably impoverished, cliché, *vie-de-bohème*

---

[1] The editor met Ayoda in Urbana, Illinois, and discussed her plans for her writing career in 1989. Since then they have exchanged letters. The quotation comes from a letter of 2 May 1991.

backdrop to life'. She worked and travelled for UNESCO in the Americas, Goa, England, studying educational systems. Disillusioned by racism and chauvinism in Europe, she got a transfer to East Africa. From Nairobi, she visited schools in Kenya, Tanzania and Uganda, basing one novella and four short stories on her East African work. She also planned a novel, *The Project*, in which a Goan teacher with a vision 'universal, outside the narrow domains of . . . society and country' makes a meaningful contribution.

Her heart weakened. She went to England, then Goa, where she died in 1972, at night, pen in hand. She felt she had failed as a writer, as she had not published. *Pears from the Willow Tree* appeared only in 1989, due largely to the efforts of Ugandan-Goan Peter Nazareth, whose faith in her and in Goan literature brought her work to public attention.

Violet resisted traditional and simplistic solutions to cross-cultural problems. She was concerned with the impact of tribalism in Africa and the inappropriate imposition of Christian mythology on East African youth maturing in a neo-colonial, westernised society. She was accepted by the Nandis, who broke tradition in allowing her to witness and photograph male circumcision rites. Her fiction based on witchcraft was drawn from interviews with Kenyan students.

KABAGARAMA, DAISY Born in Toro, Uganda, in 1951, she received her primary and secondary school training in predominantly Catholic schools. After graduating from high school, with a major area in English Literature, she taught English in a high school run by American nuns. She wrote and directed her first play there, based on the Easter story.

Daisy attended Makerere University, Kampala, and attained her BA in Social Work and Social Administration in 1975. From 1975–7 she worked in Entebbe as Lecturer in the Institute of Social Development. From 1977–81 she was a lecturer in Kampala at the Institute of Public Administration. She married and had two children.

She went to Iowa State University for further graduate study. In the period from January 1982–9, she obtained her Master's degree in Community and Regional Planning, and her PhD in the Department of Sociology and Anthropology. Her Iowa achievements are outstanding, including membership in three honour societies: Phi Kappa Phi, Alpha Kappa Delta, and Sigma Xi, and three local awards: ISU's Most Outstanding International Woman, 1986, Outstanding Leadership, 1988, and Promotion of International Friendship and Understanding, 1988. During this time she had two more children, presented several research papers, published several research articles (some on women in development) and also wrote poetry, produced, directed and acted in three of her own plays. After graduation, she taught several courses in sociology at Iowa State University, including 'Marriage and the Family', and 'Sex Roles'. She also served on the Women's Studies Program.

In 1989 she moved to McPherson College, Kansas, to teach and to act as adviser on international education, both curricular and extra-curricular. During her stay there, she had a fifth child, held national conferences, and produced a socological text on cross-cultural under-standing. She is completing a novel, *At the Cultural Cross-roads: An African Visits the U.S.* Part of the first chapter is included here – 'The Rich Heritage' pertains in large part to her own Ugandan background.

Because her mother was a primary school teacher and had to move from school to school, Daisy spent most of her childhood at the home of her maternal grandmother, Kabahenda. She was her grandmother's favourite grandchild. Her grandmother's home, with the maternal relatives around, provided stability and a 'first-hand experience of the rich heritage of her people from her grandmother, who had royal roots'.[1]

Daisy started writing as a little girl, even before she went to school. She wrote on banana leaves, or on the ground with a stick. She claims that her humour comes from her mother and grandmother, from whom she also learned that 'women with determination and opportunity can achieve their hearts' desires'. Daisy also says she experienced her grandmother's 'spiritual reverence, wisdom, and a sense of self-determination'. The wisdom and power of Karungi – the grandmother in the novel (like that of Kabahenda) delights the reader. We can see why the granddaughter, Kemigasa, eventually turns out to be 'a strong voice for other women', like Daisy herself.

MAGAIA, LINA From southern Mozambique, bordering South Africa, she dedicates her book to her parents, 'who taught me about freedom and justice' and to the former president of her country, Samora Machel. He died in a mysterious plane crash in 1986, later acknowledged to be a murder, probably contrived by South African terrorist forces allied with the RENAMO guerrillas, the Mozambique National Resistance (MNR) ravishing the countryside.

Magaia was in the capital, Maputo, during these troubled times and

[1] The quotations come from a statement by Daisy Kabagarama that I asked her to write about her early life in Uganda. C.H.B.

went to the area of a massacre to interview peasant victims of the RENAMO bandits. She named her book of the stories they related *Dumba Nengue*, after the large area on both sides of national Highway One, formerly a prosperous agricultural area of cashew and mango trees and cattle and goat herds. The subtitle is taken from a Portuguese proverb, 'Run for your life', or 'You have to trust your feet', the only course left to peasants 'after the MNR plundered their fields, burned their homes, press-ganged their sons, and raped their wives and daughters'. This work is translated by Michael Wolfers and has an excellent historical introduction by Allen Isaacman: (Africa World Press, Trenton, 1988).[1]

On 22 July 1987, the MNR bandits massacred 380 people at the coastal town Homoine, just north of Dumba Nengue. Lina Magaia left the capital and went there to talk to the abused and dispossessed peasants. They were impoverished and illiterate; she decided to tell their stories for them. The Portuguese edition of her book sold out overnight. She insisted that Mozambique was suffering, not from 'civil war', but from 'genocide perpetuated by armed men against defenseless populations'.

Magaia's stories read like journalistic accounts, brutal facts clearly stated, neither softened nor embellished nor explained away. She says, 'The events recounted here are not the invention of a sick mind with a taste for the macabre. And there are many, many more, some of them much worse.' Some of the titles in her anthology suggest her horror as she listened to the men, women and children recounting what had happened to them: 'Their Heads Were Crushed Like Peanuts'; 'They Slaughtered Bertana's Husband as if He Were a Goat'; 'Pieces of Human Flesh Fell in Belinda's Yard'; 'The Little Girl Who Never Learned to Dream'.

Magaia has particular concern for war's child victims. By 1985, 325,000 children had died in the war. Twenty-five per cent of the health clinics and 1,800 schools had been destroyed. Magaia is appalled that Mozambican children, kidnapped and brutalised by the bandits, were trained to terrorism, 'forced to kill and mutilate members of their own family'. Of herself, she says, 'I have four children. One of them . . . as a result of action by the *bandidos armados*. I gave birth to three.' Having witnessed child killings, she visualises Sonyka, her adopted child, in all the abused and slaughtered children.

---

[1] The work is also the source of information supplied here.

DEVI, ANANDA (A. D. Nirsimloo-Anenden) Born in a little village among sugar-cane plantations in Mauritius in 1957, she was three when her family moved to town, where she received her early education. From the time she was seven, she wrote busily: poetry, fairy tales, comic strips. At twelve, she wrote her first novel, and for the next two years she produced several novels of over 200 pages each. Even then she dealt with the themes she still pursues: 'destiny, death, solitude, introspection'[1]. When she was only fifteen, her story 'La Cité Attlee' won a prize in a contest sponsored by Radio France International. She was the only female writer to have her work included in the subsequent collection of the ten stories published in 1973. 'This alerted me to the importance of writing in my life.' She continued writing short stories, 'mystical, and wild about nature'. In 1977 she published her own collection, *Solstices*.

In 1975 she won a fellowship to study linguistics and anthropology in London, feeling that a writer should learn the culture of the people she writes of, and not just by 'statistics, analyses, questionnaires'. Though her academic studies temporarily interrupted her writing, she feels they enriched her understanding and disciplined her art. In 1982 she received her doctorate at the University of London. She has written critical articles in both French and English on anthropological subjects. She also writes of the Congo, having spent some years in Brazzaville. A short story, 'The Student', reflects her African experience.

Devi's collection, *Le poids des êtres* (1987), in which 'Lakshmi's Gift' appears, won an honourable mention for the Noma Award. Since then she has written three novels, *La rue poudrière* (1989), '*L'arbre-fouet* and *Le rêve Carnassier* (1991). She feels she will turn increasingly to stories of her own inherited Indian culture and themes of mysticism, destiny, and reincarnation.

Dorothy Blair, who has brought Ananda Devi to western attention and is translating some of her work, says of Devi, 'She lays bare, in dense, often poetic prose, with a pessimism bordering on cynicism, the violence, passions, the inadmissible in family relationships, the dreams and nightmares of life in the slums of Port-Louis, demythifying the Romantic vision of Mauritius'. Blair explains that the title of the collection comes from *L'exile et le royaume* of Albert Camus: '*Elle respirait, elle oubliait le poids des êtres, la vie démente ou figée, la longue angoisse de vivre ou de mourir.*'

---

[1] The citations from Devi come from correspondence with C.H.B., and from Blair from articles and letters she has sent to C.H.B.

DANGAREMBGA, TSITSI Born in 1969 in M'toko, she grew up in Mutare, Zimbabwe. Like her character Nyasha in her novel, she spent some years abroad. But the novel, she says, is not an autobiography. She identifies herself with both her main characters, Nyasha, who went to England, and Tambudzai, who was educated in Zimbabwe. Dangarembga speaks of her childhood as very sheltered: 'My parents were relatively well off by black Rhodesian standards at that time . . . Really nothing was affecting me . . . I was one of the elite of our circles, and I didn't have to think about anything.'[1] Later on, as a teacher at a mission near the Mozambique border, she became more aware of war and revolution when her best students would suddenly leave school to serve in the army.

She went to Cambridge to study medicine, hoping thus to serve her society. There she was shocked by the ignorance and ethnocentrism of those in the upper middle class academic environment: 'What am I doing here? . . . my family, my relatives are being killed, and I am enjoying a lifestyle in which people will say, where is Rhodesia?' So in February 1980, she returned to study psychology at the University of Zimbabwe in Harare. Here she found she could use her writing skills to fight political corruption, both in the student magazine, *Focus*, and in a drama she co-wrote with Robert McLaren – 'the most significant period of my creative development'.

Except for her play, 'She No Longer Weeps', 1987, and a short story published in Sweden, 'The Letter', 1985, she was almost unknown until *Nervous Conditions* appeared in 1988, for which she won the overall winner's prize for the African section of the 1989 Commonwealth Writers Prize. 'I think it gives a woman's perspective of life in a colonised African state. As a result . . . it does not focus on societal-level oppression and rebellion, but on the day to day hardships and problems that constituted existence under colonisation.'[2] As the first black woman of her country to publish a novel in English, Dangarembga feels sympathy with some black American female writers. They 'touch more of me than the white ones. The white Western feminism does not meet my experiences at a certain point, the issues of me as a black woman.' Her intended audience is 'Firstly, African women, secondly, black women, thirdly, people interested in Africa. I would hope that this latter category

[1] Unless stated otherwise, quotations from the author are taken from an interview with her by Flora Veit-Wild, 'Women write about the things that move them,' in *Black Women's Writing, Crossing the Boundaries*, edited by Carole Boyce Davies, Frankfort, Matatu, 1989, 101–8.

[2] The quotation is taken from a questionnaire completed for this publication.

would include African men in particular and black men in general amongst other interested parties.'[1]

Dangarembga feels that 'real art is honest', and as such runs the risk of being misunderstood or undervalued. Nonetheless, for the Harare critic, Flora Veit-Wild, in her review of *Nervous Conditions*, Dangarembga has painted the 'colonisation of the mind, with feminine insight, in an honest, deeply moving book'.

HEAD, BESSIE Born in Pietermaritzburg, South Africa, in 1937 in a mental hospital. Her mother, daughter of a rich white family of racehorse owners, had been committed when it became known that she was pregnant by a Zulu groom who worked in the family stable. He disappeared; eliminated, Bessie always supposed. Bessie's mother remained at the mental institution for six more years and then committed suicide. As an infant, Bessie was put in the care of a coloured foster family until she was thirteen. Then she was put in an orphanage until she finished secondary school at eighteen. Her mother's legacy provided her educational opportunities. She became a teacher, then a journalist. In 1962 she married Harold Head, a fellow reporter. Her son, Howard, was born the following year.

In 1964 she left South Africa for a teaching position in Botswana. Refused a passport, she left only with her small son (her marriage had failed) on an exile visa. From Botswana, only childless refugees were allowed to move on, so she had to stay in Serowe, reporting every Monday to the local police. Bessie Head once wrote, 'I desire above all else to be ordinary'. She sought a frail stability in Serowe where for many years she lived 'restless in a distant land', an exile without a passport, *a stateless person*. The serenity she found there was with the ordinary people in a bleak, arid land. There she gardened, sold guava jelly in the market, and typed her stories in a small hut without electricity – her sanctum, her refuge, her ultimate home.

In Serowe, Head had started to write short stories, but won little recognition for her fiction. She published her first novel, *When Rain Clouds Gather*, in 1969, basing it on her own experiences at the Bamangwato Development Farm, showing the problems of development and modernisation in this Third World agrarian society. A male South African exile works with an enlightened development expert and a strong village woman to push back the desert from the traditional village.

Head continued these interests. In 1978 she wrote, 'I am of such a

[1] See note 2 on page 196.

practical turn of mind and there is so much going on in the world today that I am very eager indeed to pursue some of the work I have already done in my novels – communal development and how people relate to it ... There is a temptation to give a writer a very airy-fairy category and for people not to see that such talent could be very useful and practical.'

The central character in Head's second novel, *Maru*, 1971, is a Masarwa (Bushman) woman, light-skinned like Head herself, and hence of lower caste. Head wrote that she 'wanted to write a novel that would be beautiful, like a fairy tale, about an ugly subject, racism' (in *World Literature Written in English*, 18/1 1979, p. 23).

In 1967 Head suffered a severe nervous breakdown, and had to fight her way back from paranoia and hallucination to sanity. Did she have the inner power to recover? *A Question of Power* (1973), 'her only truly autobiographical work', concerns this three-year mental illness, during which she was certified and admitted to the psychiatric hospital in Gaborone. Charles Larson, first to recognise her extraordinary talent, wrote: 'In her concern for women and madness, Bessie Head has almost single-handedly brought about the inward turning of the African novel.'

After fifteen years, Head finally received citizenship and was able to travel, to the International Writing Program in Iowa, and to a Berlin African writers conference. Though her fame grew, she elected to remain in Botswana. She wrote short stories, sketches, autobiographical and historical notes and interviews of the villagers. Of her short story anthology, *A Collector of Treasures*, 1977, she said it was 'much more even-keel than my other work, and reflects the rural life of which I have been a part – I have a deep affection for it as it is so deeply involved in the everyday world.' Of *Serowe, Village of the Rain Wind*, 1981, she explained, 'I have lived most of my life in scattered little bits. There is a sense of wovenness, a wholeness of life here.' Her history of Botswana and several collections of her stories and sketches have been published since she died in 1986.

Head's recognition came late, but today critics, readers, scholars are studying and collecting her work and her letters. She had many correspondents, and most quotations here come from her letters to C.H.B.

MARQUARD, JEAN Born in 1942, in her short forty-three years as a white intellectual in South Africa, Marquand made a great impact. She used her vantage point as teacher, critic, editor and writer to expose the confusion and malaise a privileged citizen may feel there. She sought to understand both the black majority and the white minority, which seemed impervious to the evils of apartheid.

She received her BA with distinction from Stellenbosch University in 1961, her honours degree *cum laude* the following year, and her MA also *cum laude* in 1966. After two more years of study at St Anne's College, Cambridge, she was awarded a BPhil.

She taught at Paarl Girls High School, lectured at the Universities of Stellenbosch and Pretoria, and was senior lecturer at Witswatersrand University until her death. In 1983 she was awarded a PhD in South African Literature there.

Marquard's research centred on South African women writers: Olive Schreiner, Pauline Smith, Doris Lessing, Nadine Gordimer and Bessie Head. She travelled to Botswana to interview the latter, who later characterised her as 'a good sort'[1]. Nadine Gordimer became her neighbour and wrote of her, 'She was a stimulating intellectual in a society that has little respect for such people. She was as uncompromising in her loathing of oppression as she was in her literary judgement . . . A rare bird – she cannot be replaced.'

When Marquard's book, *A Century of South African Short Stories* came out in 1978, she also gave a course in 'Women in South African Literature'. She said then: 'Women do not inhabit a separate world . . . Women come in contact with the whole world, including men, so one should not expect them to write only about women in their so-called world.'

Most important to her personally were her two sons, Conrad Hughes and Octavius Merry and her beloved second husband, Bruce Merry. She died leaning on his shoulder in 1984. She had a family history of cancer. 'I think Jean knew she would not make middle age . . . She just wanted to cram all her ideas and excitements into the short span which she felt was permitted to her,' wrote Bruce Merry. Gordimer recalls, 'How can I forget . . . seeing her, when she was already mortally ill and had lost her hair as a result of treatment, striding along in an African-style turban and wide bright trousers. She was splendid, in her refusal to live a half-life, whether the strictures were those of ill health or that other disease, apartheid.'

Alan Paton had been a friend of the Marquard family for 60 years. At her funeral, his son Jonathan spoke particularly of her short stories, a collection of which she left unfinished.

---

[1] The quotation from Bessie Head is from a letter Head sent to me in 1979. Those from Bruce Merry are also from letters to me. The other references and quotations come from various obituary notices and clippings sent me by the archivist at Witswatersrand University. C.H.B.

WICOMB, ZOË Born in Cape Province, South Africa, in 1948, she studied English Literature at the University of the Western Cape. She continued her studies in Britain, at the University of Reading; she then studied literary linguistics at the University of Strathclyde in Scotland. She has taught English at both secondary and university levels. When in 1991 she moved back to South Africa to teach at her old university, she found the relocation traumatising, after so many years living and working abroad. She missed her family left behind.

She started to write short stories when she was teaching abroad and raising her daughter. 'As for the short story, I have little to say except that the form was dictated by both material conditions and my fear of writing. Working at the time without the legendary room of my own, always prepared for the interruptions of a young child and for other legitimate claims of the kitchen table, the short story, after a day's teaching, seemed more manageable and somehow less presumptuous to tackle. I found its limitations, both in length and subject matter, attractive. I could pretend that I was simply messing about with words, that I wasn't doing something as embarrassing as "writing" and nevertheless after a while found to my surprise that I'd produced something with which to tinker. The process of tidying it up and finishing it off could be tackled as an exercise, matter-of-factly, like any job; the final story would give me the confidence to do another, as a chapter of a novel never could – the insecurity and anxiety induced by writing would necessarily lead to abandoning a larger project.'[1]

The resulting volume, *You Can't Get Lost in Cape Town*, 1987, a combination of reminiscences and impressions by a fictional Frieda Shenton, builds into a sequential narrative. Frieda grows up in a coloured district, becomes the first non-white scholarship student to attend a white secondary school, feels fragmented as she studies and works her way in the canteen of the coloured university. She goes to London, and returns to her home country with new and sometimes unsettling perspectives. She is formed by her culture and yet, distancing herself, not a part of it. As Wicomb says, both the story episodes and the gaps between are relevant, revealing Frieda'a growing self awareness as, on occasional visits to her South African parents, she rediscovers her own roots, her family and her people. '*You Can't Get Lost in Cape Town* started as a compromise between novel and short stories, but I soon came to see the gaps between stories as an integral part of the work.'

[1] The quotations come from letters by Wicomb to C.H.B., and from 'An Author's Agenda' by her in the *South African Review of Books*, Feb/May 1990, p. 24.

Wicomb's strengths are many. She is concise, and in a few words can paint a meaningful portrait or suggest the subtlety and the complexity of a human relationship. As teacher and educator, she is no snob, and encourages others to write despite their restraints and fears. 'Political oppression invariably means linguistic oppression, and for marginalised groups like black women who are doubly bound, it is difficult to break through the silence.'

Wicomb resists the idea of a writer's agenda. 'As a writer, I do not have an agenda. But like everyone else I write from a political position, as, amongst other things, a South African and a black feminist. This position informs my writing just as my material situation as teacher, mother, or member of a nuclear family affects my practice.' Perhaps because she does not propagandise, her work is balanced. She is incisive, often ironic, yet at the same time warm and captivating. Her fascination with language, too, is evident in 'Bowl like Hole,' included here and the first story of her book.

FUGARD, SHEILA Born in Birmingham, England, in 1932. Her South African doctor father and her Irish mother moved the family to South Africa when Sheila was eight. She was educated there, and attended the University of Cape Town. She had studied theatre and was working as an actress in Cape Town when she met Athol Fugard. He says now she was the 'decisive factor' in his turning to drama as his life's work.[1] Both were writing short stories and poetry when they met in 1956 and became engaged. Sheila's conservative father objected to their marriage since Athol had given up university, worked as a common sailor, and at best, he thought, could become only a 'hack journalist'.

Nonetheless Sheila and Athol married, worked in experimental theatre, and lived frugally. She directed his first play, in which both had roles. In 1958 they moved to Johannesburg where he worked as a court clerk, and they visited black writers in Sophiatown. Both felt the need for free theatre and for fiction that could deal realistically with black oppression. They produced other plays by Athol. The black amateur actors were teachers and labourers, both literate and illiterate. At rehearsals, Sheila said, 'I would have to buy them hamburgers and we had very little money'. Lack of recognition and hand-to-mouth living characterised much of their early married life.

[1] Most quotations are taken from Mel Gussow's 'Profile' of Athol Fugard in the *New Yorker* (December 20 1982). Nkosi, *The Transplanted Heart*, 1985, p. 117, knew Sheila as an actress. Other information comes from correspondence between Sheila and C.H.B.

They moved briefly to England in 1959 but looked for work in London theatre in vain: Sheila typed for a department store; Athol house-cleaned. In 1960 the Sharpeville Crisis at home and Sheila's pregnancy led them to return to Port Elizabeth, where their daughter Lisa was born. The following year Athol's *The Blood Knot* aroused international attention. Local black actors persuaded the Fugards to form Serpent Players for them. Lewis Nkosi remembers Sheila's work with this company: 'She created out of flimsy gestures and bare words a whole world of living people.' Despite curtailments, harassments, and the jailing of two actors, Athol continued to write and produce his plays.

In 1967 Athol was ordered to choose between leaving South Africa on an exit visa or remaining there sequestered without a passport. They stayed. Athol dedicated *Boesman and Lina* to Sheila. 'Boesman . . . focused on Lena who is, after all his life . . . immediate enough to be beaten, derided, and worst of all, needed.' They could not attend the New York showing, of course, but the play was so popular that 4,000 people signed a petition demanding Athol's reinstatement. He got his passport back within a year. They went to India in 1981 for the filming of *Gandhi* (Athol played Smuts) and were touched by the mass poverty there.

They now divide their time between Carmel, New York, and Port Elizabeth. Both centre their work in South Africa. Sheila's fiction treats the history of the people and their diversity. Her first novel deals with a mental breakdown; the second, with race relations from a historic perspective. Her third, *A Revolutionary Woman*, portrays a local English-speaking teacher in the Karoo Boer area who works with coloured students. 'Crossing the River' shows a flash-flood emergency which unites the races in a brief moment of shared emergency. 'Lace' is based on an actual recent incident which occurred near the Fugard's cottage, a 'retreat' in the Karoo area where they work.

KARODIA, FARIDA Born in a rural community, Aliwal North, in South Africa in 1942, her first novel, *Daughters of the Twilight*, reflects her own childhood background, as does the cross-cultural marriage between her Indian father and her South African mother. Karodia attended local primary and secondary schools, and graduated from Coronationville Teacher Training College in 1961. For three years she taught at the Coronationville High School in Johannesburg.

In 1967, after her short failed marriage, she went to Zambia with her year-old daughter, Anesia, to teach at a High School in Livingston. After three years there, the South African government unexpectedly revoked her passport. Left a *stateless* person, she joined her mother in Swaziland for nine months, waiting for Canadian approval to emigrate there in 1969.

Her teaching certification and experience proved insufficient to qualify her for a place in the Canadian educational system. Karodia did odd jobs, wrote radio drama for CBC, and took further education courses at the University of Calgary, graduating in 1974. She resented the professional discrimination she encountered as a 'non-white' (a South African term like Hitler's 'non-Aryan', created to negate all but the 'chosen race'). She went to British Columbia to teach at the Golden Secondary School to gain the required 'Canadian experience'. She then returned to do graduate work at Calgary. In July 1988 she wrote, 'The only clear recollections I have of this period are years of writing, writing, and rewriting . . . everything on the periphery faded. I can't even remember what jobs I did to support myself and my family during this time.'

Nonetheless, Karodia persisted. In a letter dated April 1988 she wrote, 'I found myself fighting a war on both fronts, a woman and a non-white. I managed, however, to raise my daughter and established a career as a writer . . . I always told myself that there was little in terms of indignity and prejudice that I could not endure because I had encountered the worst aspects of it in South Africa.'

Karodia's first novel, *Daughters of the Twilight*, 1986, concerns two sisters who live, as she did, in the family store in a small country neighbourhood. The mother and grandmother portrayed resemble her own in their strength and 'positive influence' in a survival struggle. The novel was recommended for the Fawcett Prize. One of the three judges was Buchi Emecheta, who championed the novel.

Karodia went back to South Africa briefly in 1981, but found little change. Her second book, *Coming Home and Other Stories*, 1988, shows her skill in portraying both various rural protagonists from the despised non-white ethnic groups and also those from the ruling classes of Dutch and English descent. Her coloured, black, 'Asian' or Indian, Boer and English characters are painted with irony and pathos.

Her third novel, *A Shattering of Silence*, is set in Mozambique during the Portuguese colonisation. Karodia is working on the film script for *Daughters of the Twilight*. Like other emigrés, she is turning for her fiction to her present Canadian environment, where, at last, she has found a kind of peace. 'For the first time in my life I feel I belong somewhere' (letter, June 1989).

Her years of careful writing and rewriting and her ability to empathise with all kinds of people she has met make her work varied, provocative, and compelling.[1]

EL SAADAWI, NAWAL Born in 1931 in the Egyptian village of Kafr Tahla. The eldest daughter in a relatively poor family, she worked her way through primary and secondary education, and later through medical college. She graduated in 1954 and went to work in the rural area she grew up in, feeling keenly the inequalities in education and income women suffered there. She wrote short stories, and later, novels and treatises. Becoming Minister of Public Health in the Egyptian cabinet, Saadawi spoke out against the bureaucracy there. Her study of Arab women, *The Hidden Face of Eve*, brought her international attention, but also persecution and harassment at home, which continues even today.

In 1972 she was removed from her government position, and made to relinquish her job as editor of *Health* magazine after the publication of her *Women and Sex*. During the ten years that followed, her books were banned in Egypt and several Arab countries. Meanwhile she wrote five more books on the situation of women, several works of fiction, and gave lectures abroad. Many readers came to know of her through her account of her own excision when she was six, and the resulting psychic and physical traumas she endured.

In 1981 Saadawi was arrested under Sadat, and imprisoned for three months, being released after his assassination. Her accounts of her seizure and imprisonment appeared in *Index to Censorship* (4/85) and in her *Memoirs from the Women's Prison*, 1986. Her novel, *Woman at Point Zero* (1983) is inspired by a psychiatric interview she conducted with an imprisoned prostitute under a death sentence for murder. At the International Women's Conference in Copenhagen in 1983, she provoked serious discussion of female circumcision and excision in Africa and the Middle East.

Despite bannings and censorship, Saadawi's Arabic writings, both studies and fiction, have been widely read and discussed. In 1982 she founded the Arab Women's Solidarity Association, over which she still presides. She has travelled and lectured widely. In the United States in 1983 she was keynote speaker for a conference in Urbana, Illinois, 'Common Differences: Third World Women and Feminist Perspectives,' organised by Evelyne Accad, who speaks of her as 'such a vibrant and

[1] Much of the biographical material comes from Karodia's letters and telephone calls to C.H.B.

warm person'. Her work is now appearing in English translation and is thus available in the anglophone world. Thirteen of her works have also been translated into thirteen different languages.

Her own life, her strength in combatting violence and abuse, her personal faith in her own sexuality and marriage, have brought illumination and hope to women all over the world. She writes feelingly of her devoted husband, who has translated some of her books, and of her son and daughter. She lives in Cairo, although she has often been boycotted by the government-controlled media. At times armed guards have circled her home to protect her from assassination.

So far, she has written twenty-seven books, 'with lucidity and daring on subjects which are considered taboo in the Arab world'. She says, 'Writing a short story sometimes is more difficult than writing a novel. Anyway I write both short and long stories, and it is the subject itself that chooses its shape.'[1]

DJEBAR, ASSIA (Fatima-Zohra Imalayen) Born in 1936 in Cherchell, Algeria, her family belonged to the Muslim middle class. However, since her father taught in the French-colonial educational system, he was atypical both in his knowledge of French and in sending his little daughter to be educated in French schools. The dilemmas of language and cultural overlay she experienced when young were to form the subject of much of Djebar's later fiction. They also provoked her to much self-examination and questioning which again has had an effect on her writing.

She was a brilliant student at the Lycée of Slidia, and again at the Sorbonne where she specialised in history and geography. In 1955 she was the first woman to be admitted to the Ecole Normale Superière at Sèvres. She married during the Second World War and went with her husband, Ould-Rouis, to teach at Tunis. Throughout her life she has been a teacher, scholar and researcher in both history and linguistics.

Djebar has tried various alternatives to the problems her bi-cultural status has forced upon her. Her interest in Algerian women and their concern for greater freedom has been paramount in her fiction. She published her first novel, *La soif*, at the age of twenty. In the next ten years she published three more novels and became known as the most prominent woman in Maghreb literature, recognised as deserving equal

---

[1] Many of the details of Saadawi's life and views come from vitae materials and letters she sent the editor, and David Bruner's interview with her in Cairo in 1986. Evelyne Accad said of her 'She is such a vibrant and warm person' (letter, 21 April 1983 to C.H.B.).

recognition with Mohammed Dib, Driss Chraïbi, Mouloud Feraoun, and Katib Yacine. Her student, critic, and friend Mildred Mortimer affirms Djebar's eminence, saying she best shows '*la réalité féminine dans toute sa complexité*'.

Her early novels deal with sequestered, upper-class Muslim women, somewhat shallow, and ignorant of the situation of their poorer sisters. They are romantic idealists day-dreaming an idyllic future. She showed, however, that the Algerian war forced both upper- and lower-class women to greater freedoms, greater powers, and greater awareness and compassion for each other.

Djebar returned to her own country to teach history at the University of Algiers, writing little during her eleven-year stay. She studied the effects of bilingualism and published *Women of Islam*, photographs and commentary, in 1961. She produced two films, *La nouba des femmes du mont Chenoua*, a documèntary of interviews with women (1979) and *La zerda ou les chants de l'oubli*, a musical documentary of Algeria in revolution. She translated Nawal El Saadawi's *The Hidden Face of Eve* from Arabic into French. In 1980 she brought out a short story collection.

Drawn by her publishers, by a large and appreciative francophone reading public, and by a certain freedom to champion greater liberty for women, she moved back to France. She is currently working on a four-novel series to be called *Quartet*. The first two volumes, *L'amour, la Fantasia*, and *Ombre Sultane* are already available in French and in an English translation by her friend and critic, Dorothy Blair. The excerpts about her childhood in this collection are taken from the first volume. Here she alternates her own personal reminiscences with descriptions of the historic resistance by Algerian women to the 1930 French conquest of their country. She commemorates these forgotten women, '*sœurs disparues*', and implicitly likens them to the peasant women who took part in the Algerian Revolution of 1954, whose oral narratives she herself records here.

The second novel, *Ombre Sultane*, is a domestic narrative of two women, an emancipated westernised wife and a traditional sequestered one, sequential wives of the same man. Djebar uses the friendship that develops between the two wives as a symbol of an eventual joint effort by other Algerian women to rid themselves of their psychic and societal fetters. The projected third and fourth volumes of *Quartet* will depict problems of contemporary Algerian women, who were freed to work outside the home by the exigencies of the war, but were expected to return to confinement and the veil after hostilities ceased.

Evelyne Accad summarises Djebar's development as a writer: 'Her earliest works focus on selfish and individualistic revolt; then she turns to political and social commitment; the understanding of the importance of one's body and the relationship of the couple; and finally to the feeling of greater prudence in the face of women's problems. In an authentic and courageous process, the desire for truth opens mouths that have been closed far too long.'[1]

HALIMI, GISÈLE Born in Tunis in 1927, she was the second child of a Jewish mother, Fortunée, and a converted Beduin father, Edouard Taïeb. She adored her father, despite his harshness and his disappointment that she was a girl: 'Such a packet of problems and natural inferiorities.' He would not even acknowledge her existence until two weeks after her birth. He felt her own and her sister's education should be sacrificed to maintain her elder brother at the French Lycée. Her parents made her feel guilty for surviving her younger brother and for outdistancing the elder one in studies. Later, however, her father felt great pride in her accomplishments. Her mother continued to complain that Gisèle should stay at home with her children in a conventional wifely role.

Another ambiguity plagued her. When she rejected the confines of her Islamic faith, and the expectation of a passive, enduring womanhood, she went to France with a scholarship for law school at the Sorbonne. She had dreamed that French civilisation would mean liberation. 'I surrendered to the invasion of the French genius.' When she discovered that this very France had perpetrated torture on Algeria, she felt bewildered and betrayed. 'The shock was terrible.' But she chose her course – to defend the oppressed, even those of the Algerian rebel forces who had confessed to murder and genocide. She proved that their confessions were extracted under torture and hence were invalid.

Gisèle Halimi is an extraordinary woman. Her autobiography clearly portrays her inauspicious Tunisian background, unlikely to produce a woman of acknowledged importance and influence. Yet she has become a world figure as an advocate, and *avocat*, for human rights. 'It was not easy to accommodate to the ambiguity of my life,' she wrote. She has

---

[1] Djebar is widely recognised by francophone readers in France and in the Maghreb. Evelyne Accad's *Veil of Shame* (1978) and her *Contemporary Arab Women Writers* (Monograph 5, Institute for Women's Studies in the Arab world, Beirut University College, 1985) quoted above praise Djebar. Mildred Mortimer has written extensively about Djebar. Jean Déjeux published a full-length study in 1984. Only most recently, however, have her works appeared in English.

felt compelled to fight oppression, colonialism, racism, and particularly violence (domestic abuse and governmental torture). She has found happiness in sharing with 'mavericks, non-conformists. And among these, *women*, who are the most exposed. Women whose movement made me what I am – an individual – equal and different.'

Halimi's bravery and initiative has made her a well known figure in French justice. She was a friend and colleague of Simone de Beauvoir, with whom she helped found an association for establishing abortion rights, *Choisir*. Sartre's friend and lawyer; she loved him as a 'just man'. She was in contact with many of the celebrated men and women of the time.

Halimi is also a fine writer. *Milk for the Orange Tree* is a tribute to her father, concluding with his death. In it she traces her own development frankly and astutely, giving the reader a very human self-portrait. Her reminiscences are episodic, candid, intimate, and moving. She speaks of her pleasure that her lawyer's robe was full enough to conceal her pregnancies. In difficult trial cases, she would finger and fray the buttonholes of her robe so compulsively that each night she had to sew them up again. She was anxious lest Simone de Beauvoir, who refused to have children, should find her own small son badly behaved. She writes of the harrassment and threats she endured – even risking death knowing it would leave her children unprotected – after her first marriage failed.

Of Sartre, she writes fondly: 'I saw through him. Even when he pretended to behave like everybody else and to get annoyed, in order to please me . . . His overwhelming concern: writing, creating with words.' Of herself she says, 'I accepted, basically, Sartre's system of ethics. I knew I was free. God did not exist, and if, as one of Sartre's characters says . . . "This is even at times quite inconvenient", there were days when the absence of God elated me with my own responsibility.' In the chapter included here, she shows the elation she felt when, as a small child, she put 'God on probation' and won.[1]

SEBBAR, LEÏLA Born and raised in Algeria, her French mother and her Algerian father were both teachers. She pursued her university education first at Aix-en-Provence, and then in Paris, where she lives today. Her research interests centre on the colonial concept of the '*bon nègre*' in eighteenth-century colonial literature, and on nineteenth-

---

[1] I am indebted to Dorothy Blair and to her excellent introduction and translation of *Milk for the Orange Tree* for the information on the life of Halimi. The quotations from Halimi's text are on the following pages: 205–6, 100, 153, 153, 310, 293.

century education for girls. In addition to her fiction, she writes for literary journals, broadcasts on French television, and documents photographic books.

Although she has written five novels, many essays (some autobiographical), stories and articles, she is just beginning to be recognised in the West[1]. Sebbar often chooses to portray the second-generation North-African immigrants known as '*beurs*' – usually women, often juvenile rebels who leave their own traditional families to inhabit a kind of subculture in France. A favourite character, Shérazade, appears in several novels. At seventeen, Shérazade 'flees the suburban housing project for Paris, possessed only of lots of nerve, green eyes, brown frizzy hair, and a Walkman.'[2] Her adventures constitute a picturesque narrative involving petty thieves, vigilantes, truckers, terrorists, and runaways.

Sebbar's style transmits the uncertainties of the illiterate or semi-literate immigrants, caught between two cultures, two languages, two religions. Her women characters are often sharp observers, with the keen memory associated with the oral tradition. In stream-of-consciousness style, the protagonist seems to talk to an *alter ego* or to an absent person, as in *Parle mon fils parle à ta mère*. 'I think my style of using the spoken language – the language of emotion – is to be inside the character . . .', Sebbar said in an interview with Nancy du Plessis in 1988.[3]

In the collection, *La Négresse à L'enfant*, Sebbar tells several stories in the inner voice of her character, sometimes in counterpoint to the observations of a group of women fellow-workers – a kind of passive chorus which interprets the main character's confusions and predicaments.

[1] Some of Sebbar's novels are now appearing in English translation by Dorothy Blair. Such leading critics of Maghreb in literature as Mildred Mortimer and Evelyne Accad praise her fiction. (See Mildred Mortimer's *Journeys Through the French African Novel*, 'Running Away: Leïla Sebbar,' Chapter 6 'Women's Flight,' Portsmouth, Heinemann, 1990, pp. 177–194.)

[2] Nancy du Plessis, 'Leïla Sebbar, Voice of Exile,' *World Literature Today*, Vol. 63, No. 3, Summer 1989, p. 416.

[3] Nancy du Plessis in the article cited in note 2 draws from her own interview with Sebbar in a letter, part of a continuing literary correspondence with Nancy Houston, published by Stock in Paris as *Lettres Parisiens*. The citation here is noted as No. 7, November 1988.

Nancy du Plessis in a letter to C.H.B. 21 December 1989 wrote, 'My efforts with Sebbar's work are based on my strong feelings that it is important to have cross-cultural communication.' Sebbar herself has written that she is *ravie* to find D. K. Bruner's translation '*excellente*'.

CHEDID, ANDRÉE   Born in 1920 of Lebanese-Syrian-Egyptian stock, she grew up in Egypt loving its past, its history, its mythology and its recorded wisdom. As a child she often spent holidays in France. At the American University in Cairo, she wrote her first poems, using English and a pen name to see if she could attract readers on her own. She met and married Louis Chedid, a medical student. When he finished his training, they went to Paris to live, as she had always longed to do. She has a son, a musical performer and composer, a daughter who is an artist, and six grandchildren. She has won many prizes for her literary works.

Chedid is an expatriate by choice, but her love of Egypt and the Middle East permeates her work. She builds bridges, not barriers, between the ancient African world and today's western world. 'I live in Paris by choice, because I have loved this city since my childhood . . . But my writing is less a matter of nostalgic return to the past . . . than it is a need to experience the . . . pulsations, movements, chants, misery and joy, sun and serenity, which are inherent to the Middle East' (*L'autre* and Knapp).[1]

She is truly unique, like her character Kalya, in finding her cross-cultural roots a source of joy and breadth. 'Hybrid, why not?' asks Kalya. Chedid's friend and fellow writer, Evelyne Accad, writes in *Sexuality and War*: 'Unlike many North African writers, such as Driss Chraïbi, Albert Memmi, Abdel-Kebir Khatiri, and Marguerite Taos-Amrouche . . . who have described how divided they feel about being a mixture of cultures, how torn and unhappy it causes them to be . . . Chedid insists on the positive aspects of such hybridisation, affirming cosmopolitanism and the enrichment, tolerance, and openness it brings.'

Chedid's characters often belong to antiquity, but reflect issues of today. Her fictional biography of Nefertiti, for example, reveals the historic queen as a woman seeking equality and self-determination. Chedid writes in 'The Future and the Ancestor', 'Sometimes we bend beneath the fullness of ancestors. But the present that shatters walls, boundaries, and invents the road to come, rings on.'

Chedid is further remarkable in winning acclaim in many genres. Her *œuvre* includes twenty volumes of poetry, ten novels, five plays, several collections of short stories, and recently films. There is continuity throughout her work: the need for love, for understanding, for peace not

[1] Quotations are from Bettina Knapp's *French Novelists Speak Out*, from Chedid's own introduction to *L'autre* (translated quotation by C.H.B.) and from Chedid's poem from women in *Women of the Fertile Crescent*, ed. Kamal Boullata, p. 12.

war, for help not violence – from ancient pre-Christian eras to the continuing Lebanese war. 'Writing is a demanding work, with great windows of joy,' she says. Her work reflects affirmation, bridges between the past, the present, and a hoped-for future of common understanding. Her novel, *A House Without Roots*, 1985, ends tragically in the death of a child by a sniper's bullet during a women's peace march in Beirut. Nonetheless, the possibility of future accord through mutual understanding is there.

'Death in Slow Motion' first appeared just after the start of the Lebanese war and is included in Chedid's latest anthology, *Mondes Miroirs Magies*, 1988. The lead story portrays an orphaned and maimed child victim of the war. Chedid rewrote it as a novel in 1989, *L'enfant multiple*, with a more positive resolution. On the frontispiece is written, 'from tears to laughter.' She is, however, never facile nor sentimental. She knows first-hand the misery, poverty, desperation in lands where women are exploited, where peasants suffer unheeded, where war devastates the innocent. 'Let the memory of blood be viligant but never void the day.' Writing short stories is 'Close to poetry . . . I want to keep my eyes open to the suffering, distress and the cruelty of the world, but also on its light, its beauty.'

In 1991 *Sud* published a collection of tributes to Chedid from forty critics and colleagues, *Andrée Chedid. Voix multiple*.